THE ACCIDENTAL OFFICE LADY

THE ACCIDENTAL OFFICE LADY

Laura Kriska

CHARLES E. TUTTLE COMPANY
Rutland, Vermont & Tokyo, Japan

Published by Charles E. Tuttle Publishing,
an imprint of Periplus Editions (HK) Ltd.

LCC Card No. 97-60125
ISBN 0-8048-2105-4

First edition, 1997
Second printing, 1998

Printed in Singapore

Distributed by:
USA **Charles E. Tuttle Co., Inc.**
Airport Industrial Park
RR1 Box 231-5
North Clarendon, VT 05759
Tel: (802) 773-8930
Fax: (802) 773-6993

Japan **Tuttle Shokai Inc.**
1-21-13 Seki
Tama-ku, Kawasaki-shi
Kanagawa-ken 214, Tokyo
Tel: (81) (44) 833-0225
Fax: (81) (44) 822-0413

Southeast Asia
Berkeley Books Pte Ltd.
5 Little Road #08-01
Singapore 536983
Tel: (65) 280 3320
Fax: (65) 280 6290

Tokyo Editorial Office:
2-6, Suido 1-chome,
Bunkyo-ku, Tokyo 112, Japan

Boston Editorial Office:
153 Milk Street, 5th Floor
Boston, MA 02109, USA

Singapore Editorial Office:
5 Little Road #08-01
Singapore 536983

To
The Office Ladies

Contents

Acknowledgments

FOR THEIR SUPPORT AND KINDNESS DURING my time in Japan, I would like to thank Shigeyoshi Yoshida, Mieko Ogiwara, Yumiko Shoji, Hiroko Kanno, Kumiko Hashimoto, Yasuko Kodama, Akiko Onoguchi, Kayoko Furokawa, Ayako Nishiyama, Yoko Sashi, Michio Iwata, Tetsuo Chino, Toshiro Yamada, Moritaka Higuchi, Tom Umeno, Koji Arinami, Rika Takeuchi, Masakazu Iino, Tokiko Iino, Eric Peabody, Bret Anderson, Susan Insley, and Scott Whitlock.

I am also grateful to the following friends and family members who provided encouragement and various kinds of support during the writing of this book: Le Anne Schreiber, Richard Locke, Leila Phillip, Alden Matthews, Laura Grenning, Alex Cox, Bobby Rahal and team, Marcy Mowrey Gauch, and especially Patrick Gunn, my brother David, and my parents Brian and Sally Kriska.

Prologue

A WEEK AFTER GRADUATING FROM A SMALL liberal arts college, I was working in an automobile factory in Ohio. In the weld shop I applied thick black sealer between small metal parts and then fused them together with a hydraulic press. On the assembly line I pressed penny-sized bits of adhesive into six precise points on the car's metal frame before it moved down the line. In the paint shop I held tacky rags in both hands and had ten seconds to wipe the entire white body clean to prevent lint from messing up the color coat. Every day my feet throbbed inside a pair of steel-toed boots, and streaks of dirt marked the white cotton uniform with the red patch that said "Honda of America Mfg." More than once I had to remind myself what I was doing here—that this was all part of my training to be the first American woman to work in Honda Motor's Tokyo headquarters.

When people heard I was on my way to work in Japan they always looked surprised until I told them where I came from. I was born in Tokyo during my parents' assignment as missionaries, and my first words were

Japanese. If they still didn't believe that a fair-skinned redhead could have Asian roots I would offer to show them the bottoms of my feet where, I'd say jokingly, "it says 'Made In Japan'."

After two years in Tokyo we returned to Ohio and lived like the other families in Grandview Heights except that my mother filled the kitchen cupboards with colorful Kutani pottery, my father lugged around complicated Canon camera equipment on family vacations, and once a week we ate bowls of sticky white rice with chopsticks. Growing up, I used certain phrases and words without really knowing they were Japanese. *"Tadaima,"* I'd say, walking in the door after a day at school. *"Okaerinasai,"* my mother would reply, welcoming me home. *"Itadakimasu,"* the whole family said before digging into a hot dinner; it was a convenient, one-word way to get around saying grace.

I took my first trip back to Japan with my family when I was sixteen. We traveled and visited Japanese friends that I knew only through the decorative New Year greeting cards they sent. Most of them, Takeuchis, Uchidas, and Abes, had known me as an infant. They treated us to elaborate feasts as we sat shoeless on the floors of their small homes.

At sixteen Japan excited me. My thirteen-year-old brother rebelled against this strange place where his knee-high tube socks and ragged baseball shirts didn't fit the norm. On our first day in Tokyo my parents took us out to lunch at a restaurant on the top floor of a large department store. Without glancing at the menu my parents both ordered the deluxe sushi plate. My brother and I ordered spaghetti with meat sauce.

After the first few days my curiosity began to outweigh my uncertainty and the few words I knew helped me navigate my way. I discovered a sense of place, of coming home—the narrow streets, thin paper sliding doors, fresh-smelling tatami mats, and delicate cardboard lunch boxes folded into the shapes of flowers.

I started to study Japanese formally at Denison University after returning to the United States. The dark, curvy lines of the phonetic alphabet represented a secret code, and I practiced writing the forty-six symbols over and over, quizzing myself on any white space that presented itself to me: a place mat, the back of an envelope, or a blue book for an English exam. I loved learning to read all over again like a child stringing together syllables and discovering new, recognizable words.

I signed up to spend my junior year at Waseda University in Tokyo. But before going to Japan I got a summer job working at the Honda manufacturing plant in Ohio. I wanted to be a translator, but after only two semesters of Japanese I could barely read a sushi menu. The only thing I was qualified to do was to be a lifeguard at the Honda Sports Center. It was there that I met Mr. Yoshida, who was both an alumnus of Waseda and Honda's vice president in Ohio. He took an interest in my study of Japanese and encouraged me to get a part-time job with Honda during the exchange year.

After that summer I arrived in Tokyo with a list of people Mr. Yoshida had suggested I call, and was hired as a weekend Welcome Lady at the Honda headquarters showroom. I worked with ten glamorous Welcome Ladies who maintained flawless manicures and taught me to humbly say "Please accept this stupid gift" as we distributed complimentary pens to potential customers.

During that year everyone called me Kiki. It was a

nickname that I made up for myself before going to Japan. My given name, Laura, would have been all right, but I rationalized that it would be good to have a name without the "L" sound that in Japanese sounds more like an "R," turning my name into "Rora." The truth is that I wanted a cute, attractive name. Laura sounded so boring, but Kiki sounded full of energy and fun.

The year at Waseda was a year of discovering new territory. I joined the university judo team and, with bruised shins and a broadened back, earned my brown belt. Seaweed-covered rice balls and hot canned coffee from vending machines became staples of my diet. When I finally learned to read train maps and station signs, the geography of Japan suddenly opened up into an inviting web of well-marked paths that took me all the way from the northern mountains of Hokkaido to the beaches of Okinawa. I found a Japanese boyfriend and some days spoke Japanese exclusively. Japan became my playground, a place where I was safe to fearlessly explore and reinvent myself.

After I returned to Ohio for my senior year, Mr. Yoshida hired me to work at Honda as an intern for a month. This time I had more to offer than lifeguarding skills and worked as his assistant, translating press releases and writing articles for the company newspaper. On the last day he offered me a job working at Tokyo headquarters, to start after graduation. It would be the first time an American woman would be sent to headquarters for a long-term assignment. I couldn't believe his offer, and accepted without even asking about the salary.

He explained that I would go to Tokyo for two years, after which I would return to the United States and continue working for him. The first year in Japan would be spent working in the executive office of Honda Motor Company as an assistant to one of the senior managing directors, Mr. Chino, who had just been promoted after seven years as president of American Honda in Los Angeles. Mr. Chino had requested a bilingual assistant because part of his new responsibilities included all of Honda's North American operations. My second year would be spent rotating through various departments at the headquarters—sales, public relations, and finance—to help me understand the organization and prepare me for work back in America.

From the beginning, Mr. Yoshida emphasized that I was joining the company, not just starting a job. After I had accepted his verbal offer, he sent me a half-page letter confirming my start date and salary. He wrote that Honda was pleased that I would be joining the company and that they hoped I would find my career with Honda both challenging and rewarding.

Mr. Yoshida set up an orientation schedule beginning a week after I graduated from college. He wanted me to be prepared when I arrived in Tokyo, so he decided that I should spend the summer studying the operations in America—starting with a month on the assembly line in the Ohio factory. After that I traveled to the offices in New York, Detroit, and Washington, D.C., and then spent six weeks in Los Angeles.

During the three-month training period I met with Mr. Yoshida regularly to talk about the company and its theories of business. He asked me to write daily reports about all the different departments I visited, not just to make sure I had learned something but because he was interested in my observations. He wanted to know my opinion about what I saw and how things worked. When we were in different cities I would fax him my reports and he would respond the next day, writing his comments in scrupulous English with the penmanship of a calligrapher. He treated me as the adult I aspired to be.

I knew very little about what it would be like once I arrived in Tokyo—the company, the job, and where I would live. Mr. Yoshida assured me that Honda would help me get settled. I sent a list of questions to the manager of the executive office, who replied with a vague, one-page letter saying that we would talk about things more after I arrived. The lack of information didn't bother me too much. What I didn't know I filled in for myself, relying on my memories of life as an exchange student and as a Welcome Lady—when strangers had asked to take my picture and invited me to their homes for dinner because I could speak Japanese.

Mr. Yoshida had been grooming me and I'd been grooming myself: I straightened and styled my unruly red hair and bought suits and matching high heels. A prim gold-plated watch replaced the leather thong and beaded bracelets I had worn around my wrist for the past four years. Two local newspapers interviewed me for front-page profiles, and my head filled with glamorous images of my job as the first American woman to work at Honda's headquarters.

Working at Honda was my dream job. Although I knew almost nothing about manufacturing, I did know Japanese. I knew that words would be my passport to understanding the company and Japan. What I didn't know then was the geography of this unexplored language—the phrases of assimilation, the words of compromise, the messages of rebellion and acceptance I had yet to learn.

Note: For this book I have relied on journals I kept while in Japan, letters I wrote home, and my memory. Some of the conversations recorded here are re-creations. Some names have been changed to protect the privacy of the individuals concerned.

Uniform

1 ON MY FIRST DAY OF WORK AT HONDA'S headquarters in Tokyo, I walked into the seventh-floor Administration Department and stared into a black-haired sea of Honda employees. The Japanese men were dressed in dark business suits, but the women wore blue polyester knee-length skirts and matching vests. I was shocked to see only women in uniforms. They looked like tall Girl Scouts, missing only merit badges and knee socks.

More than one hundred desks and at least as many people filled the wide-open office space, and considering the number of people it seemed suspiciously quiet. Two women approached me looking like paper cut-out dolls in blue uniforms, white blouses, and black, shoulder-length hair. Nothing about them seemed particular enough for me to grasp; if they were to turn back into the crowd of people I felt sure I would never find them again.

In polite Japanese one of the women asked me to follow her. We walked down a long, empty hallway. No one spoke. We stopped in front of a closed door and one of the women knocked timidly. Then she opened the door which led into a small, dingy storage room; brown cardboard boxes stood along the windowless walls. The women effortlessly slipped off their shoes before stepping up onto a low landing. I imitated their actions.

Without saying a word, the two women began digging around in the boxes; when I realized what they were looking for, a shiver ran up my spine. The boxes were full of uniforms. All I wanted to do was run away from the room; but I had to stand there pretending not to hear them discuss my waist size.

I was wearing a new cream-colored suit—a light wool, tunic-style Liz Claiborne design I had purchased just weeks before at Nordstrom with one of my first paychecks. A pretty beige briefcase was slung over my shoulder, a graduation present from Grandma Mozelle, and I wore matching beige pumps. I had tried to mold myself into the image of an international corporate woman—an image that did not include polyester.

I hadn't minded wearing a uniform when I worked on the assembly line in Ohio. Everyone there, including the president, wore the same white coveralls with a red name patch on the front. The only problem I'd had then was that the newness of the clean, stiff cotton betrayed me as a temporary college kid, so I'd had to make liberal use of black sealer paint to give myself a broken-in look.

There had been times in my life when I actually welcomed uniforms. In elementary school I idolized my neighbor Kiva Guss who was a Grandview High School cheerleader. Every Friday I watched her leave home wearing a smart blue and white pleated skirt and a sweater with our school's roaring bobcat emblem on the front. Wearing the uniform was part of my motivation to try out for the cheerleading squad when I got to high school. I wanted the uniform to set me apart from the other girls. I wanted it to tell everyone that I was part of an elite and talented group.

"Please, take it," said one of the women handing me a skirt as though it was the latest design from Issey Miyake. The material was thin and insubstantial. This uniform offered no expression of status—it sent an entirely different message. It said, "I'm just a woman; don't take me seriously and don't treat me with respect because I am as replaceable as this polyester."

I could see by the woman's expression that I was expected to wear the uniform; my resistance would not be understood. But I felt like I should put up some kind of fight. I wanted to formally register my displeasure before submitting. Shouldn't someone take note that I was consciously making a choice to fit in here? I wanted credit for compromise, but instead a got a perfunctory smile. I took the skirt behind the privacy curtain to change.

The skirt was simply cut and had a zipper in the back. As I got ready to step in, I noticed a small paper tag attached to the waistband. In Japanese characters it said "Ms. Tanaka." She must have been the employee who had previously wore this uniform. I wondered if she had retired from work to marry. Had she done her time and, like so many women, lived with her parents to save money for her big wedding day? I knew that she had not been promoted out of the uniform because all women, no matter what job they did or how long they had worked at Honda, wore the same uniform.

I did not want to follow in Ms. Tanaka's footsteps

even though I didn't know where they would go. I was twenty-two and new to this corporate world; but I felt certain that if she had started by stepping into this polyester straitjacket her footsteps would lead someplace that I didn't want to go.

I stepped out from behind the privacy curtain dressed in Ms. Tanaka's discarded uniform. My clones smiled pleasantly. "It looks fine," one said as the other nodded in agreement. They gave me two uniforms to take home along with an oatmeal-colored long-sleeved blouse which I noticed was not mandatory. They were both wearing short-sleeved, nonprescription blouses of their own.

When I got back to my hotel room I put on the entire uniform and laughed hopelessly at my hideous reflection. The exaggerated collar of the blouse touched my chin, and the holes of the vest constricted my arms. My image was nothing like I had anticipated. As if to capture this point of departure I used my self-timing camera and took a picture.

*　*　*

It had been the same month two years earlier when I had arrived under very different circumstances as a twenty-year-old exchange student to spend my junior year at Waseda University. On that first night in Tokyo, I had gone with a small group of students to explore local bars. We immediately discovered that if we spoke a few words of Japanese, red-faced, drunken businessmen would buy us beer. We went from bar to bar drinking free beer and practicing our textbook-inspired introductions. That night, I learned that in the eyes of many Japanese I was singularly intriguing because I did not have black hair but could utter Japanese syllables that made sense.

My particular group of exchange-student friends, like me, were continually searching for the quintessential Japanese experience. Unlike some of the other Americans, we were not interested in re-creating a Little Los Angeles or Little Ann Arbor on the Waseda campus. We were the kind of exchange students who immediately started drinking green tea and earnestly tried to eat everything—from spaghetti to yogurt—with chopsticks.

We found inherent value in participating in almost any activity that involved Japanese people who did not speak English—activities like camping with the 4-H Club or practicing grueling martial arts that we never would have considered doing in America. In our minds, going to Tokyo Disneyland with other exchange students ranked much lower than attending a traditional tea ceremony dressed in full kimono with one's host family. An adventure at a love hotel was in and of itself a valuable cultural experience, but going there with a new Japanese lover was considerably more interesting than going there with an old beau visiting from Missouri.

This authenticity-ranking applied to our choice of everything from extracurricular clubs to part-time jobs. When I got my job working as a weekend Welcome Lady in the Honda showroom I felt I had exceeded the authenticity quotient in every way.

In preparation for my job, Honda provided a two-day training course for me on how to be a Welcome Lady. I learned how to graciously accept business cards and how to delicately decline sexual advances without using the word "no." Above all, our job as Welcome Ladies was to smile and create a friendly atmosphere for the customers. The Welcome Plaza was a place for them to relax. The most expensive item a visitor could buy was a rum raisin ice cream cone at the California Fresh snack counter.

The eight Welcome Ladies were in their early twenties. They wore an outfit that reminded me of the television show *The Jetsons:* blue short-sleeved tops with pink piping that flared out at the waist, white skirts, and high-heeled white pumps. Manicures were a requirement, but no rings were allowed. All the women had the long, well-coifed hair that comes only from hour-long styling sessions. Their makeup and glossy pink lips were flawless and checked every hour. All day we smiled and greeted customers and handed out brochures. On special occasions, the Welcome Ladies stood on platforms next to sparkling new Honda products and used the soft, agreeable tones of formal Japanese to explain its features into a microphone.

I was treated as a guest by the women and sometimes even by the customers themselves. The Welcome Ladies included me in after-work drinking parties, took me on day-trips, and told me secrets about turbulent and clandestine love affairs. Young men in thousand-dollar leather riding gear and schoolgirls wearing sailor-suit uniforms asked to have their pictures taken with me and requested that I autograph their Honda brochures.

At six in the evening the thank-you-and-goodbye soundtrack played as we ushered all the visitors out the sliding glass doors, bowing and smiling sweetly as though it pained us to bring the eight-hour workday to a close. After the doors were locked and the bright lights dimmed, all the Welcome Ladies lined up in a row facing the showroom manager. With our hands clasped gracefully, we continued to smile as the manager made a few closing remarks. We listened politely, as though with great interest, then bowed to him in unison saying, "*Otsukaresama deshita*, You are the tired one."

The Welcome Ladies then retreated into the dressing room, where a shocking transformation took place. They shed the Joan Jetson costumes and put on expensive, funky black dresses. They concealed their pink lips in deep red tones and reapplied eye makeup several shades darker. Checking to make sure their cigarettes were pocketed, the women emerged from the Welcome Plaza purged of their girlishness.

I enjoyed watching this transformation, and I admired the women for it. Their new appearance was rebellious and in a way explained how they could generate eight continuous hours of sticky-sweet pinkness to strangers and then listen nightly to a patronizing speech from the manager on how we would have to try harder to be more friendly the next day.

During the year of weekends that I worked as a Welcome Lady, I never went beyond the first-floor Welcome Plaza of Honda's Headquarters. I knew there was a bank of elevators that transported people to the building above, but I had no idea what it would be like.

* * *

"This is an intelligent building," a young woman from the Personnel Department said as she handed me a schedule for the next six days. "We will begin your orientation with a tour of the headquarters," she explained.

I sat at a table in the center of the seventh-floor Administration Department across from this woman, who was dressed exactly like me in blue polyester. All around us was a buzz of activity: phones ringing, people moving around and in between aisles of desks and cabinets that gave some order to the huge open office space. I had hoped that wearing the uniform would have at least helped me blend in, but instead I felt curious eyes watching me and sensed people wondering, "Who's that redhead in the uniform?"

The orientation schedule was meticulously organized into daily and hourly columns according to the twenty-four hour clock. Lunch at 13:00, a lecture at 14:30, and the end of the workday at 17:30. Each event on the schedule included a room number and a list of participants' names.

Just as Mr. Yoshida had promised, the woman told me that the Personnel Department would help me get settled in Tokyo—set up a bank account, review company policy, and, most importantly, find a place to live. My understanding was that I would choose from two or three apartments found by the Personnel Department. I was familiar enough with the city to have an idea where I wanted to locate, but I had never looked for my own place so I was glad to have their help. As I was a foreign employee, the company would also pay my rent. I assumed there would be a ceiling on how much could be spent, so I asked the woman how much was allowed.

"Oh, you don't need to worry about the amount," she said. "We've already found a place for you to live."

"What?" I asked in English, hoping that I had misunderstood her.

"It's all settled. We'll go visit the apartment later this week," she said and pointed to the schedule. "See here. 'Visit apartment in Nerima.'"

I was stunned. Nerima was over an hour away from

headquarters by train, including several transfers. But more than the location, I couldn't believe that I didn't have any choice in the matter—especially with something as important as my home for the next two years. The woman explained that another foreign employee had recently been transferred to a facility outside Tokyo and that I would be taking over the recently vacated apartment. It was obvious from her explanation that the Personnel Department had taken care of absolutely everything.

*   *   *

Honda's intelligent building was like a self-reliant city. In addition to eight business floors, a cafeteria, and the Welcome Plaza on the first floor, the building housed a travel agency, a bank, and a dry-cleaning service. One floor had a health clinic including a pharmacy and dental office; there was an exercise room, a coffee shop, a VIP restaurant, a gift shop, and a formal Japanese tatami room.

What made the building intelligent was the internal computer system that operated like a network of nerves throughout the building. Communication between the intelligence network and the employees took place through a magnetically coded identification card. So that attendance and overtime could be monitored, every day employees ran their identification cards through an electronic sensor located on each floor. The network went up the center of the sixteen-story building like a spinal column. Other sensors throughout the building controlled air conditioning and lights. The cash registers in the coffee shop and cafeteria were also in the link, so all purchases were recorded on the identification card and then automatically deducted from the employee's monthly paycheck.

The woman from Personnel who explained all this to me was Ms. Uno. She was in her mid-twenties and spoke cautious English, carefully articulating each syllable. She didn't make the usual language mistakes like replacing the L sound with an R and calling me "Rora" or telling me it was time for "runch." Often, before speaking, she would pause, and her eyes would dart around the room as though she were searching for the correct words spelled out on the walls.

I learned that Ms. Uno had been hired right out of college as one of the first career-path female employees at Honda. Unlike most women who were hired as clerks, she was trained along with the male employees. She spoke fluent French and English and, compared with the other women I had seen on the seventh floor, had an unparalleled flair for wearing polyester with style.

Ms. Uno patiently guided me through my first days of work. She seemed confident and well organized. My admiration for her grew, and like a friendless camper I attached myself to this knowledgeable counselor. Our first days consisted of a series of meetings with managers in the company who taught me about the history of Honda and company policy. My Japanese wasn't good enough to understand the lectures, so Ms. Uno acted as a translator.

The first lecture was on the "History and Management Philosophy of Honda." A man in his fifties from the Training Department met us in a large conference room on the fifteenth floor. We gathered at one end of a long table, the speaker on one side, myself opposite him, and Ms. Uno in between but just out of the speaker's direct line of sight. From the moment the meeting started I saw a side of Ms. Uno that disturbed me.

"Wouldn't you like to sit here?" she asked the speaker, motioning to another chair that looked more comfortable. "Shall I order some coffee?" she asked him, waiting for his nod before placing the call. When we started the meeting, she sat somberly, as though banished from conversation, and quietly translated his words. She seemed to withdraw into herself, occupying the smallest space her body could possibly manage. When the lecturer stopped for a break she asked if she could clean his ashtray. Her comments were barely acknowledged with smoky nods. I couldn't understand why he was treating her this way. The scenario was repeated every time a new manager showed up for a lecture.

During one lecture I stopped the speaker to ask a question. Not only was I curious, but I thought that an informed question would show the speaker that I was interested in his subject. Later, Ms. Uno told me that I had been rude.

"When you ask a question you need to be more polite," she said. "Next time use this phrase first: *'Mōshiwake gozaimasen ga, chotto kikitai to omotte orimasu.'*" She recited this phrase again: "I'm terribly sorry to interrupt, but I was wondering if I could ask you something." It seemed as familiar to her lips as her own name. Over and over again I repeated her until I had mastered the unfamiliar sounds.

The apartment situation still concerned me. Even though I hadn't even seen it, I wanted to resist it. I wanted a choice. Corporate authority already determined how to speak, what to wear, and how to behave. When would my opinion count? I was perfectly willing to give up space in order to live closer to the city. As long as I could find a place within the budget I didn't think it was the company's business where I lived. I couldn't move into the Nerima apartment without at least voicing my dissatisfaction, so I had a talk with Ms. Uno and let her know that I was unhappy with the idea of living way out in Nerima. If this was the only choice, I told her I would look for an apartment on my own. She sucked in her breath and looked at me as though I had announced that I had decided to leave the country.

Ms. Uno looked distraught as I explained my feelings, but she agreed to ask her boss about it. She timidly approached a man sitting at a cluster of desks and bowed her head repeatedly as she spoke. The man hardly looked up from what he was doing. Ms. Uno's shoulders were hunched, her head was down and her hands were clasped. Again I felt disturbed by her subservience. The man barked a few words and Ms. Uno retreated, walking backwards. She sat down at the table and reported his response in English. "You will take the Nerima apartment," she said, shaking her head. "This is the rule." Suddenly I noticed that the armholes of my uniform seemed unbearably tight.

It seemed like every time I approached the Personnel Department I left feeling disappointed. One day I asked Ms. Uno how to order my business cards. I had purposely delayed having a card made while I was still in the U.S. because I wanted one with both English and Japanese. She deferred to her boss for an answer. Through her he told me that I wouldn't be needing a business card. None of the other women working in the executive office had business cards, so I wouldn't get one either. I protested and tried to argue that surely in the next two years I would be in situations where having a business card would be useful. "What if someone gives me a card and I don't have anything to give back?" I asked him. He handed me a few generic cards that said "Honda Motor Company, Ltd." with a blank line underneath where a name could be written. "Use these," he said.

In the evenings after orientation I returned to the President Hotel located just around the corner from headquarters. After a day of speaking in Japanese the hotel lobby offered the illusion of escape, where guests sat in European-style antique chairs reading the *International Herald Tribune* and a corps of bell boys dressed like a marching band called me "Madam."

The only illusion my room offered was that of being in a cell. The room seemed to be a complete unit, as though every piece had been perfectly engineered to fit into place. Although the bed was designed for one person no taller than five and a half feet, it took up two thirds of the room and touched three of the four walls. A small nightstand with a lamp touched the bed and was connected to a narrow desk which took up the fourth wall. On the desk was a mini entertainment center consisting of a compact twelve-inch television, along with a tea set and complimentary tea bag. Next to the desk, a small luggage rack loomed over a pair of beige plastic slippers.

In a small closet-sized room was the unit-bath. It was one continuous piece of putty-colored plastic with a drain in the center of the floor making it look like what you might find on an airplane if the bathrooms included a half-sized tub and shower. Like a one-man band with the drum, cymbals, and banjo all included, the unit was so compact that I could shower, brush my teeth, and flush the toilet all at the same time.

I couldn't do much in my room except lie on the bed and think. Usually I brewed my complimentary tea bag and worried about work. Besides the uniform and the way women were treated, the apartment situation troubled me. Taking the apartment represented total compliance. I felt the corporate walls forcing me into a mold as though I were trapped inside a Fisher-Price playhouse, in which each piece of furniture fit perfectly into its assigned space and had a single hole for a peg-shaped doll. I didn't want to be that doll, and the more threatened I felt, the more I wanted to resist.

I decided to call Mr. Yoshida and ask his advice. He didn't take sides but suggested that I present specific and convincing reasons to the Personnel Department as to why I wanted to live somewhere besides Nerima. He thought I should find an alternative apartment and gave me a general idea of what would be a reasonable rent. Because I was thinking about living near my parents' friends, he also thought I could make the argument that living there would be safer for me. Mr. Yoshida said he would call the Personnel Department the following week if I wanted him to, but I got the feeling that he thought I should try and work this one out on my own.

I called one of my mother's Japanese friends. She welcomed me to Japan and asked how everything was going. I told her that things were great and that I would soon be looking for an apartment in her neighborhood. She offered to help me look, and we made a date to meet.

When I hung up I was suddenly overwhelmed with

sadness and started to cry. I thought about calling a friend in America, but it seemed so far away and I wasn't even sure that I could explain my feelings. I didn't want to admit to anyone, especially to myself, that my dream job was not everything I thought it would be. I felt more alone than ever before. My head ached from crying, so I swallowed a packet of bitter Japanese aspirin powder, took a bath, and ate an entire chocolate bar.

The headquarters building stood on one corner of an intersection in Aoyama, a chic business district in Tokyo where wide streets house boutiques, cafes, and show-rooms. The Honda building was less than two years old and was the most modern-looking concrete high-rise on the block.

The front of the building protruded out toward the corner. Each of the sixteen floors had a window running round it that sat back from the smooth, gray stone sur-face of the building, making it look like a modern bunker. The entryway was clad in austere steel and glass. It was easy to miss the understated sign above the sliding glass doors that said HONDA.

On the corners across the street to the right and left of headquarters were similar tall concrete buildings. Kitty-corner from Honda was a conspicuous gap in the landscape. No building or construction existed—only a six-foot high, moss-covered stone wall. In this bustling commercial district, the empty corner stuck out like a gaping hole in a smile.

The stone wall circled an area bigger than the size of a hundred football fields. It belonged to the Imperial Family and housed an immense garden, a guest palace, and lots of wide-open space. Commoners were not per-mitted inside the walls and were even discouraged from viewing the grounds. When a thirty-two-story building across the street from the garden was built, a special agreement was made to prevent people from looking inside the wall. Not a single window exists on the entire north face of that building.

With help from my mother's friend, I found an apartment in her neighborhood that was within my budget and only a thirty-five-minute subway ride away from headquarters. I presented my case to the Personnel Department, emphasizing, as Mr. Yoshida had suggested, that I be allowed to live close to a family friend who would surely be helpful in case of an emergency. Ms. Uno's boss was unsympathetic but said he would consider my request. I went back to my hotel room that night feeling entirely at his mercy. There was nothing more I could do. I had decided that I wouldn't bring Mr. Yoshida into the battle; it was clear to me that this was the first of many to come.

When I got back to my hotel room I put on my favorite baggy pants, put my hair in a pony-tail, and walked around the neighborhood looking for ice cream. The cool, dainty scoops didn't seem like enough on the hot September evening, so I ate three.

The next day Ms. Uno told me that we wouldn't be going to visit the Nerima apartment because her boss had decided I didn't have to live there. Arrangements would be made to rent the apartment I had found.

My new apartment wasn't quite finished when I moved in one Saturday morning with two large suitcases. The apartment was on the first floor of my landlord's house. Like many homeowners in Tokyo who wanted to profit from high real estate prices, the family had recently renovated their lower floor into two small apartments.

The apartment had two rooms which were measured using the standard dimensions of a tatami mat. A single mat is about three feet by six feet, making it easy for me to fit my whole body into the space of a single mat. The front room had a blond hardwood floor and was measured as a six-mat room. The other room was four-and-a-half mats and had a tatami floor.

I sat in the tatami room enjoying the quiet and sunshine that filled the apartment. Sliding paper screens softened the light coming through the windows, and the brand-new mats smelled green and fresh. All morning, workmen and the landlord's children had been trekking in and out of the front door, which still didn't have a lock. It was lunchtime and everyone had taken a break, including me. The landlord's sister had brought me some food, which I laid out on top of a blue suitcase like a picnic: seaweed-covered rice balls, glazed doughnuts, and a can of iced coffee.

I looked around and admired the space—the hardwood floor was flawless and the kitchen gleamed. Next week I would pick out furniture from a leasing company. I would also be getting the equivalent of $2,000 from the company to buy dishes, appliances, and other start-up items. It seemed like so much money.

Just by moving to Japan I got a fifteen-percent raise and a per-diem allowance. I knew the raise was given to any employee who accepted a foreign assignment, but I didn't feel that I had done anything to earn it. The extra money was supposed to compensate for the sacrifice of living overseas, but I *wanted* to live here.

It wasn't as though Japan was a Third-World, hardship assignment where I couldn't drink the water or get medicine. In many ways Japan seemed more advanced than America. The streets were safe for a single woman at night. Subways and trains were clean and ran on time. The taxis were impeccable—drivers wore white gloves and covered their car seats with lace doilies. Even the bathrooms at headquarters were exceptional: every sink had a mouthwash fountain and many toilets were equipped with an electronic bidet. I liked the polite way salesclerks treated me even in places like the drugstore where I had gone to buy powdered aspirin. The clerk had said, "Please take care of your health." I felt my living standard had improved.

A man from the Administration Department accompanied me to the Tokyo Lease Company. I paged through several brochures, examining tables and refrigerators. It was hard to make choices because I didn't know exactly how much I was allowed to spend. The Honda man would not tell me what the limit was. He weaseled his way around my questions, holding his authority like the gavel of a parent who makes all final decisions. I didn't understand his attitude. He acted as though I couldn't be trusted to make my own choices.

While I was looking at a low Japanese tea table with two floor chairs without legs called *zaisu*, I heard the Honda man discussing my situation with the man from Tokyo Lease. Suddenly the two of them were deciding what items I should have. I couldn't believe it. Ignoring me, they made a list and even started to decide what color scheme would be best. My stomach tightened. Maybe they thought I didn't understand. Maybe they thought that I wanted their help, but they didn't even look at me, let alone ask for my opinion.

I wasn't sure how much authority I had. I felt my cheeks getting warm. "Excuse me," I said, interrupting them. "I think that maybe I would like to make some suggestions." The Honda man looked shocked, as though he wasn't used to having a woman tell him what she thought.

The first thing on their list was a bed. "I don't have room for a bed," I told them. "I'm going to sleep on a futon." They were both incredulous: an American sleeping on the floor? "It is much more practical for the space I have," I explained. The Honda man acted as though I needed his approval for every item. I finally persuaded him that I was going to buy a futon, but I had to agree to lease a sofa that opened into a mattress just in case. We haggled over the number of chairs and where to fit in a washing machine. I insisted on having a clothes dryer, which the Honda man felt wasn't necessary. He was crazy if he thought I was going to hang my laundry out to dry like a virtuous Japanese housewife who fervently believed there was some inherent value in clothing dried naturally by the sun. I felt like telling him to shut up. If I wanted to have an apartment without a single chair, or a dryer instead of a microwave, then it was up to me.

When I showed them the picture of the tea table they both laughed. "You want *zaisu?*" the Honda man asked, as though I had requested a water bed filled with goldfish. "It will fit perfectly in the tatami room," I told him. He acted as though without black hair and hundreds of years of Japanese ancestors, I couldn't really want to sit on a *zaisu* or sleep in a futon.

I exhausted my immediate cash supply after buying a few things for the apartment. My bank account wasn't set up for international transfers and I hadn't received the $2,000 set-up allowance yet, so I found myself with less than ¥5,000 (the equivalent of about $35 at the time) to last for two weeks before my first monthly paycheck. I had already purchased a train pass so I could get to work; I really only needed money for food. I asked Ms. Uno if it would be possible for me to get an advance on my next paycheck. She didn't know and said I should ask her boss directly.

"Be very polite when you ask him," she counseled. The thought of imitating Ms. Uno's obedient posture and subservient behavior made me feel ill, but he was the only one who could authorize my request. Ms. Uno helped me practice the solicitous words, *"Mōshiwake gozaimasen ga, chotto onegai ga arimasu keredomo . . ."*

When I saw her boss hunched over his desk I felt like abandoning my plan. The thought of surviving on $35 for the next two weeks seemed like a more appealing option. By going to him I felt as though I would be admitting my unworthiness as a responsible adult, that my request would prove I was incapable of making good decisions or budgeting money. Approaching him made me feel like a little girl asking for a nickel to buy some candy. I heard myself reciting the words and conforming to the role.

"I'm sorry to be such an inconvenience, but I've run out of money and I would like to make a request for a small advance on my next paycheck."

He thought about it for a moment, shook his head, and said, "That would be very difficult." It was the Japanese equivalent of saying no.

I felt like an idiot, but I didn't know what to do. My anger got confused with doubt, and I simply bowed and thanked him for his time. I had been selfish, I told myself. I couldn't depend on the company to always bail me out. His cursory indifference immediately erased my earlier feeling that I deserved some credit, and even a little respect, for getting this far on my own. Instead I started to feel like he had been treating me—like my voice didn't matter.

Later in the day, after I got over feeling foolish, I approached one of Ms. Uno's colleagues who was the most popular man in the department because he was so genuinely friendly. When I told him about my predicament he immediately checked the petty cash supply and graciously offered me ¥70,000 (about $490 at the time), asking if that was enough.

One evening I made a delightful discovery—a *sentō*, or public bath house, just blocks away from headquarters. The small building was stuck between small wooden homes. I was astonished to find an area still untouched by modernization located so close to some of Tokyo's highest-priced real estate. A blue-tiled porch and a small cloth banner hanging outside modestly announced the establishment as a bathhouse.

While an exchange student I had gone to a *sento* with a small group of American women—we all wanted to baptize ourselves into the Japanese world. We spent most of our visit laughing nervously at the man who took money and could see into the women's bath. At this *sento* a woman took my ¥500. I left my shoes outside in a wooden slot and put on a pair of pink plastic slippers. The changing area was only the size of a family room in an American home, and had a smooth wooden floor. There were several chairs in the center of the room, with well-worn, sunken cushions. On the walls were several wooden shelves with old wicker baskets for clothing. I took one of the baskets and stripped.

Through a sliding glass door I could see a few women

in the white-tiled bathing room. The steamy room echoed the sound of women's voices and the soft rush of running water. I walked into the bathing room carrying my towel cloth discreetly in front of myself. The warm moisture of the room embraced me.

I sat down on a blue plastic stool in front of a pair of spigots and grabbed a yellow bathing bucket. Cold and hot water gushed out of the spigots and filled the bucket in seconds. I poured bucket after bucket on my head, drenching myself and letting the water spray all over. Every splash was a release.

As I soaped my body and washed my hair at the spigot, I listened to the echoing chatter. Other than a few prepubescent girls with their mothers, the women were wrinkly and saggy. These women, I imagined, were probably regulars and had likely been coming to the *sento* since they were young, when the public bath was their only bath.

I felt soothed by the warmth of the room and comforted by the community of women. After I was all clean, I walked to the soaking pools in the back of the room. Three deep, tiled pools held water of varying temperatures: hot, extra hot, and super-extra hot.

I slid into the hot pool without stirring up the water and sat still until my body adjusted to the cooler water at the bottom of the tub. The heat swallowed me completely. Leaning my sweating head back against the wall, I felt my muscles release my bones. My head felt light and I let go of every worry: the frustration of being treated like a child, the language, the uniforms, Ms. Uno's boss. Everything was still, and I felt no impulse to rebel. For a moment I was at peace in my body.

I got out of the tub and went back to the cold water

spigot, filling the bucket with icy water. As I doused my steaming body my skin shrieked. My head tingled and every pore was in shock. I kept pouring the cold water until my skin felt numb. The coldness became heat, and I felt totally refreshed. When I got into the extra-hot soaking pool I didn't even feel the heat of the water. I repeated this cycle several times.

When I returned to the spigots for the last time I noticed a middle-aged woman with a young girl, maybe her daughter. They were talking while the young girl washed the woman's back. The woman smiled at me and said in Japanese, "You didn't get your back very clean, did you? You're supposed to bring a friend to wash it."

I smiled back and said, "Today I'm alone." She pulled her stool behind me and said, "Well, I'll wash it for you."

She soaped my washcloth and started to rub my neck. I bent my head down to my chest and held my arms folded together. Her strong movements made my shoulders shake. I let go of my arms and let my body feel everything.

"It's a good feeling, isn't it?" she said. "Oh, you'll certainly sleep well tonight."

I could feel the washcloth sliding up and down my back. Each vertebra of my spine felt like it had been loosened. The tension from my body was released, and I crouched over with my arms hanging to the floor. The woman filled a bucket and poured warm water over my shoulders. A rush went through my entire body. She poured again.

Office Ladies

2 Five high-pitched, cheerful voices rang out simultaneously, "*Hishoshitsu de gozaimasu.* Hello, this is the executive secretariat." Each secretary had a phone on her desk, and when the red light flickered and the bell rang, every available hand immediately reached for a receiver. They were like television game-show contestants racing to push the buzzer first.

At first I assumed that the secretaries were competing with one another; then I realized that no one kept track of who answered telephone calls. It was a group responsibility. The group made sure that the phone didn't ring more than once.

This new team was unlike any group I had ever experienced. For one thing, in matching uniforms, all ten of them looked alike. Each one was under five feet tall and weighed less than a hundred pounds. They had straight, shoulder-length dark hair and fair complexions; coral-colored lipstick painted their interminable smiles.

The executive secretaries looked like more studious

versions of the Welcome Ladies. They too were in their twenties and greeted me with smiles even though their polite introductions were interrupted by self-conscious giggling.

From the beginning they treated me with gentle uncertainty, as though at any moment I might explode into unintelligible, blithering English. Although I was one of the youngest, and clearly the most inexperienced, I felt as though my native language threatened them— that if I spoke in English they would feel obligated to converse with me. I made an effort to speak only Japanese.

The only English speaker in the group was a man who was the president's personal assistant.

"My name is Tsutomu Umeno, but you can call me Tom," he said with a cheeky grin when we met. The women tittered with approval. His voice was hearty and friendly. Tom looked to be in his early thirties and wore an elegant white suit coat, gold cuff links, and an expensive watch. When I commented on his English skills he told me he had spent a year at Stanford and later had worked in the Philippines.

Tom explained that he was the only male secretary in the group, but unlike the female secretaries, it was his job to attend the president wherever he went, whether it was the Tokyo Auto Show or a factory in Brazil. Tom acted as translator, public-relations man, and gofer.

He pulled out a Cross pen and drew an organizational chart of the "executive secretariat," as he called it, on a piece of notebook paper. There were eleven women, including me, and five men. In addition to the manager of the department, two of the men were responsible directly to the entire executive board of directors for special projects. The other man was the assistant manager, Mr. Higuchi, who I already knew was responsible for the daily activities of the secretariat.

Before coming to Japan I had been told by Mr. Yoshida that the executive office was a special group within Honda. It had its own floor in the headquarters, unlike any sales or administration department. Our group was directly responsible to the thirty-seven men who made up the Board of Directors of Honda Motor Company.

During the first weeks of work I tried to get to know my colleagues by joining them for lunch. The women usually split into small groups according to age. One of my first lunches was with the youngest group, women in their early twenties.

I placed my tray next to my colleague Ms. Kodama. Two other women from our office sat across the beige formica table in the company cafeteria. Several women from other departments wearing the same blue polyester uniforms were seated next to them with trays or box lunches from home. Over five hundred employees filled the room.

"Oh, you're having fish today?" Ms. Kodama exclaimed within hearing of everyone at the table. "Are you sure fish is all right?" she asked with a concerned smile.

I assured her I liked fish. Then she commented on my selection of rice and miso soup even though it was the same meal she had selected.

"Do you like bread or rice better?" she asked me, deliberately emphasizing each syllable.

"I like them both," I told her. I had been through this conversation many times as an exchange student with people who had never met or conversed with a non-Japanese person. As a student I had felt obligated to answer the questions I knew would come next. Did I eat bread or rice for breakfast? Did I eat with chopsticks or a fork? What Japanese foods did I hate? I knew the routine so well that I could answer without having to pause to think. I wanted to remind Ms. Kodama that I had lived in Japan for a year, but instead I kept quiet and tried to enjoy my meal like the rest of the group. I cracked open my wooden chopsticks and began to eat.

"Oh, Rora-san, you use chopsticks so well!" she praised me. Then she wished me good luck in eating the fish. Ms. Kodama reminded me of my host mother as an exchange student who would reward even my smallest effort with exaggerated praise. When I had finally learned enough Japanese to write her notes she would return them to me, corrected with red check marks and smiley faces. The continual approval made me feel like a dim child.

Another day two senior members, Ms. Ogiwara and Ms. Shoji, invited me to go out to lunch. They were older than most of the secretaries and were in their late twenties. In the office both of them showed a level of self-confidence and maturity that I would later recognize as common to Japanese women who remained single beyond the traditional marriage deadline of twenty-five. They were both good-humored but decidedly un-silly, another characteristic I found appealing.

They took me to a small noodle shop called Ezokko across the street from headquarters. As at many restaurants in Japan, the main dishes were displayed as plastic replicas in a glass case, so making a selection was simple. Both Ms. Ogiwara and Ms. Shoji immediately put me at ease by not trying to help me order a meal, and just asked me what I was going to have. We ordered, paid at the door, and then edged inside to find three seats together. Small wooden tables packed the narrow shop. Waiters in white aprons yelled orders across the customers' heads to the cooks wearing white hats behind a long counter.

Everything about Ms. Ogiwara seemed small except her personality. "You can call me Ogi," she had said when we first met. A wide, cherubic grin lit up her heart-shaped face when she laughed; she giggled heartily, sometimes using her hand to cover her mouth. But when she couldn't contain her amusement her whole body would react; she would bend over at the waist and swing her thick mane of hair.

Ms. Shoji had a more formal presence. Neat bangs and straight hair sharply framed her strong triangular face. When she smiled she exposed what the Japanese called yaeba, a single cuspid tooth that jutted out slightly in the opposite direction of her other teeth. The minor irregularity was considered appealing, like a beauty mark, and not something to be corrected by the orthodontist. Ms. Shoji was poised and dependable, the kind of person who had probably been a straight-A student since first grade.

Three steaming bowls of noodles arrived at our table.

"One corn ramen, one *gyōza* ramen, and one pork ramen," the waiter said, placing the jumbo-sized bowls in front of us. The lip of the bowl was the size of my whole face.

"Would you like some garlic?" Ms. Shoji asked, lifting the lid of a small ceramic dish. The aroma of freshly minced garlic made my mouth water and I added a heaping spoonful to my broth. With garlicky steam covering our faces we dug into the noodles, slurping loudly to let the air cool the hot broth as we ate.

Neither Ms. Ogi nor Ms. Shoji commented on my skill with chopsticks or marveled at my noodle-slurping ability. We talked about work and the directors. I told them that I felt my Japanese was improving already and that I had recently been dreaming about work in Japanese.

"Sometimes I dream about work too," said Ms. Ogi. "That's when I know I am working too hard!"

Ms. Shoji nodded in agreement. "When one of my directors shows up in my dream and then I see him the next day at work I want to say, 'Hey you—I have to see you all day long so stay out of my dreams!'"

We continued to talk about work, which led to something I had been wanting to ask.

"What did you hear about me before I arrived?"

"Mr. Higuchi told us that a young American woman would come to work with us. He didn't give us many details, but everyone was very curious," Ms. Shoji said.

"Since we had never worked with someone from America we were all a little nervous," admitted Ms. Ogi. "Mr. Higuchi said you could speak Japanese but we didn't know how much. Since we don't speak English well we were concerned that we wouldn't be able to communicate."

"Also, some people thought that maybe you would be a big, pushy American career woman who would take over!" Ms. Shoji said and laughed.

"When we saw you for the first time and you smiled and greeted us in Japanese, we thought 'She's so nice, just like an American OL,'" Ms. Ogi said.

"An OL?" I asked.

"An office lady."

I remembered the term from college. Office Lady was the Japanese version of a Kelly Girl—young and semi-educated, lacking specific skills. OLs usually joined a company after graduating from high school, and worked for three to five years before retiring to get married and have children.

For many women in Japan, this stage of life was the high point of financial freedom. Since most women live at home until marriage they have few expenses. Most of an OL's income is saved for her wedding day, but a regular portion is used for her own enjoyment—expensive restaurants, stylish clothing, and overseas trips.

I looked across the table at Ms. Ogi and Ms. Shoji and noticed their designer leather wallets sitting on the table. They fit the OL description, as did the others in our group—they were all unmarried, most of them lived at home, and they had disposable income to buy nice things like expensive jewelry and designer handbags.

I had imagined myself as something very different. I carried a backpack, my wallet was made of nylon and velcro, and I had no plans for early retirement. Even though before coming to Japan I'd had very little idea of what kind of work I would be doing, I expected to be more than an OL. But since I had never been hired for a full-time job before, I hadn't questioned it when Mr. Yoshida was vague about my job.

Asking too many specific questions had seemed unnecessary and even petty. I wanted to act like a professional. I had high expectations of myself, and I thought Mr. Yoshida did too. Why else would he have sent me to work on the assembly line in Ohio for a month and on a two-month tour of the North American offices with a company car and an expense account?

Only a few months earlier I had been asked by the dean of my college to give the commencement speech at graduation. In her introduction to my speech, the dean had proudly told my peers that I had been hired by Honda to study various methods of production in Japan. I'm sure no one in the audience that day, including myself, pictured me with a group of office ladies who wore polyester uniforms and served tea to Japanese executives.

The OLs' workday began and ended in the same place—the pantry. It was hidden behind a one-way window that looked out onto the tenth floor. It was a place for women only—a place to drink coffee, reapply lipstick, and look at fashion magazines. In the mornings the pantry had a relaxed atmosphere, but once work started, the pantry functioned like a factory, with workers assembling tea cups and saucers, washing utensils, and generating refreshments.

The rectangular pantry was the size of a suburban American kitchen, with cabinets above and below a counter that circled the room. On one side of the room there were two sinks and two smooth-top stoves. The opposite counter held coffee makers, thermoses, shelves for wooden saucers, and a heating appliance for hand towels. In the corner was a full-sized refrigerator, something I had never seen in a Japanese kitchen. The cabinets were filled with cups and pots for Japanese and English tea. There were stockpiles of tea and coffee, and cans of low-calorie Coke Light and Florida orange juice. In the center of the room was a narrow table with two stools.

In the morning the women arrived on the tenth floor already dressed in their uniforms. Carrying petite designer purses, they would walk into the pantry and chime, "Good morning." Greetings and gentle nods were passed around the room like neighborly handshakes at church.

Even though work didn't officially begin until 8:40 A.M., the women immediately started to organize the pantry. They filled large thermoses with mugicha, barley tea, that would be used throughout the day. Others put away dishes and got cleaning rags ready in a bucket.

Through the darkened one-way window I could see our work area, the *hishoshitsu*, which literally means "room of secrets." "Executive secretariat" was Tom's translation. He told me he thought it sounded more impressive than "secretarial office."

Our work space was set behind a beige reception counter. Desks were clustered in groups of four to six desks, pushed together to form *shima*, or islands. The desktops were completely clear, with the exception of a phone on each desk. There was a rule at Honda that everyone had to clean off his or her desk before going home every night, so all desk supplies and paperwork were stored away in cabinets and on chair seats.

I watched the secretaries retrieve their supplies from hiding places. Each woman had some type of pastel-colored box filled with pencils, glue, heart-shaped note paper, scissors, erasers shaped like animal crackers, and sometimes a pen that had lemon-scented ink or an automatic pencil with a pink charm dangling from the end. Each island shared common supplies, usually in a cigar box covered with stickers. There were no personal items:

no family pictures, no mugs or flower vases. The desks were devoid of character; if a secretary wasn't sitting at her desk I couldn't identify whose it was.

For ten or twenty minutes the chores in the office were attended to. The women used white cleaning rags to wipe the desktops and clean the receivers of each of the two dozen telephones. They sharpened pencils from the desks in the executive office and made sure that all the cabinets were unlocked. After each OL had organized her desk and taken care of her chores, she would return to the pantry for a communal cup of coffee or tea. Because there were more than two people, the two stools would remain unused. Instead, everyone stood or squatted next to the table while they talked until 8:35, when the jingly morning exercise music started playing over the public-address system.

"All right, everybody, let's begin by swinging our arms over our head," instructed the peppy recording in Japanese. The secretaries ignored the directions but hurriedly emptied their cups and washed them. "Touch your toes, one, two, three, four!" The women scurried from the pantry to the executive office and back to their desks, aware only of the minutes remaining until the music stopped.

By this time the *buchō*, or manager, would be sitting at his island in a cloud of his own smoke. The other men usually arrived later in the morning because of late-night responsibilities to the executives. Tom and the other men took turns staying late until all the directors had gone home. Because some of the directors had responsibilities in countries halfway around the world in different time zones, it wasn't unusual for at least one of them to stay at the office until after midnight.

At 8:40 A.M., when the official work bell sounded, all eleven secretaries were obediently sitting in their assigned seats, hair freshly combed, vests buttoned up, and smiles caffeinated for the day.

"*Ohayō gozaimasu,*" said the *buchō.*

"*Ohayō gozaimasu,*" a chorus of sopranos replied.

The morning meeting began with a recitation of each executive's schedule. The chairman's secretary, Ms. Mori, started. "Today the chairman will have a meeting with the Belgian ambassador at 2:00 P.M. At 4:00 P.M. he has an appointment with the accounting manager. This evening he has a dinner meeting with the president at the Advisor's Building." Down the line, each secretary read her schedules aloud so everyone would be aware of the day's events. The *buchō* often made administrative announcements and then concluded the meeting.

The directors started arriving after 9:30. One by one they filed off the elevator and passed the reception desk to get to the executive office. They were quiet, slight figures in dark suits. Sometimes they acted as though they didn't want to be noticed, but that was impossible. As soon as one was spotted by a secretary she would ring out a greeting in a loud, cheerful voice to alert all the secretaries. The others, from whatever position they were in, conversation or work, would immediately follow her greeting with an even louder, more cheerful "*Ohayō gozaimasu!*" The executive would keep walking, maybe nod his head and utter a barely audible "*Ohayō.*"

For a week I observed my fellow OLs at work, rushing to answer the phone and patiently analyzing the piles of mail that were delivered six times a day. They served tea and cleaned ashtrays, they washed cups and then started all over again.

I had not been asked to serve tea, but I knew there was no way to avoid it. Every morning I watched as Ms. Ogi prepared to meet with each of her directors and review his schedule for the day. She balanced a jade-colored tea cup on a red lacquer tray in one hand and held the schedule book in the other. All the secretaries repeated this routine for each executive. Tea was served mid-morning to whoever was at his desk, and again in the afternoon. If an executive had a meeting or returned from an outside event, tea welcomed him back.

I already knew that green tea in Japan was more than a beverage. It was a hobby, a culture, a way of life. My host mother, like many Japanese women, had practiced the art of tea ceremony. Every week, for years, she went to class and rehearsed the delicate, meditative move-ments of tea preparation.

Once, my host mother had invited me to accompany her to a formal tea ceremony. She spent two hours wrap-ping me up in a three-layered kimono. Magnificent pur-ple and red flowers embroidered the outer garment. I also wore *tabi*, white cotton socks, geta, wooden clogs, and an elaborately tied obi around my waist so I could move only in short, shuffling steps. My host mother had to show me how to walk with my toes pointed in, heels apart. The obi prevented me from leaning back. All I could do was sit with my back straight. I felt like an exquisitely packaged Japanese doll that couldn't play; I could only watch.

But even knowing the historical and cultural impor-tance of tea, I felt about serving it like I did about the uniforms. Why was it restricted only to women?

In high school I'd had a teacher who would routinely ask only the girls in the class to fetch him a daily cup of water. Some girls felt honored by his attention. I felt sickened. On one occasion he asked me and a friend of mine to get his drink. We went to the drinking fountain, spit in his cup, filled it with water, and then served him.

*   *   *

The executive office was adjacent to our office. From the double doorway I could see the entire room, which was about the size of two tennis courts. A long row of windows spanned one wall. There were no walls or room dividers interrupting the open space because all thirty-seven directors of Honda Motor Company shared one office.

The chairman, president, vice presidents, and senior managing directors, a total of eight men, sat in a row furthest from the entrance with their desks facing the window, the most prestigious location. Their plain wooden desks had no distinguishing features. Each one had a beige telephone and a flimsy corporate phone directory hanging on a yellow plastic adhesive hook. The desks were so close together that it would be easy to pass things back and forth without even standing up. The only difference I noticed was that the chairman's and president's desk-chairs had high backs.

Anyone below the level of senior managing director had to share space at one of three oblong tables in the front of the room where each director had an assigned seat. Their names had been taped to their places at the table so the secretaries wouldn't get confused. Each director kept his work in one of the wooden cabinets that surrounded the perimeter of the room, but lower-level directors had to share.

On the otherwise anonymous tenth floor, there was

one highly privileged space—the Mr. Honda Room. It was a utility closet-sized room located off the executive office. The room was reserved for Mr. Honda's visits. Paintings and photos of him drinking beer with other retired executives decorated the sparse walls. Even though the founder had retired, he maintained an almost sacred status within the company.

In the lectures about Honda I had learned that its founder, Soichiro Honda, was one of the few living legends in postwar Japanese history. At the age of 81 he was still the flamboyant maverick who had created Honda Motor Company in 1948, contrary to the wishes of the Japanese government, with little more than war-surplus engines.

Born in 1906, Soichiro Honda grew up with a fascination for mechanical things. In his youth he had worked as an apprentice in an automobile repair shop and later established his own piston ring manufacturing company. He had little formal education, but a great passion for learning. After World War II he met Takeo Fujisawa, a businessman looking for a promising investment opportunity, and together they built Honda Motor Company into a twentieth-century industrial player in the international motorcycle, power equipment, and automobile market. In 1973 both Soichiro Honda and Takeo Fujisawa retired and were named Supreme Advisors to the company.

Sometimes during the morning rush I would go into the executive office pretending to check something because I wanted to see what it was like. I watched the secretaries interacting with the executives, noting that their body language often conveyed what kind of relationship they shared. Some directors barely paid attention to secretaries and just barked orders. Others treated the secretaries almost as equals. No matter how casual or serious the interaction, I noticed a particular similarity in the way all the women treated the men—as though they were mother and son.

In the pantry after work the women would complain or worry out loud about a director, and the others would console her. "He's so impatient. He's always making his own appointments and then doesn't tell me. And why doesn't he ever call when he's out of the office?" they would say. The secretaries knew the directors' schedules as intimately as the feeding schedule of a baby. They knew if a director was taking medication, and worried if he didn't eat his lunch or if he seemed tired.

When a director went on a business trip in Japan or overseas, he usually brought back some kind of gift— cookies, rice crackers, or candy—for all the secretaries to share. Boxes of treats filled the table in the pantry, and our tea breaks included anything from traditional sea- weed-wrapped rice crackers to Godiva chocolates wrapped in gold foil. Later I learned about the private gifts that certain directors brought back—scarves, leather wallets, and perfume. Although the gifts were not entirely a secret, no one wanted to flaunt special atten- tion.

After three weeks of general observation, the office manager Mr. Higuchi called me into the executive con- ference room to talk about my assignment. He handed me a one-page document in Japanese with my name written in Roman letters at the top.

"I've made up a list of your job responsibilities," he said.

It was the first job description I had seen since accepting the job. He had divided the tasks into four categories. First, I would be Mr. Chino's secretary, starting out as an assistant secretary and moving up to a main secretary. Second, I would be in charge of all English-language correspondence. Third, I would work as a receptionist as I learned other skills, and fourth, I would provide English language advice to all the directors.

"I want you to focus on the job of receptionist and take care of the English correspondence," Mr. Higuchi advised. "Then later, when you are ready, we will start training you for the secretarial job." He didn't mention anything about when that would start.

I remembered that I had been so excited about joining Honda that I had accepted the original job offer in Ohio without even knowing the salary. But the prospect of working as a receptionist with the hope of becoming a main secretary did not sound promising. There was no mention of what the secretarial job actually entailed, but I had observed enough to know that it didn't mean delving into special project research or attending meetings with executives. I felt as though Mr. Higuchi wanted me to prove my ability at monitoring the front desk so that maybe one day I could serve tea too.

I had to admit that even receptionist skills were challenging because they were all in Japanese. I couldn't even answer the phone properly. But I was disenchanted with the thought that these tasks made up the core of my job. Was this why I had been sent to Japan in the first place? At least Mr. Higuchi's written list inspired in me a sense of purpose, but the overarching goal of becoming a good tea-serving secretary was discouraging.

His list also included five goals to keep in mind

throughout the training. One, learn the operations of the executive secretariat; two, learn Japanese; three, learn the way Honda operates in Japan; four, study the approach to public relations; and five, study Honda's philosophy. These basic ideas appealed to my hopes for a higher purpose, and I embraced the Zen-like quality of his direction. It gave me hope that some day I would be given more sophisticated assignments. I desperately wanted to believe that I had a significant role, that I was good for something more than monitoring attendance.

Immeasurable as the goals were, I earnestly went about pursuing them. I started to keep daily lists of all the new Japanese words I learned and asked my colleagues to explain unfamiliar phrases. Every few days I sent Mr. Yoshida a fax describing my duties and reporting on events. He responded promptly, which gave me a feeling of importance that I didn't get from doing the tasks themselves.

I threw myself into organizing all the English mail. Part of the job was to filter junk mail from legitimate mail, but I had to do more than just filter it. If an envelope was addressed to a specific director, his secretary felt personally responsible for it even if it was a computer-generated invitation to buy millions of dollars of personal life insurance from a guy named Buddy. As a result, I first had to weed out the junk and then I had to persuade each secretary to throw it away.

One of the first letters I read was from an American woman. She wrote to the president of the company warning him of a plot to use gamma rays in conjunction with Sputnik to destroy the Japanese. The letter went on for twelve pages detailing, among other things, what pop astrologer Jeanne Dixon had predicted for the year.

I usually knew a letter would be interesting when I saw that it was simply addressed to: Mr. Honda, Main Post Office, Tokyo, Japan. One letter came written on rumpled paper in elementary-school script. It was from an American man saying that he had written Honda about an engineering idea. He had since moved, but had heard from a friend in his old neighborhood that a Japanese-looking person had been in the area. The man figured that it was Mr. Honda looking for him and so he wanted us to have his new address.

Another amusing letter came from a young Californian woman who sent a set of holistic, psychedelic love poems to the president. She wrote of her special mission to serve him in *any* way possible and kindly included nude photos of herself posed next to a waterfall. Although the president and other executives might have been entertained by these scandalous letters, they never even heard about them because it was my job to throw them away.

Some of the English correspondence demanded serious attention. Mixed in with the junk and freak mail were letters from international government agencies and legitimate customer comments. During the first week I came across a letter that had been set aside by one of the secretaries because she didn't understand it. The letter came from a United States federal agency inviting Honda's president to a meeting in America with other guests including the President of the United States. By the time I got to the letter, however, the event had already passed.

Although I had successfully avoided having to serve tea, I received special tea-brewing training from the president's secretary, Ms. Onoguchi.

"You make sure the teapot is completely dry," she

said, giving the inside of the pot an extra wipe with a towel. "Then sprinkle in the tea leaves so that they cover the bottom of the pot." I watched as she visually measured the dry flakes, which had a fresh, earthy aroma.

"Then, pour in the hot water and let it steep. If you don't let it steep long enough the tea will be too weak, kind of a light yellow color. If you let it steep too long it will be too dark and bitter." While the tea brewed, she selected a cup from the cupboard.

"This is a special tea cup with a lid," she explained. "Usually only the president uses this cup. It keeps the tea extra hot." The cup had no handles and sat on a wooden saucer.

"The special secret for delicious tea," she said, taking the cup in her palm, "is to heat the cup before the tea is poured in." She poured plain hot water into the cup, swished it around for a moment, and dumped it out into the sink.

"When the tea is ready, you pour it into the warm cup and place the lid on top. That's all there is to it." She poured the clear yellowish liquid. It smelled sharper than the caramel-colored Lipton tea I drank with milk.

Ms. Onoguchi, like the other women, had been making and serving tea for years, and every time she prepared a new cup for the president she followed the same, detailed procedure.

As the weeks passed, sounds in the office began to make sense. I got great satisfaction from figuring out Japanese words, recognizing faces, and practicing how to write everyone's name. Even the daily routine gave me comfort.

At home I had started to develop my own routine. I broke in the new leased furniture, spread brightly colored cushions on the floor, and tacked family photos to my tiny refrigerator. The housing allowance helped me acquire appliances, but I needed a Japanese-English dictionary to learn how to use them.

Every night I wrote down questions about the appliances and consulted my colleagues in the pantry the next morning. I figured out how to record a message on the answering machine, but I didn't know how to retrieve one. My new rice cooker had only one switch, but the rice still turned out hard. I even drew a diagram of the washing machine settings so my colleagues could teach me which one was the delicate cycle.

The most challenging appliance was the one I had bought on a whim, an electric bread maker. After struggling to read the directions, translating the recipe and converting metric measuring units in order to use my American measuring tools, the first few tries were disastrous. Instead of bread, the maker produced hard, mealy clumps of dough. I took my problem to the pantry for consultation. I learned where to find yeast in the supermarket, and Ms. Ogi bought me a measuring cup that correctly converted everything to metric.

One Monday night I decided that I finally understood how to do it. I carefully measured the flour directly into the machine and sprinkled the dry yeast in a little pool of milk and melted butter. The entire cooking process would take four hours. My goal was to wake up to a fresh loaf of warm bread, so I set the timer to start at 2:00 A.M. I was almost afraid to go to sleep, worried that maybe I had miscalculated the amount of yeast or programmed the timer incorrectly. When I went into the tatami room to sleep, I closed the sliding door that separated the two rooms wondering what I would find the next day.

I woke up at 5:30 A.M. on Tuesday feeling the excite-ment of a Christmas morning. Cautiously, I slid open the door as though expecting the entire living room to be filled with an enormous loaf of bread. Instead, the room was filled with a sweet aroma. I ran over to the bread maker and popped open the lid. Inside was a benign, square loaf with a toasty brown crust waiting patiently in its warm home. I was so excited that I ate a piece right away and went back to bed.

I took the loaf to work. By then the crust had sunk a little, but the secretaries praised my efforts. After my ini-tial excitement, I decided that it tasted like homemade bread made by a robot. There were two odd holes in the square loaf, one in the base and one on the side, where the cooking devices had been lodged. But we ate the goofy-looking mass anyway and talked about how to cure hiccups.

Ms. Ogi spent time explaining some of the general secretarial duties. We went into the pantry where the women made tea and took breaks. On the wall were var-ious schedules and lists written in some kind of code. Ms. Ogi pointed to one of the papers. "This is the morning chore list. Every morning two people arrive before work to do these jobs. We rotate each week so we only have to do it about once a month."

She explained that "A" chores included unlocking doors, turning on the computers and video monitors, checking the meeting rooms, and making sure that the cologne bottle in the men's bathroom was full. The "B" job was to file the eight daily papers into the newspaper rack.

"Each person in the office has a single letter code name that we use to simplify the lists. My code is the letter M because my first name is Mieko." She showed me all the code names, most of them Roman letters, each encased in a small circle. "This one is Ms. Shoji's name," she said, pointing to the letter Y with a circle around it. "The Y is from her first name Yumi." Another list showed the codes for all thirty-seven directors. Ms. Ogi explained that the secretaries used the codes for all interoffice memos because writing the full names took too long.

"Of course, you need to have a code name too," Ms. Ogi said. I wondered if I should tell her I already had a code name in Japanese—Kiki. But this was the professional world, and Kiki sounded silly to me. The uniform alone took away much of the professional image I had hoped to present. I was already resigned to being called Rora, so I agreed when Ms. Ogi suggested using the phonetic symbol for "RO," which was one of the easiest in the language, a simple square. In Japanese kanji characters the square symbolized mouth. She pulled out a scrap of paper and handed me a pencil. I drew a small square and circled it.

"That's it," Ms. Ogi said. "I'll make a memo and pass it around the office to tell everyone that you are □." I was in the club.

I decided to host a Halloween party for the group, thinking that it would help me get to know more about my colleagues than just their names. When I passed out invitations everyone immediately accepted. My dilemma of what to cook was solved by El Paso taco supplies from the international grocery store, which were twice the price of the same thing in America, but worth it because I wanted to prepare something unusual. I used every dish and plate and maneuvered my few furniture items to make sitting room for eleven on the floor.

All the secretaries, except for Ms. Mori, arrived together on a Friday after work. I was shocked to see how sophisticated the women looked wearing dresses and skirts—an improvement over the juvenile uniforms. Everyone brought a mask or hat as a costume, except for Ms. Shoji who was in full costume with a frilly white maid's apron and hat. Ms. Ogi wore a cone-shaped orange paper hat and a gold mask.

Everyone was curious about my apartment, especially since most of them lived with their parents. Even though the space was so small that a full tour could be given by standing in one place, it was roomy by Tokyo standards. The kitchen area was against the wall of the entryway, but space was so limited that the mini refrigerator was in the living room right next to the television. As in most Japanese homes, the toilet was located in its own closet-sized space, and the shower and *ofuro* bathtub were next to it in a small, tiled room.

Someone made the suggestion of removing the sliding door that separated the two main rooms. Sitting on cushions around two low tables, we drank wine out of paper cups and tried to eat tacos with chopsticks. We took turns trying on each other's masks and hats. I passed around a pair of glasses with an enormous nose and bushy eyebrows and mustache attached. My prim colleagues were transformed into something that resembled Groucho Marx in Japanese drag.

We talked about Halloween in Japan. Although everyone had heard of it, they didn't really understand its significance. I explained the custom of dressing up and trick-or-treating; it was a practice completely foreign to

Japan. Halloween had been imported via Hallmark in the recent past and was aggressively marketed with jack-o-lanterns and skeleton costumes hanging in shop windows.

After about an hour, Ms. Mori showed up.

"I'm sorry; I had to work late," she said with contrived fatigue. Everyone rushed to greet her and offer pity, but something bothered me about her. I had noticed something different about her compared to the other women, but I couldn't name it. It seemed rather cynical of me, but I sensed that she had created the overtime excuse as a way to get attention.

As part of the trick-or-treat theme each woman brought a treat to share. We settled in the tatami room with tea and a table full of desserts—an Oreo cookie pie, gourmet chocolates, sweet potato cakes, and rice crackers. I lit candles and put on some James Taylor music. Our festive mood mellowed, and soon we were talking about men and who we thought was good-looking at the headquarters building.

"Rora-san, who do you think is handsome?" Ms. Ogi asked me.

"I haven't seen too many men under fifty years old," I joked.

"You're right. The only men we get to meet on the tenth floor are the senior citizens in the company who come to see the executives," Ms. Shoji replied.

"That's why we're all still single," Ms. Ogi added, and everyone laughed.

Someone suggested the name of a man in the Overseas Service Department and everyone agreed he was handsome.

"*And* he's not married," another woman offered, and

they all giggled. I got the impression that they didn't often talk about things like this with one another.

Questions about boyfriends were bounced around the circle. No one had a boyfriend, or admitted to having one. The atmosphere was so warm and intimate I almost wanted to make up some romantic long-distance love affair to share.

Finally the question came around to one of the senior members, Sashi. She was in her late twenties and as petite as a twelve-year-old girl. Even in high heels she wasn't five feet tall.

"Hmm, well . . . ," Sashi said to the group. Everyone became very quiet. "To tell you the truth, I do have a boyfriend." Squeals of discovery and delight exploded from the group. "Really? Who is it? Does he work at Honda?" The questions poured forth and Sashi put her head down, covering her face with both hands in embarrassment. "Come on, tell us! How serious is it?" The enthusiasm was palpable. I sensed that her confession was unplanned.

"Well," she continued, as if in pain, "actually, we've recently decided to get married." The room again exploded with mirthful glee, and I thought Sashi would jump out the window to escape. "Tell us how you met him. Who is he?" the group demanded.

"Well, we met picking strawberries."

"How romantic. How sweet!" chorused her envious colleagues.

"It was a company event last year. He works in Research and Development. His name is Nakata." A few women nodded in recognition.

I noticed that she wasn't wearing an engagement ring and asked if she had one.

"Oh, yes, I have one, but I'm much too embarrassed to wear it," she told me. "What would the directors say?"

It was after eleven when I saw Ms. Ogi reach for Ms. Shoji's maid hat. She put it on her head and started to gather dishes. Without a word, the other women stood up and began cleaning. An assembly line formed in the kitchen to wash, dry, and put away the dishes. Others wiped tables, shook out floor pillows, and put the left-over food in plastic containers. I moved around answering polite questions. "Rora-san, where do you put the bowls? Do you have any empty grocery bags?"

Two women replaced the sliding doors; another found the vacuum cleaner and swept the tatami floor just like my host mother used to do each night before rolling out the futon sleeping mats. I looked at the small entry-way that had been filled with a pile of shoes and saw that all eleven pairs had been reorganized in pairs and reversed so that the toes pointed toward the door. Three white bags of garbage were lined up neatly against the washing machine, tied with exacting knots, waiting to be taken out on trash day. My apartment looked better than before the women had arrived. Even outside the tenth floor the group proved they worked well as a team, but it was odd to me that they seemed to know little about each other's lives.

* * *

The Halloween party helped me understand more about the organizing principle of our office—hierarchy. It was evident in the way people treated the symbolic leader of the secretaries, Ms. Mori. At the age of 29, she had worked for Honda for eight years and had the most seniority in the secretariat. She was as thin as a bird. Her shiny black hair hung straight to her shoulders and feathered bangs crowned her forehead. With traditional Japanese beauty traits—almond-shaped eyes and a smallish mouth—she was considered one of the most beautiful women at headquarters. Like all the other secretaries, Ms. Mori was single, but unlike the others, she lived alone.

Sitting at the reception desk with my back to the group, I could hear Ms. Mori's shrill voice above all the others. When she called to the other secretaries for information it came across as a demand rather than a request. Her use of polite language sounded sarcastic. She didn't speak rudely or make directly condescending remarks; rather, her disdainful tone seemed to say, "I have the most seniority here and everyone will acknowledge it."

As secretary to the chairman, Ms. Mori held one of the most prestigious positions for a woman in the company. In fact, her role was unprecedented. Ms. Shoji told me that no woman had ever before directly assisted a chairman. When the current chairman had been promoted he had specifically requested that Ms. Mori continue as his secretary. Tom Umeno accompanied him to events and out of the country, but Ms. Mori was his main support.

To the directors Ms. Mori always offered a pleasing smile and graceful compliance, but among the secretaries she maintained an air of superiority. She didn't easily give away favors to her colleagues. She was clever and bright, and I admired the way she dealt with many of the management-level men in our company who could be boorish and sometimes treated the secretaries poorly. She had an amazing knack for disguising her demands in polite language, as if to subtly remind them that she was their link to power.

A secretary could make things difficult for middle managers who needed access to the executives. A secretary could also do helpful things—like making a phone call to warn a department manager that an executive was on his way down for an impromptu visit. The smarter managers gave Ms. Mori regular attention and often complimented her when they visited our office.

According to Mr. Higuchi's plan, I would eventually take over Ms. Mori's position as Mr. Chino's secretary. Even though she would still be managing three other directors, I guessed that she might not want to give up Mr. Chino. I admired the control Ms. Mori maintained, but resisted getting too close. I didn't want to become part of her secretarial hierarchy. Having no place in the hierarchy made me feel exempt from the rules that defined work and relationships. No one asked me to come in early to prepare cleaning rags. If I arrived early, I spent my time talking or reading the week-old *Wall Street Journal*. I didn't mind taking my turn doing the "A" and "B" chores, but I wanted my work to be hierarchy-free. It was the same with my relationships: I liked being able to join the various groups for lunch. I didn't want to be categorized simply by my age.

I wanted to be an honorary member the way I had been as an exchange student with the Welcome Ladies and on the Waseda judo team. My coaches and teammates treated me like a member of the group, but they'd had different expectations of me than they did of other members.

On my first day of judo practice I had noticed that all of the thirty men on the team had cauliflower ears. Their smooth ear-folds were plump and puffy like a twisted bun. The ears are badges of courage in judo, I was told—proof of toughness. The initiation started in junior high school when upperclassmen boxed the ears of their juniors during grappling practice. As the initiation continued week after week, the ears would swell with liquid and the lobe would start to separate from the skull. Even if cold compresses were applied, the ears would throb and sounds would be muffled. By the time the boys were in their second year of junior high school, their lobes were hardened for life—hard as a knuckle with no loose flesh, just smooth, unmoving tissue.

My initiation into the judo team was much less painful. I had to fall—*ukemi*. My entire first week of practice was spent doing this. While the others practiced, I stood in the corner of the dojo flinging myself onto the green mat while the two white ends of my belt swung wildly with each *ukemi*.

After a year of being a member of the judo team my body reflected my earnestness and I earned my brown belt, even though I was without status and without cauliflower ears. I noticed that my blouses felt tighter around my shoulders and back. I had never measured my strength before, only my weight. I could do one hundred push-ups in a row and found immense satisfaction in throwing men twice my size. Judo gave me a physical thrill that I had never known playing basketball or running track. Judo also gave me a sense of belonging that I'd never had on the court or on the field.

I wondered if I would ever feel the same way about the executive secretaries. This was a new kind of team, but one that already demanded more conformity than I had ever been expected to give. What I had seen so far on the tenth floor made me think that my indifference to the hierarchy was going to have to change. I was going to have to play according to the rules of this corporate team, but I wasn't sure what those rules would be. Where were the cauliflower ears on these dainty women?

Every day the secretaries attended to the same tasks: arranging meetings, writing in three schedule books, rescheduling meetings, erasing and rewriting in the schedule books, arranging transportation, procuring tickets, rearranging transportation, exchanging old tickets for new, tabulating expense reports, securing appropriate signatures for expense reports, preparing for guests, preparing guest rooms for guests, greeting guests, preparing tea, serving tea, cleaning up guest rooms, and washing tea cups. No matter how many times the task had been repeated or how seemingly unimportant it was, the secretaries treated each job as a significant duty.

A secretary entered the company as an assistant and would most likely continue to operate in that capacity until she left. The women didn't complain about the mundane tasks or wish for promotions and more interesting work. Like a new mother of a child, each woman accepted her role and the obligations that went with it. Just as their diligent phone answering skills had impressed me, their overall attitude and approach to Office Lady work confounded me. I both admired their dedication and rejected their obedience.

I wanted to belong to this group, but I wasn't sure about the sacrifices it might require, like treating Ms. Mori as a queen. I thought of myself as an individual before I thought of myself as part of any group. After working in the secretariat for two months I still didn't get excited at the thought of making the perfect cup of tea. Simple tasks such as sharpening pencils and setting out paper seemed pointless. I didn't seem to get the same sense of satisfaction as my colleagues.

My way of life was unusual to them. I wondered what they thought about the choices I had made. They seemed curious about me in the way one is curious about a contortionist. I felt sure that not one of them would have wanted to leave the comfort of the group and trade places with me. I felt the same way about them.

Ms. Mori

3 IT WAS A QUIET AFTERNOON AND MOST OF the directors were out of the office when Ms. Mori announced that it was time for my tea training. I had successfully avoided serving tea for months. But I knew that, as with the uniform, I had little choice. If I refused to serve tea, I wouldn't be seen as a team player and would surely isolate myself from my colleagues.

The other women didn't seem to have the same aversion to serving tea. Questioning why only women served tea would have been like asking them, "Why do only women have babies?"

I had accepted the inevitability of this task coming my way, so when Ms. Mori made her announcement I didn't resist. She recruited two junior-level secretaries to help. The four of us went into one of the guest rooms used for social visits. The room looked like a den in an elegant home; four handsome leather chairs were placed around a square marble coffee table. The two women sat down obediently.

"The first thing to learn is how to enter the room," Ms. Mori instructed. She was holding a lacquer tray with two empty tea cups on wooden saucers. "Before you enter the room, you must knock." She walked out and closed the door. I heard her tap lightly before gently opening the door as if entering a sanctuary. "*Shitsurei shimasu*. Excuse me, I'm sorry to interrupt," she said and proceeded into the room.

"The next thing to consider is the order in which to serve the tea. It depends on who is visiting and if he is more important than Mr. Chino. You never serve Mr. Chino first if the guest is more important."

"But how do you know?" I asked.

"If you don't already know before you walk in, you can tell by where they are sitting. The most important place is the seat furthest away from the door. If Mr. Chino is sitting there, then you can serve him first, but if the guest is sitting there, serve him before you serve Mr. Chino."

"What if there is more than one guest?" I asked.

"Then you serve them in descending order," she barked as if it were common knowledge. Her reply only confused me more, but I could tell she was losing her patience. She moved to the far right of Mr. Chino's chair. "Always approach the table at an angle so that you don't disrupt the conversation." In one fluid motion she placed the tea cup and saucer on the table without making a sound. Then she backed away and moved around to the outside of the guest's chair and placed the second cup. Each time she reached, she whispered, "*Shitsurei shimasu*," as if to cushion the obtuse gesture.

She held the empty tray flat against her body as she surveyed the room before backing slowly into the door.

She turned to open the door and then turned back to face the room, bowed and retreated backwards once more mouthing the refrain, *"Shitsurei shimasu."*

"Now it's your turn," she said, walking back into the room and collecting the cups. I took the tray and balanced it with one hand.

"Use two hands," she instructed. I proceeded to the table. "Be more discreet. Keep your head down," she said.

When I got close to the table, I grabbed one of the saucers and placed it next to one of the women. "Don't get so close," Ms. Mori cried "You don't want to interrupt them." I started to place the second cup in between the two women, but Ms. Mori stopped me. "Never go in between when you can go around."

When I finished the task she told me to do it all again, this time starting from outside. I collected the props and left the room. Staring at the closed door, I felt my stomach tighten and had a powerful urge to turn and walk away.

What was I doing here? The months of training in America before coming to Japan seemed meaningless at that moment. I thought back to the month working on the assembly line in Ohio on the morning shift. Working on the line was tiring and repetitive, but at least I had felt useful.

Five months and eight thousand miles later, I was practicing how to serve tea in blue polyester and high heels. What would the dean of my college say now if she saw me dressed like a Girl Scout and using my language skills to apologize for entering the room? My only solace was that no one from America could see me.

I knocked on the door and quietly made my entrance.

"Don't forget to bow when you enter and exit," Ms. Mori ordered from her observation point in the corner where she stood with her arms crossed. I performed like a trick monkey and bowed. Holding my breath, I went through the motions, handling each saucer as though it were antique crystal and moving as though I were in pain—my head bent and shoulders hunched. Each time I opened my mouth I wanted to scream, "I hate this!" but instead I whispered Ms. Mori's requisite phrase, "Excuse me, I'm sorry to interrupt."

When the task was completed, I bowed, repeated, *"Shitsurei shimasu,"* and softly shut the door as I left the room. Tears rushed to my eyes and I couldn't stop the waves of disappointment. I ran to the supply closet and cried.

Ms. Mori monitored the secretarial office from her corner desk like a queen bee watching over her hive. With a single glance she could check on what the other secretaries were doing and see where the executives were. She was keenly aware of everyone and made it her business to know everything that was going on.

Her power was sometimes subtle, often direct, and influenced all the secretaries. Ms. Kodama, like the other women, regularly deferred to Ms. Mori. I watched one afternoon as Ms. Kodama and Ms. Mori made plans for a joint meeting of their executives. When the secretaries worked together to coordinate events usually the senior secretary took the initiative, but Ms. Mori always waited for others to approach her and only responded when she was ready. No one would dare make preparations without her.

That day Ms. Kodama approached her, effusing polite tones, and asked Ms. Mori which meeting room should be reserved. Ms. Mori curtly replied, "Oh, it doesn't matter. Any room will do." Ms. Kodama bobbed her head until her shoulders jiggled and said, "Yes, I understand."

Later Ms. Mori checked the meeting room schedule. "Oh, this won't do. We can't have the meeting in *that* room. The chairman hates to have meetings there," she cried out so everyone in the office could hear.

Ms. Kodama leapt from her desk practically trembling. "I'm so sorry," she said to Ms. Mori. "I can change it to another room," she offered. Everyone listened with their heads bowed over their work.

"Yes, please move it and notify everyone of the change."

Ms. Kodama bowed her head and smiled. She was one of the youngest in the group. When she had wished me luck eating the fish at our lunch together, I thought her excessive giddiness was a nervous reaction to being around me. But she was bubbly and enthusiastic and cheerful all the time—so much so that I thought no one took her seriously.

When others might casually greet one another saying, "'Morning," Ms. Kodama would bow with her hands together and recite, "Good morning." When she laughed she squinted her eyes and cupped her cheeks with her palms like a little girl in gleeful delight. She made cute nonsense sounds as if she were entertaining a baby and liked to flash peace signs. But when I mentioned my thoughts about her silliness to another secretary, she remarked, "Oh, Ms. Kodama is just cute. I think she brightens up the office."

Ms. Kodama was considered *kawaii*, or cute, perhaps the highest compliment possible for a young, unmarried woman. She and the other women kept pink quilted makeup kits and toothbrushes shaped like teddy bears in the bathroom cabinet. Some wore frilly bows in their hair and carried tissue paper in terrycloth sachets. Part of being *kawaii* was a cheerful, perky attitude.

But there was something more to Ms. Kodama's constant smile that bothered me. It was insincere. I couldn't understand how she could smile with bubbling glee and bob her head as Ms. Mori criticized her within hearing distance of the whole office. I didn't believe it when she smiled with sweat trickling down her cheeks after running down to the travel agency to buy a train ticket for her director, who had decided at the last minute to attend a meeting out of town that he had known about for weeks. Her enthusiasm wasn't convincing when she forfeited the stool in the pantry to Ms. Mori after a ten-hour day, squatting next to the table with her lukewarm tea saying that it didn't matter, she wasn't really that tired. Ms. Kodama was an expert in showing only her public self—*tatemae*.

All the women displayed it. *Tatemae* was deferring to Ms. Mori when you knew it wasn't her business. It was having to eat lunch with her and smile and make small talk for an hour. *Tatemae* was joyfully calling twenty people to reschedule a meeting because your director had forgotten about the meeting that you had discussed with him that morning. It was keeping quiet when the directors called you *kanojo*—meaning "Hey you"—in the executive office because they didn't know your name even though you had been working there for six years. *Tatemae* was saying that it was probably best that your friend had decided to retire from the company because she wanted to do other things, when you really knew she just couldn't take the sexual harassment from her boss any more.

The public face for women was cooperative, energetic, pleasant, and non-confrontational. I wanted to shake Ms. Kodama's jiggly shoulders and say, "Aren't you angry? Why don't you do something besides smile stupidly when Ms. Mori humiliates you in front of everyone?" When Ms. Kodama showed *tatemae* there was no room for anger or passion or even mild frustration. To me this made all of her actions suspect. How could I know when she, or anyone else, was sincere?

The private self, *honne*, was somewhat of a mystery to me. I laughed with my colleagues and we talked superficially about things other than work—families and hobbies. I assumed they were showing their *honne*, but they rarely talked candidly about their personal lives or complained about work. No one ever said negative things about their colleagues, even Ms. Mori. If I mentioned something about her, the others would silently nod their heads to acknowledge me but didn't offer their own thoughts. I was used to being much more open with my feelings and opinions, especially if I felt frustrated. I expected to find solace in mutual and shared pain, but it didn't take me long to learn that expressing negative *honne* would only get me into trouble.

I ran into a man from Tokyo Broadcasting System who was working on a program about Honda worldwide. I had met him several times in the United States while I was preparing to come to Japan. He knew of my unusual assignment and was always very friendly and encouraging. When I saw him this first time at headquarters he greeted me warmly and asked how things were going. I said that there had been ups and downs and told him that I'd had problems with housing, but that I was happy with the way things had worked out.

The next day Tom Umeno called me aside and rebuked me for being so personal. The TBS man had confided in Tom that he had been surprised by my frank response. Tom suggested that I might be looking for media attention and that I should be careful because TBS might try to do a story on how Honda was not treating me well. I felt betrayed in what I had assumed to be a private conversation, but knew that by expressing my *honne* I had only betrayed myself.

Every Monday after our morning group meeting I quietly disappeared into a narrow side room next to our office. From the outside it looked like a broom closet, but inside was the only private space on the tenth floor. The room had a chair, a desk, and an olive-green telephone with beige buttons and direct access to international phone lines.

The telephone was my umbilical chord to America—my connection to another life where people understood me without effort. I felt private and secure in the small, dark room. It was the only place in the intelligent building where I felt safe to be myself and express *honne*.

Monday morning in Tokyo was Sunday evening in Ohio, and for an hour—at a dollar a minute—I would talk with my parents. My father would tell me about the latest Arnold Schwarzenegger movie he had seen, and my Mom and I would groan simultaneously; then we would talk about whom they had seen at church and news from relatives.

I usually made a list of things to tell them—reporting on life in my neighborhood, telling how an anonymous recycler had returned a bag of combustible garbage to my front door because I had put it out on glass-recycling day. I gave them updates on my language lessons and stories about work.

After the call I would slip back into the office, usually going to the pantry first before making my way back to my desk as if to obscure the obvious absence. Mr. Higuchi and I had a tacit understanding that I was permitted to use the phone to call home once in a while. The Japanese tendency toward vagueness was, in this case, to my advantage. Everyone knew where I had been but no one said anything about it, even though no one else made personal calls from the private phone room.

If I received a business call during that time a message would be taped to my desk with a little circled letter at the bottom indicating who had taken the message. Ms. Mori was the only one who wouldn't take a message. If she answered a call for me she would knock on the phone room door and cordially say, "Rora-san, you have a call," to which I would courteously request that she take a message. It was clear that she disliked my special privilege, but *tatemae* prevented her from saying so.

I was surprised one Friday afternoon when Ms. Mori invited me to take a break with her. The two of us had just finished serving coffee to twenty guests and so we rewarded ourselves in the pantry. We got our drinks and sat facing one another on the stools. I asked her where she came from in Japan and she laughed saying, she was from *inaka*, the boondocks. She told me that after high school she had come to Tokyo to attend secretarial school and then started to work at a Honda dealership. After two years she had been promoted to work at headquarters.

"Do you like living by yourself?" she asked me.

I told her that I was getting used to it, but that I didn't like cooking for myself.

"I always have food left over and it spoils. It's also so hard to get to the grocery store before it closes every night," she said.

"My grocery store is the same way," I complained. "I usually have to buy instant food at the convenience store."

"Me too," she said, and grimaced.

We talked about our families and discovered that we were both the eldest in the family and each had a younger brother. Our conversation was easy and friendly. I could hardly believe this charming woman sitting across from me was the bossy manipulator I had thought her to be. Through our conversation I realized that we were really very similar, both willful and used to having things our own way.

I saw the conversation as a significant breakthrough. For the first time we had shown each other respect and been genuinely friendly. I started to rethink my entire opinion of her over the weekend. The following Monday I walked into work and greeted her with a cheerful, genuine smile. She replied with a blank stare and gave me a cursory hello. I was shocked. Nothing had changed at all. Thinking back over our warm Friday conversation, I finally realized what I had missed—that it was her *tatemae* talking with my *honne*.

I was unprepared when Mr. Higuchi called me in to a meeting with Mr. Chino and Ms. Mori one afternoon after I had been working as a receptionist for more than two months. We sat in a conference room. No one asked me to serve tea, so I was certain that the meeting had something to do with me.

"There are eighteen areas of responsibility for a secretary," Mr. Higuchi began, and handed me a typed list in Japanese. There were two columns next to the list of eighteen items. At the top of one column, written in Ms. Mori's sharp script, was my last name, クリスカ, a name which no one in the office used. At the top of the other column it said "Mori," 森 in kanji characters.

"As Mr. Chino's secretary you will be responsible for some of these items," Mr. Higuchi continued. "And Ms. Mori will be responsible for others." We started going down the list checking off who would do what. Ms. Mori drew concise circles in either column to indicate which one of us was responsible for each job.

Mr. Chino and Ms. Mori followed along as though they had thoroughly discussed and agreed to all of this. I felt strangely left out, as if it were by accident that they had let me in on the plan at all. We continued down the list. I got circles in categories such as keeping the schedule, sending Christmas cards, serving tea to guests, arranging the car service and business trips. Ms. Mori's categories included managing Mr. Chino's finances and insurance. I also got the duty of managing "daily needs," which included unlocking his locker every morning and making sure all the pencils on his desk were sharp. Regardless of the types of tasks, I found it satisfying to look down my column and see all the circles. What I didn't like was a series of triangles in both Ms. Mori's and my columns.

"There are some items that you and Ms. Mori will share," Mr. Higuchi said.

"I will be involved in anything that might affect people outside the company," Ms. Mori added. She explained that we would share such duties as phone correspondence and arranging dinner and golf meetings. Although Ms. Mori's face revealed nothing, her superiority seeped through every word.

"And since you have shared duties, I think it would be best for you to move your desk next to Ms. Mori," Mr. Higuchi said. "You will need to work very closely so she can teach you the secretary job." I looked over at Ms. Mori. She smiled smugly, and I felt myself being drawn into her hierarchical hive.

There had been only one time during my judo experience that I had felt helpless within the hierarchy. It was during a week-long spring training camp held in a small town near the sea. Every day started with military-like exercise drills to increase our strength. We jogged, jumped rope, and did push-ups, sit-ups, squat thrusts, knee bends, and stair-climbing drills while carrying a partner on our backs.

Twice-a-day judo practices were held in the dojo of the local high school. It was a country school. The campus was a stretch of dirt; the dojo consisted of a roof over a flimsy wooden structure with old dusty tatami mats that had lost their spring. It was vacation time for the high school students but they came to practice too. It was an honor for them to have the Waseda University team at their dojo.

In addition to the twenty or so boys on the high-school team, there were four girls. They were all about my height but stronger, and young—maybe fourteen or fifteen—and had the hard bodies of little boys who play all day long.

I was used to practicing with my Waseda teammates, who, although much larger than me, were always careful. But these young, hard girls didn't know me. They only saw that I wore a white belt just like them. I had no particular status with them; I was just part of the judo team—the college judo team.

I was nervous about sparring with them, but I didn't want to be a wimp. Certainly I had learned something in the months I had practiced judo. I didn't want to embarrass my coach, so I played as though I belonged and then I got beat up.

When I was thrown in our own dojo by men twice my size, I never felt ashamed. But to be thrown repeatedly by a young girl was humiliating. Suddenly I had no excuse. I felt weak and stupid and useless. I felt like I had been indulged all those months by my male colleagues and that I hadn't really learned anything about judo; when it came to actually sparring with someone of comparable strength, I couldn't stay on my feet.

During the floor work one of the girls put me into a choke-hold. I was frantic and indignant. I didn't want to give up so I struggled furiously to escape. My face was to the mat, but I could hear the others grunting and exerting themselves just a step away. I was embarrassed and humiliated, and I felt my neck being squeezed tighter. Tears came to my eyes as I ground my face to the mat, but her grip just got tighter. My head was hot and sweaty. I felt panicked; it was impossible to breath. The tears started to spill from my eyes and I hit the mat twice, signaling that I'd given up.

She released her grip and I gasped for air with a choking sob. My tears flowed and my sobs interrupted the muffled grumbling of the floor work. Everyone could hear me, but I couldn't stop. I stood there choking and heaving in an open doorway looking out onto the dirt campus. I tried to gain my composure, but I had already broken a code. I had never seen anyone cry in a dojo before. My face was red and hot and puffy, and there was still another hour of morning practice to go.

Later, when the group was walking back to the dorm, one of my teammates pulled up beside me and said in a quiet, conspiratorial voice, "Kiki, you really shouldn't cry during practice." I couldn't bear to say anything because I felt like crying again. I just blinked my watery eyes and nodded my head.

Ms. Mori seemed to revel in her official position of being my instructor, and watched everything I did and how I did it. She taught exclusively by rote, just as in Japanese schools, instructing me to follow the most minute details but omitting an explanation. She told me to open the mail by slicing open the short end of the envelope and not to use a red pen to make notes to myself. But if I asked her why she did things in a particular way, she would either ignore me or say, "This is the way we do it here."

Since we now sat side by side with our desks touching, she always knew what I was doing. But if I asked her a sudden question, she would pretend not to know what I was talking about until I explained the entire situation and deferred to her completely. If I didn't preface my questions by saying, "Excuse me, Ms. Mori, may I ask you a question?" she would say she was too busy to help me. But when I went to Ms. Ogi or others who were easier to talk to, Ms. Mori would pout and take it as a personal affront.

Sitting right next to her all day long, I noticed how she maintained an almost constant dialogue with herself. "*Dō shiyo?* What shall I do next?" or "*Iyada*, yuck." Her little phrases kept me off guard because it sounded as though she was talking to me. I felt like I had to be ready at any moment to defend against one of her attacks. When she got frustrated she had mini-tantrums at her desk, exhaled dramatically, and said "Humph!" so everyone could hear.

I listened to her on the telephone making demands and bullying others throughout the company. She regularly withheld information and feigned ignorance in order to make things more difficult. Even though no one in the office would discuss her difficult behavior, I found some in the knowledge I wasn't the only one suffering.

My main job was arranging Mr. Chino's schedule and keeping it up to date in three calendars. It took time to write in Japanese in my master planner, which I then copied into Mr. Chino's datebook and into the group datebook. Every time the schedule changed—sometimes a daily occurrence—I had to correct all three books. Writing in Japanese was difficult, but my problems were private. I could quietly consult dictionaries or ask Ms. Ogi for help.

One of the worst tasks was calling people to notify them of the change. Speaking on the phone was language torture. Since I had mastered the formal phone greetings, the person on the other end wouldn't know at first that I was a foreigner. When I said my name quickly it sounded like Wada, a common Japanese name. But as I started explaining my reason for calling, I could detect the moment of recognition when I was discovered. It made me feel like an imposter. "What did you say your name is?" the caller would ask me again. "Oh, Rora-san. I understand now." Sympathetic listeners would slow down and speak in simple language; others got frustrated and hung up.

I couldn't fool anyone. I wasn't good enough. Every time I heard this phrase through the receiver I imagined that Ms. Mori was listening and laughing to herself, "See, she can't do it. She doesn't belong here."

As much as I hated talking on the phone, there was one job that I dreaded more—reciting Mr. Chino's schedule out loud during the morning meeting. Every morning when the exercise music started playing right before work, my stomach started to churn. Listening to the ritual had made it seem easy, but speaking out loud in Japanese to a room full of native speakers was terrifying.

Ms. Mori always started by reading the chairman's schedule, but she left Mr. Chino's schedule to me. When it was my turn, I bowed my flushed face into the calendar and mumbled through the long list of unfamiliar words and names. Ms. Mori's voice sounded smooth, natural, and authoritative. She was sure of the words and sure of herself. I made mistakes and rushed through as fast as I could, hoping that no one would ask me to repeat something.

As word got around the company that I had taken over as Mr. Chino's secretary, I noticed that people seemed more patient and considerate. Because I had responsibility for a director I detected a new sense of respect among my colleagues. I also started to move among the directors more freely.

Mr. Chino was especially patient and kind. Every morning I went through his schedule with him as he drank a cup of tea. I stumbled through the events, my lack of confidence causing me to switch back and forth from Japanese to English. Mr. Chino was fluent in English, and he didn't seem to mind.

"Good morning. How are you?" I would ask. Then I would begin my hodgepodge briefing. "*Kyō*, Kobayashi-san from the Public Relations *Bu* will come at *jū-ji* for an *uchiawase*," I said, meaning: Today Mr. Kobayashi from the Public Relations Department will come at 10:00 A.M. for a meeting. "He would like to *sōdan* about *rainen* strategy." (He would like to discuss next year's strategy.)

Mr. Chino's responsibilities included all North American operations as well as financial issues for the entire company. Because he spoke such excellent English, the Public Relations Department and Finance Department managers continually requested meetings and interviews for him with foreign journalists and American analysts.

I saw Mr. Chino throughout the day, letting him know when meetings were being held and where he was wanted. He was demanding, but pleasant to work for. He appreciated my efforts and often joked with me. Sometimes I made language mistakes in the entries in his schedule book. He would laugh and take out his dictionary to explain the word. Calling himself Professor Chino, he would erase the mistake and show me how to write it correctly.

Once, when he was watching his diet, we argued about which had more calories, tofu or vanilla ice cream. For some reason I insisted that ice cream had less calories, so he challenged me to a ¥1,000 bet. The next day I showed him my mistake in a calorie book and tried to pay up, but he wouldn't let me.

Another day Mr. Chino arrived before I'd had a chance to unlock his locker. I got so busy that I forgot to go through the morning routine. Later in the day he emerged from the executive office and walked over to my desk, something I had never seen an executive do before. If the directors wanted something they simply picked up the receiver on their desk and the secretaries came running. But he was standing next to my chair. Ms. Mori sat at attention, her eyes narrowed, already accusing me of the unnamed transgression that had brought Mr. Chino all the way to our area. I looked at his smiling face, and he said, "Open sesame." I was confused and on edge. "I'm sorry, what did you say?" I asked him. Ms. Mori was fuming. She didn't like it when he and I spoke in English. "My locker," he said. "It's locked. Open sesame! Ha ha ha."

Everything about Ms. Mori seemed disagreeable; even her code name ク (Ku) looked and sounded sharp. I saw her harshness in the hard strokes of her handwriting and in the tone of her voice, which seemed to penetrate every room of the tenth floor. Unlike the other secretaries who gathered in the bathroom to use their colorful toothbrush kits after lunch, I noticed that Ku kept a plastic bottle of brown medicinal liquid on the shelf. It looked bitter and thick, and I imagined that when she started to feel herself going soft she would come in for a swig.

Although I couldn't get away with much under her surveillance, I did small things that gave me private joy. I would graciously request her help but follow her directions with slight aloofness. If she was bullying me I'd pretend not to understand and page slowly through my dictionary to weaken her intensity. I imagined that with a well-timed look away from her while she was talking, I could send a vague, yet private message that said, "You don't control me."

One afternoon Mr. Chino returned from a meeting outside the office. Ms. Mori leaned over and reminded me in a condescending tone that I should take him something to drink. "The choice of what to take him is up to you," she added, as if it were a matter of great importance over which I must carefully deliberate and then ask her advice.

I knew the drink rule and I had planned to take him something; but, I decided, it may as well be something that he wanted. I followed Mr. Chino into the executive office instead of going directly to the pantry and told him about a phone call that had come during his absence. When we were finished talking, I asked him if he would like something to drink.

"No, thank you," he replied. I left the executive office and returned to my desk aware that Ms. Mori had been watching me. She knew that I had not prepared a beverage for Mr. Chino but asked me anyway, "What did you serve him?"

"He doesn't want anything to drink right now," I answered her calmly, feeling smug simply because I knew this would make her angry. Her almond-shaped eyes narrowed, and she lurched into a vigorous tirade as if berating a disobedient child.

"Did you forget that we in the secretariat always take a beverage to a director when he returns to the office?" She acted as though I had defamed the entire secretarial pool.

"I am aware of the procedure," I replied in an equally obnoxious tone. "It's completely unnecessary for you to repeat the explanation. I heard you the first time."

No one had ever spoken to her in this way in the office. She jumped up from her seat, strutted over to Mr.

Higuchi's desk, and announced, "I have something to discuss with you." With a huff she stomped out of the room.

I felt momentarily gratified and then guilty. I was afraid I was going to be in trouble, but no one said anything. Mr. Higuchi didn't follow her and he didn't say anything to me. Eventually Ms. Mori returned, but she ignored me.

For the rest of the afternoon tension split our connected desks as though a steel wall had been erected. I listened to her "Humph"-ing and talking to herself in high-pitched yelps. I purposely slowed down and tried to pretend that nothing was wrong, but my guilt outweighed the temporary satisfaction. I knew I would never be able to do my job without her help and that I couldn't continue sitting next to her like an enemy, so I asked her to come into a conference room to talk. She reluctantly agreed.

We rolled two large chairs away from the conference table and faced each other—Japan on one side, America on the other. There was something humorous about the two of us sitting in chairs that dwarfed us, in the conference room of one of Japan's largest companies. We looked as though we had come to the negotiating table to settle an enormous dispute between nations—as if the future of Japanese-American relations could be boiled down to two secretaries fighting over a cup of tea.

"This is Japan," she exclaimed. "You should do things our way!"

"I am just trying to do a good job," I said.

"But you are new. You have many things to learn."

"You're right. But because I am new and because I am not Japanese I sometimes need extra explanation."

"When you are learning, you can ask how, when, where, or what, but not why," she said.

"Sometimes it is hard for me to understand why things are done a certain way. I need to know why, so that I can understand and do a good job."

Ms. Mori was right. I was in Japan and I was supposed to do things her way. I felt I didn't have any choice but to apologize for not always understanding. I was sincere when I told her that I really wanted to learn from her and wanted us to get along better. She seemed much less agitated after my apology, and I thought we agreed to start communicating better. When we left the room I felt hopeful that we had started to build some common ground.

On Monday morning I went to work with an unusually enthusiastic attitude. I felt certain that our disagreement and frank discussion would lead to the start of a new relationship in which we would communicate openly. Maybe we'd even be able to become friends.

When I sat down at my desk, Ms. Mori didn't even acknowledge me. She acted as though nothing had changed—the wall was still between us. I had thought that it was possible to bridge the gap between the private *honne* and public *tatemae* selves. But I had been wrong. Nothing had changed.

Her surveillance and interrogation of everything I did was paralyzing. I hesitated before doing any task, afraid that she would lash out at me. Sometimes when we disagreed, I escaped to the pantry, hid my face in the refrigerator, and ate chocolates to sweeten my bitter feelings. My colleagues were no help. They took her criticism and unpredictable moodiness in stride. Once or twice Ms. Ogi made a vague comment, saying, "Some people just have a different way of doing things," and "If I were you I wouldn't get upset by certain people." Her meaning was clear, but I yearned for something more substantial.

The only place I found comfort was on the sixteenth floor, which housed the most elegant guest rooms and where there were three women whose singular task it was to serve tea to Honda's most important guests. They had a lot of free time, so I would sneak up to see them. I always used the stairs, not the elevator where Ms. Mori could watch me from the monitor.

The women on the sixteenth floor were not employed by Honda but were hired through a temporary-staff agency. They had no loyalty or *tatemae* where the secretariat was concerned, so they didn't hold back their feelings about Ms. Mori and agreed that she was a terror. In the room where they took their breaks one wall was covered with magazine pictures of Caucasian male models in various states of undress. There they listened to my complaints and poured tea for me.

Ms. Mori harassed them as well, using video monitors on the sixteenth floor to watch them. One day she had a fit because a light in the hall was turned off. She made a series of curt phone calls to the sixteenth floor, to which the women responded with less than enthusiastic action.

There was no true escape from Ms. Mori, and every day I felt the pressure she created. Her behavior was as unpredictable as her moods. She was sitting at her desk when I got to work and was often still there when I left. She even showed up in my dreams. Sometimes I just couldn't take her manipulation, but I hid my *honne*, my private self. I would hide somewhere—the storage room, the stairwell, or a bathroom stall—and cry.

One day when I got to work I noticed that everyone

was there except Ms. Mori. The possibility that she had taken a day off hit me, but I couldn't allow myself to indulge in such a glorious fantasy. I prepared for work while listening carefully for the beep of her identification card sliding through the time clock. When the exercise music started to play I felt my heart leap. No one was ever that late. But I continued to hold out. I couldn't bring myself to ask anyone where she was; I just reveled in possibility. The last notes of the music played and I prepared myself to see her rush in at the last minute, out of breath and apologizing profusely to the manager. Then Ms. Shoji came over to Ms. Mori's desk and pulled out the chairman's schedule. "Ms. Mori is on vacation today," she said to me. I nodded and then pretended to reach for something under my desk. It was the only way to conceal my smile.

Sisters and Uncles

4 I WAS SITTING ACROSS FROM MR. HIGUCHI watching a thin film form on my café au lait. We were in the company coffee shop on the sixth floor; it was my first visit. The shop was simply one end of the cafeteria that had been partitioned off by a row of leafy green plants. It had a parquet floor and a dozen or so modern-looking black tables with matching chairs. A wall of windows looked out on to the busy Aoyama intersection and beyond to the west side of Tokyo.

Since space in the headquarters building was limited, the sixth floor turned into open work space during non-meal hours. The cafeteria became a huge study room where employees could spread out their papers and work undisturbed for hours at a time. But drinking coffee in the shop during working hours was conspicuously casual, so regular employees like me only came here at the invitation of their bosses. The shop was filled with dark-suited managers sitting knee to knee around the small tables and smoking cigarettes. I was the only woman in the shop not serving drinks.

"So Rora-san, how are things going?" Mr. Higuchi asked me. "Are you having any problems with your work?"

"Everything is fine," I said, keenly aware that I didn't want to say anything about Ms. Mori. She had been there for eight years and I couldn't imagine that anything would change just because I told Mr. Higuchi that I felt frustrated. On the contrary, I was afraid of what might happen if Mr. Higuchi were to tell her that I had complained. "Ms. Ogi, Ms. Shoji, and the others are very helpful," I said.

"That's good. Very good. How about your apartment? Do you have everything you need?"

"It's fine. I think I have finally figured out how to use all my appliances, but sometimes my rice still turns out a little hard."

"Do you wash the rice thoroughly?" he asked. "You have to soak the rice in water for twenty minutes before you cook it. That way it can absorb water and it will be soft."

Mr. Higuchi regularly handed out useful information and gifts. When I first arrived in Japan, he had taken me to the company health clinic and personally introduced me to the head physician, giving me the doctor's home phone and beeper number in case of an emergency. When I moved into my apartment he gave me a digital world clock that showed what time it was in all twenty-four time zones. "This is so you don't wake up your Mama-san and Papa-san when you call them in Ohio," he told me.

His sentences often began with the phrase, "I have a

friend who gave me . . . ;" then he would distribute travel coupons, special sale invitations, free tickets to concerts, and passes to art openings. He was generous with all the secretaries and liked to make sure that everyone was happy—that's why he had brought me to the coffee shop.

"How about friends? Are you making any friends outside the secretariat?" he asked.

"I don't really have the chance to meet people outside our office," I said.

"Well, how about joining a club?" he suggested.

"What kind of club?

"Honda has many clubs for the employees, things like tennis and skiing. I think joining a club would be a good way to meet people."

"When I was an exchange student I was in a club," I told him.

"This is the same thing except that it's organized by the company. What club were you in?"

"Judo."

"What! You were on the judo team? Are you kidding?" he asked, laughing in disbelief. I nodded. "Wait until I tell Mr. Chino that he has a judo player for a secretary!"

"Does Honda have a judo team?" I asked.

"Maybe there is a martial arts club at one of the factories, but I think that most of the clubs at headquarters are more like hobbies. I'm sure you will be able to find one that you like." He laughed to himself again. "Mr. Yoshida should have warned me that he was sending a martial artist to my office!"

I asked around and discovered that almost all the secretaries belonged to one of the company clubs. When I expressed an interest in joining one, I received invitations to try out several, including yoga, flower arranging, tea ceremony, and basketball.

My inflexible joints made yoga painful, and I couldn't appreciate the art of spending two hours arranging a bunch of flowers when they looked fine to me after about two minutes. Tea ceremony was out: not only was I sick of making tea, but I couldn't bear to sit with my legs tucked under me for hours. Basketball was my last hope. I had played guard all through high school and even in college, and for the first time I suspected that my five-foot-three-inch height might be an advantage.

* * *

On a Wednesday after work my colleague Ms. Kodama and I took a taxi to a nearby junior high school gym to meet the other basketball club members. She showed me into a musty, windowless locker room. The facilities looked abandoned: a cold, dusty concrete floor, rusty metal lockers, and a single spigot in a closet-sized shower room that produced only cold water.

We changed into shorts and T-shirts. I slung my high-tops over my shoulder on the way to the gym and shuffled behind Ms. Kodama. We were both wearing blue plastic slippers that we had exchanged our street shoes for at the entrance because only basketball shoes were permitted on the floor of the gym. I sat down on the court with a handful of other players and laced up my sneakers.

The gym smelled earthy, and the thumping of basketballs on the floor brought back memories of hours of after-school practices and games. I had started playing basketball in elementary school in the recreation department's Saturday-morning girls' league. Almost all the girls in my class had played. At the beginning of the season we were divided up, based on height, into groups of seven or eight. Each team made up a name to go with its assigned T-shirt color: Black Magic. Blue Diamonds. Yellow Zingers. I proudly wore my T-shirt to school as often as I was allowed.

The familiarity of being back on the court was seductive, and I could hardly wait to play. I picked up a basketball and started to dribble. The rough texture felt good to my fingertips.

By 7:30 twelve men and four women were gathered on the court. Except for three tall men, I felt relieved to see that I was about the same size as most of the players. When the club leader called for warm-up exercises everyone ran into a large circle formation spreading across the court. I hurried to find a place. Then the leader called out an exercise. The entire group responded like school children and counted out loud with each bend and stretch. After ten minutes of knee bends and jumping jacks we lined up for drills: ten minutes of right-handed lay-ups, another ten minutes of left-handed ones. The others were joking and talking. I was wondering when we would get to play.

Next we did shooting drills from the base line and then from the top of the key, first on the right, then on the left. We did passing drills, dribbling drills, and finally free-throw practice. By the time we had finished warming up, there were only thirty minutes remaining for the game. The long delay seemed absurd, but I felt well prepared to play.

As two men began picking teams, I noticed Ms. Kodama and the other two women walking over to an equipment closet where they pulled out a large scoreboard. I continued to stand mid-court watching the remainder of the men divide into teams. The two groups lined up for the jump ball. Without moving from my place I realized what was going on. "Just a minute," I said. Everyone looked as though they were noticing me for the first time. "How come none of the women are playing?"

The club leader was holding the ball. "We play first. You women can play after we're done," he said, and turned back to center court.

I didn't have time to think, but my impulse found a voice that had been silenced in the office. "We don't have enough women to play," I said.

Irritated by the delay, he turned back and said, "The women always play for ten minutes after we are finished."

I stared at the ball about to be propelled into the air. I couldn't believe that I had come all the way here and sweated through more than an hour of drills just so I could have the privilege of playing scorekeeper on the sidelines. "Ten minutes! Does that seem fair?" I wanted to scream.

Instead I turned and started walking to the door. He wasn't my boss; this wasn't work. There was no way I was going to put up with this nonsense in my free time. No way.

"Wait a minute," another man's voice shouted. "Why don't we all play?"

I was startled and turned around. Nobody else said anything.

"Yeah, there are only four women so let's all play together," the man said.

I didn't know how the other women felt so I made a

suggestion that those who wanted to play should play. The man turned to the women who sat on the floor next to the scoreboard and asked, "Do you want to play?"

All three of them immediately jumped up and shouted, "Yes!"

We quickly re-chose teams and played for the remaining time. It was a short but fast game. I ran up and down the court, totally absorbed by the speed and competition, and by the end of the game even the club leader was breathing hard.

Before we left the gym, all the members gathered in a small circle in center court. The club leader made a few announcements concerning an upcoming tournament. Then he turned to me and a young man who was also attending for the first time.

"Thank you for visiting our club," he said. "We are called the Uncles." He pointed to his shirt which said "Uncles in Tokyo" in English. "As part of our Uncles tradition we ask each newcomer to introduce himself and entertain us."

The young man seemed to understand this odd invitation and immediately stepped forward with his hands to his sides. "My name is Kameyama. Please call me Kame." Then, looking at me, he said in English, "Kame means turtle. I am Mr. Turtle." Turning back to the group he continued in Japanese. "I currently work in the assembly department of the engine factory. I am a very poor basketball player so please forgive me. I look forward to getting to know you." He bowed deeply and then gave everyone a shy grin.

"I would like to entertain you with an impression of a song I think you know." He named the song and everyone seemed to recognize it. "Please clap along," he instructed. The group started to clap in rhythm, and Mr. Turtle threw his arms into the air. His shyness vanished as he leapt into a song-and-dance routine, twisting and gyrating with vigor. Twirling and kicking his legs, he sang the Japanese lyrics as if he were Elvis incarnate. The group cheered when he finished with a bow.

Cold sweat was trickling down my back, and the expectant stares sent one message: "Does she know what to do?" Ms. Kodama prompted me with an encouraging look. I felt lost. How was I supposed to entertain everyone? I couldn't even juggle very well. I stepped into the circle of silence and said, "My name is Laura, but you can call me Rora like roller skate," making a joke out of the homonym. The group laughed with relief. "Whew, at least she understands Japanese," they seemed to say.

"I arrived this year to work in the secretariat," I said, adding a bow. The group clapped politely and waited. "Umm. I come from the state of Ohio, near Canada and the Great Lakes. I am twenty-two years old and I have played basketball since elementary school—but I'm not very good," I said, imitating Mr. Turtle's humble remarks.

"I am not such a good entertainer and my Japanese is poor," I said, stalling for time. Then I suddenly got an inspiration. "But one thing I can do very well is speak English."

Before anyone could protest I burst into a rapid-fire description of my hometown, my family, my shoes, and anything that I could think of in English.

"My name is Laura and I grew up in a town called Grandview which is a suburb of Columbus, Ohio, and I have one brother and his name is David and he is very tall and he likes to play basketball. I bought some new shoes so I could play here today, but they were very expensive so I wish that I had my old basketball shoes that I think are in my closet at home in Ohio. And when I was young my feet were too small and narrow, so I couldn't get Converse tennis shoes which everyone thought were cool and called Chucks; I had to wear Keds, these yucky, girly shoes with pointed toes."

The group looked on with interested, yet confused, expressions, as though I were speaking in tongues. I talked and talked for what seemed like several minutes in exactly the kind of blithering English that I suspected my secretarial colleagues feared. Most of it was nonsense, and it probably sounded to them the way their conversations sometimes sounded to me—somewhat familiar but just out of reach. I slowed down at the end and said clearly, "I am glad I could entertain you with English because I have been practicing it for twenty-two years." I bowed, and the group clapped wildly, seemingly impressed that I was fluent in my native tongue.

Later I saw how fitting it was that I initiated myself into the club using nonsense language, because the basketball court was the one place where my language skills didn't count. At work I often felt frustrated because I couldn't express the complexity of my feelings with my elementary language skills. My experience was that of an adult, but my language was still that of a child. On the basketball court I could eliminate this gap because, as in judo, words didn't matter; playing did.

After basketball practice, everyone went to a *robata-yaki*, a pub-like place to eat and drink. All sixteen of us squeezed around two short wooden tables with our legs snugly folded on the tatami floor. One of the women in the group took charge of the menu and ordered huge mugs of draft beer for everyone. Ms. Kodama and the other women teased the men about smoking, which was the first thing most of them did when practice was over. She was more animated than I had ever seen her in the office. For the next two hours we drank beer and ate skewered grilled chicken, spicy bean sprouts, boiled soybeans, roasted beef and asparagus rolls, and rice balls.

I talked with Mr. Turtle and the other players. I also met the man who had spoken up on the court. He told me that when he was young his parents had sent him to an international school in Tokyo where he had been a minority. He knew what it was like to be left out.

I got home sometime after midnight feeling full, slightly drunk, and pleasantly exhausted. It was then that I realized that I had forgotten about work and Ms. Mori for the entire evening. Being an Uncle was a good thing. I could hardly wait until next Wednesday.

* * *

"Today's specialty is jam tea," Ms. Ogi announced in a high-pitched voice, pretending to be our waitress. She and Ms. Shoji and I were in the pantry taking a break. It had become more and more usual for the three of us to be together for lunch or tea.

"Jam tea? What is that?" I asked.

"It's the latest in tea-drinking," she said, handing me a glossy women's magazine. The picture showed cups of English tea with a different kind of jam spooned into the bottom of each.

"You *must* try it," Ms. Ogi pleaded. She could hardly keep a straight face.

"I agree, we must!" Ms. Shoji replied, and we broke out laughing.

Ms. Ogi studied the photograph and said, "I've never made this before, but let's give it a try."

She spooned some raspberry jam into a steaming cup of Earl Grey tea. The oozing red glob at the bottom of my cup sweetened the tea, but looked disgusting. As we drank the unusual beverage Ms. Shoji told us that she would be going to her family home in Gunma Prefecture for the weekend.

"Our family runs an inn at a hot-springs resort, and my sister and I take turns going home to help," she said. I had been to an *onsen* during my previous stay in Japan, and enjoyed it immensely.

"I love going to hot springs," I told her. "We don't have them in Ohio, so I had never been to one before I came to Japan."

Ms. Shoji told us that her mother ran the inn but that her grandfather had started it in the early 1900s.

"It's a beautiful place in the mountains called Sarugakyo," said Ms. Ogi. "All the secretaries went there a couple of years ago to ski."

"That must have been wonderful," I said.

"Yeah, wonderful if you don't have to work!" Ms. Shoji joked.

"Hey, why don't you take us with you next time you go home. We can help you!" Ms. Ogi suggested.

"Would you really be interested in going?" she asked me.

"Of course; I would definitely go. I've never been to a Gunma hot spring."

"Autumn is such a beautiful time there. The leaves are changing and you can pick apples," Ms. Ogi said.

For the next few weeks, during coffee breaks in the pantry, we coordinated our schedules and made plans for a trip. I hadn't felt so excited about anything since coming to Japan.

On a Saturday morning in late November Ms. Shoji, Ms. Ogi, and I boarded the bullet train bound for Gunma, about two hundred miles northwest of Tokyo. Sitting knee to knee on fuzzy blue seats, we each brought out a little bag of treats to share. The train rode so smoothly I felt as though I were sitting in a parlor having breakfast. Various announcements played over the loudspeaker, first in Japanese and then in English, announcing the train stops and exact time of arrival at each station.

Soon after the train departed, the conductor came by to check our tickets. Dressed in a vanilla-colored suit with dark stripes on the shoulders, he looked like an official version of the Pillsbury Doughboy. Even his shoes and cap were white. Stopping at each bay of seats, he politely requested to see each passenger's ticket: "Excuse me, honored passenger. May I be so rude as to ask to see your ticket?" His language was as mechanical as his movements, and he swiftly cruised through our car.

We munched on banana muffins that I had baked for the trip.

"Does your mother want you to come home more often than once a month?" I asked Ms. Shoji.

"I used to go home more often. My father passed away three years ago, and right after that it was very hard for my mother."

"I see," I replied.

"It's all right now," she said, nodding with a smile. "What do your parents think about you being so far away?"

"They miss me, of course. But since they also lived in Japan they are excited that I have this opportunity."

"My parents don't miss me at all," said Ms. Ogi, "because I've been living with them for almost thirty years! I've never been away from them for more than a few weeks."

"What about your brothers and sisters?" I asked her.

"Both of my older brothers and one older sister are married and live nearby. My parents already have three grandchildren. They were quite old when they had me."

"They will probably be sad when you get married and leave," I said.

"Oh no, they'll be so happy to see me married they won't miss me at all," Ms. Ogi laughed.

"Do your parents pressure you to get married?" I asked her.

"Not any more. I think they've given up. When I was around twenty-five my mother tried hard to get me to marry. Most women are expected to marry by then. But now I think she understands that I won't get married to just *anyone*."

"My mother is still hopeful," Ms. Shoji said. "Since neither my sister nor I have married, she is putting pressure on me to do it first."

"What about your mother?" Ms. Ogi asked me.

"I don't think she is worried," I answered.

"And what about your younger brother?"

"He is still in college."

"But once he is out of college, won't they start thinking about your marriage plans?" Ms. Shoji asked.

"I don't think that will matter. I'm sure they only want us to be happy with the person we choose. Getting married by a certain age isn't so important."

"That style of marriage is becoming more popular in Japan; we call it *renai* or a love match," Ms. Shoji said.

"What other kind of match is there?" I asked.

"An *omiai*, or arranged match," she said.

"Do you mean men and women still marry people they don't even know?"

"Well, a long time ago, perhaps around the time of my grandmother, an arranged marriage meant that they didn't know each other, but now the *omiai* system is used to simply introduce people—an arranged way to meet someone," Ms. Shoji explained.

"So you don't have to get married to that person?"

"Of course not. There is a go-between who knows both parties and thinks they could be a good couple. The parties agree to meet based on the advice of the go-between," she said.

"Who is the go-between?"

"The go-between can be someone like a relative or employer who knows the person well," said Ms. Shoji.

"In my case, my mother's neighbor arranged an *omiai* for me. She is determined to see me get married and shows my picture to everyone!" added Ms. Ogi.

"What picture?" I asked.

"Usually men and women have a formal picture taken around the age of twenty, and it is used specifically for *omiai* purposes. The go-between shows the picture and describes the person to the prospective partner. Both men and women also print up a personal resume describing their education and background. The go-between will show this resume along with the picture, and if the prospect is interested then an official meeting, an *omiai*, will take place," Ms. Shoji explained.

"So what happened at the *omiai?*" I asked Ms. Ogi.

"I went with my parents to meet the man and his parents and the go-between at a coffee shop in a fancy hotel. We all talked and then the adults left, so we could go out alone," she said and rolled her eyes.

"Well, what happened?"

"Usually," Ms. Shoji interrupted, "following the meeting, both sides tell the go-between whether they would like to continue seeing one another. We don't have to say we want to get married right away, but of course eventual marriage is the goal."

"So after that one meeting you have to decide whether you could marry this person or not?" I asked.

"Well, I guess so. If you don't think you could marry the person then you tell the go-between no, and you don't see each other again," Ms. Shoji replied.

"What happened? Did it take you a while to know what you thought of the man?" I asked Ms. Ogi.

"No. I knew from my first impression that I didn't like him," she snickered.

"Why do people use a go-between?" I asked.

"For several reasons; the first is to find a partner. Sometimes, especially for young men who spend most of their time working, it's hard to find someone to ask out. A go-between will search on their behalf and find a woman with a similar background and interests," Ms. Shoji said.

"Another reason is to make it easier if one person doesn't want to continue the relationship. The go-between can help prevent conflict," Ms. Ogi added.

"So how common is it?" I asked.

"My friend met her husband this way," Ms. Ogi said.

"As women get older and their prospects become fewer, they feel more anxious to marry. Most of the women in the secretary group have participated in *omiai* at least once, and some even more!" Ms. Shoji explained.

"What do you think of *omiai?*" I asked her directly.

"My mother has encouraged me to do it, and I've tried. Some people think that at my age I should just keep trying until I find a husband, but I'm not so eager. What do you think?" Ms. Shoji asked me.

"I guess I might try it, but there is something about it that would make me feel, well . . . kind of desperate. Do you know what I mean? Like you can't find your own boyfriend."

"Yes, I see what you mean, but maybe in Japan people don't worry so much about that because everyone does it."

We paused in the lobby of the Sarugakyo inn and slipped off our shoes before taking a step up to the landing where slippers waited.

"Welcome!" Ms. Shoji's mother greeted us in a loud, boisterous voice. She looked nothing like I had imagined a marriage-pushing mother to be. Wearing casual slacks and a colorful sweater, she was taller than all three of us. She wore bold makeup and had a reddish tint to her hair. In America she would have been the type to throw open her arms and hug me to her ample breast. Instead she bowed and said, "I am so happy you are both here. Ogiwara-san, it's been such a long time! How are you?"

She introduced us to her mother-in-law, who looked small and frail next to her sturdy daughter-in-law. "Grandma, this is Rora," Ms. Shoji said.

"I can't speak English; I'm sorry," the grandmother said without looking at me.

"It's all right," Ms. Shoji explained, "Rora can speak Japanese."

"*Konnichiwa. Hajimemashite,*" I said, introducing myself.

"Oh, what a relief; I was so worried. Your Japanese is so good," the grandmother replied, and bowed again.

The ceiling of the lobby was exceptionally high and opened into a long room. A knobby green carpet covered the entire lobby floor. A few pieces of furniture and some plants made up a sparse sitting area in the front of the room. We walked through the lobby and passed a small counter with five stools with a sign that said "Petite Balcon."

"This is a noodle shop where guests can buy lunch," Ms. Shoji said.

"Where is the name from?" I asked. "It looks French."

"It is. It means small balcony. European culture was so popular in Japan in the early 1900s that my grandfather gave the noodle shop a French name."

Beyond the noodle shop was a gift store packed with boxes of local specialties such as sweet bean cakes, pickled vegetables, and other souvenirs.

"Before we leave we'll stop here to get *omiyage* for the other secretaries," Ms. Shoji said.

As an exchange student I had bought *omiyage* for my host family every time I went on a trip. Food was the most popular gift, but *omiyage* could be any token present given to the people left behind. Any place I visited in Japan had special *omiyage* shops just like this one.

"I heard that in Tokyo Station there are places where you can buy *omiyage* from all over Japan, so if someone forgot to buy a gift he can buy it on his way home," I said.

"I also heard that married men use this when they

sneak out to meet a mistress when they are supposed to be on a business trip," said Ms. Ogi. "They buy these *omiyage* to take home to their wives!"

We left our bags in an office and started a tour of the inn. After a few minutes I felt disoriented. We went up an elevator, crossed a passageway, walked through sliding doors, and went down some narrow stairs. I felt as though I had stepped into an Escher painting.

"How many guests can stay here?" I asked as we passed room after room.

"There are fifty rooms, so at the most we can have two hundred guests," Ms. Shoji answered. "Most people come here on company trips from Tokyo or other cities for overnight stays. They come here to get away for a night, eat, bathe in the hot spring, drink saké, and sing karaoke with their colleagues."

"Does Honda have company trips?" I asked.

"Of course, but since it's such a big company each department usually has its own trip. The secretariat will take a trip sometime."

I didn't know how excited I would feel about spending the weekend with all of my colleagues. With Ms. Ogi and Ms. Shoji I felt I could show my *honne* and relax. If Ms. Kodama and Ms. Mori had been here I would have felt different.

After exploring the inn we walked around the neighborhood. Ms. Shoji's elementary school was at the top of a hill. The austere school building looked deserted. Ms. Shoji told us about her school days and having to walk her sister to school. There were some monkey bars in the abandoned playground and I tried to demonstrate the flipping contests we used to have in grade school.

Ms. Ogi gripped a bar that was as tall as her head, and when she tried to swing her leg up, it got stuck.

"I'm a little out of practice," she gasped as we helped her down. "I don't think I've tried that for twenty years!"

On a nearby road we saw signs for an orchard inviting us for *ringo gari*, apple picking, and *kaki gari*, persimmon picking. The apple orchard smelled sweet and earthy, and plump, light-skinned Fuji apples hung from branches. We took turns steadying one another on wooden ladders and climbed up among the fragrant leaves.

"Let's eat one now," Ms. Ogi said climbing down with a Fuji she could barely get her hand around.

A flat wooden board was set up with knives. Ms. Shoji sliced the apple into two hard, white halves.

"Oh, this is a good one," she announced. "Look how big the *mitsu* is. It's the clear section around the core." She handed me a wedge and pointed to the crisp golden center. The fragrance made my mouth water, and I took a bite of sweet fruit. It was the most delicious apple I'd ever eaten. "Here," Ms. Shoji said. She pushed a bowl of salty peanuts toward me. "It's most delicious to eat these together."

Our last stop on the tour of the town was Cycle World. It was an outdoor track that had a dozen different types of cycles for rent: bicycles, unicycles, and cycles propelled with arm peddles. We raced around the four-hundred-meter track switching from recumbents to old-fashioned velocipedes with front wheels four feet tall. I was laughing so hard that I fell off the arm peddle cycle, just as Ms. Shoji was taking a picture of me. I hadn't felt so playful since coming to Japan.

Dressed in thin cotton robes, Ms. Ogi and I followed Ms. Shoji to the hot-spring bath on the lower floor of the inn. Walking down the stairways past curved corners, I felt like we were exploring a mystical dungeon. The *onsen* was like the *sentō*, public bath, but much larger and more elaborate. In a small tatami-mat room, we left our robes in bowl-sized wicker baskets and approached a sliding glass door that opened up into what appeared to be a wall of steam. I could hear the magnified echo of trickling water. Dim lights gave the space a cave-like feeling, and warm steam enveloped my naked body.

Walking through the steam, I began to make out shapes. Blue-green tile covered the ceiling, walls, and floors. Curved archways opened into connecting rooms. I followed Ms. Shoji to a large room with a shallow pool. A white statue of a Greek goddess stood in the center where water sprang forth from a small fountain.

Using small plastic buckets, we bathed at spigots that stuck out of the wall. After we were thoroughly clean, we entered the steaming hot spring water and sat completely still.

"Oh, this feels so good!" exclaimed Ms. Ogi.

"It feels like home," Ms. Shoji said.

"I can barely stand the heat," I uttered.

The water was almost too hot, and I tingled all over. Soon I felt my muscles relaxing and my eyelids droop. I stretched my head to my shoulder and heard a satisfying, knuckly crack.

Ms. Shoji's house was connected to the inn. I sat on the floor of the living room wearing a *hanten* padded jacket over my cotton robe. My body, still steaming from the bath, felt well insulated from the cold evening air. I took a drink from a frosty glass of homemade *umeshu*, or plum wine. The light, tangy liquid cooled my throat. While Ms. Shoji and her sister were in the kitchen making dinner Ms. Ogi sat across from me dozing, and I watched television. An episode of *Little House on the Prairie* was on in Japanese. Michael Landon as Pa spoke like a gruff Japanese man. Laura Ingles and her sister Mary ran through the fields of Walnut Grove calling to one another in Japanese. In a strange way it all seemed to make sense.

I had seen almost every episode of *Little House on the Prairie* and I'd read all the books, so it was strange to hear Japanese language coming from these familiar characters. I wondered how Japanese people saw them. Surely some of the meaning would be altered by the translation. Laura Ingles didn't seem quite as tough and tomboyish when she fell into a creek and yelled out a polite Japanese phrase.

Ms. Shoji's mother came into the living room dressed up in a silk kimono. With her face neatly powdered in white and her hair combed tightly into a bun, I hardly recognized her. All of her ample curves had been snugly bound flat by the stiff kimono material. She greeted us quickly before rushing out the doorway toward the inn.

"Where is she going?" I asked Ms. Ogi.

"She must formally greet the guests. It is a traditional greeting not so common any more. This," she paused, "is a very special place."

We talked late into the night like college roommates. The air had become much colder. Without central heat, the bedroom was icy cold, and I could see my breath. Slipping under a heavy, thick quilt, I snuggled deep into my futon, Ms. Shoji on my left and Ms. Ogi on my right.

I felt warm—a deep-down warmth from the hot

springs, the layers of robes, and the new connection with Ogi and Shoji. There was something about our growing friendship that reminded me of my childhood and the ritual of becoming friends. In my hometown neighborhood, friendship was signified by swapping clothes. My best friend Maria and I exchanged everything—our socks, bell-bottoms, macramé belts, and T-shirts. But when we traded, we weren't trying out new styles; we were trying on new identities—we wanted to explore what it was like to be someone else.

Throughout the weekend, playing, eating, and bathing with Ogi and Shoji, I felt like I was echoing my past in a new language. I was discovering a part of myself in my new friends. That night I went to sleep and dreamed of having sisters.

Conformity and
the Helicopter Ride

5

IN ADDITION TO TAKING TURNS DOING THE "A" and "B" chores, each secretary started the day by cleaning the directors' desks with a white terry-cloth rag from the cleaning bucket in the pantry. One day as I put my own rag into the cleaning bucket I noticed something odd about the other rags. Uncertain about my observation, I carefully watched the next morning as each woman selected a rag and then returned it to the storage bucket after completing her task. I peered into the bucket and was again amazed that my observation had been correct. Every single white rag had been precisely folded and twisted in the exact same manner.

Conformity was at the center of almost everything we did: the way we answered the phone, the rule against anyone having an individual business card, and the uniforms. I understood what Mr. Yoshida had meant about the tenth floor being different from other departments. In the entire headquarters, ours was the most conservative floor because we supported the executive directors of Honda Motor Company. We provided stability and support for the directors who dashed off to meetings across the country and traveled overseas for weeks at a time. We were home base.

But even though conformity seemed like unconscious behavior for most of my Japanese colleagues, I started to realize that others in the group, like me, consciously compromised to fit in.

Another secretary, Ms. Ishii, had also recently joined the executive secretariat. Although she had worked at Honda for over two years, she acted like a timid freshman and hesitated before doing anything. She crept softly around the office as though the floor were made of thin ice and a single misplaced step would send her crashing into oblivion. Her voice was small and whispery, and when she laughed she'd hold her perfectly manicured hand over her mouth to suppress even the slightest sound.

One day Ms. Ishii and I took a coffee break together in the pantry. I sat on one of the stools and she crouched next to the table holding her tea cup in two hands. I opened a box of chocolate-covered macadamia nuts—a frequent gift from directors who had been on overseas business trips. Ms. Ishii told me that she had majored in French literature in college. Since she and I always conversed in Japanese, I asked her if she spoke French.

"I studied, but I can't speak it well," she answered. Then, as if to tell me a secret, she lowered her voice and said in perfect English, "I lived in Queens for about four years."

"What? You can speak English?"

She looked away from the table, embarrassed at my surprise. "I can't speak it very well," she said with excellent pronunciation. "I attended an American junior high and high school because my father worked in New York City."

I was shocked that Ms. Ishii hadn't spoken with me earlier. I had already been here for three months, struggling to understand and communicate, and Ms. Ishii had never offered to help me or even to speak with me. Even my attention to her ability seemed to be truly, almost painfully, embarrassing.

Her behavior helped explain a proverb that was supposed to explain Japanese social behavior: "The nail that sticks up will be pounded down." I had heard this in college, but I hadn't understood it as I was experiencing it now. Ms. Ishii helped me see that conformity was a choice for my colleagues just as it was for me, only they had been doing it all their lives.

The English skills of most of the secretaries consisted of junior high school reading ability and elementary verbal skills. "Howdoyoudo Iamfinethankyou," was one word in our office, and this level of proficiency established the group norm. Even though Ms. Ishii could converse like an adult in English, she hid her skills so she wouldn't stick out.

Conformity had become less and less important to me as I had grown older. Even during my most conformist period as a high school cheerleader, I had tried to distinguish myself from the other girls. During my senior year I was the only cheerleader who was also in the band and on the basketball team. Sometimes during football season I filled in for missing members of the marching band. After cheering for the first half of the football game, I would change into my band uniform for the half-time show and feign playing an instrument while I marched to balance out the formations. After the show, I would change back into my pleated skirt and saddle shoes for the remainder of the game.

During basketball season I cheered for the boys and played with the girls. Some days after school I would go from cheerleading practice straight to basketball practice, but I didn't mind—I reveled in being the only cheerleader who could sink a free throw and carry a tuba.

It was precisely the nonconformist path that had brought me to Japan. While most of my college friends had made plans to study in Europe in their third year of university, I was the only one from our college to go to Japan. I made the choice to work for Honda partly because I didn't want to conform to traditional Midwestern expectations. I didn't want to move to Chicago or New York and start an entry-level job with a well-established advertising or investment firm—not because it wasn't appealing, but because most of the people I admired in college were doing that.

The irony of my situation was that now conformity was the only path toward acceptance and success in my job. I wanted to be part of this group, but as the expectations became clearer, the more uncertain I felt about my ability and willingness to conform. My success on the tenth floor depended on my ability to smile, serve tea without spilling a drop, organize junk mail, and cheerfully anticipate the needs of any executive who walked into the room.

But I wanted more. Mr. Yoshida had made it clear that as part of my assignment I would experience Honda's international operations: visit factories, attend international functions, and see the company firsthand, not just from brochures on the tenth floor. All the training in

America would make sense to me if I had opportunities to explore other parts of the company. I wanted to reach out of the secretariat, but I didn't know how I could experience work outside the executive office and still be an accepted, effective member of the group.

One afternoon Mr. Higuchi called me into a conference room.

"The Quality Circle Convention will be held at the end of this month at the Suzuka factory," he told me. "I think it would be a good opportunity for you to observe an international event. Although it is unusual for a secretary to leave the tenth floor, Mr. Yoshida wants you to see many parts of the company. But it is important that you don't stand out. Do you understand what I mean?"

I nodded and listened quietly while he described the trip details and my responsibilities. Quality circles were groups of self-organized employees who suggested improvements, from technical assembly-line operations to personnel policies. Mr. Higuchi explained that every year Honda's best circle groups from around the world gathered for a convention to share ideas and, particularly, to reward employees for their efforts. This year over three thousand employees from fifteen countries would participate.

He told me that I would take the bullet train to the Suzuka factory on the Friday before Saturday's convention and that my job would be to assist Tom Umeno.

"Tom will be accompanying the president, who will be giving a speech. You should check with him in case he needs your help, but basically you will be free to observe the activities. After the convention you can return to Tokyo with Tom."

At the end of our discussion my boss produced a gift. "Here, this is for you."

I opened the package. Inside was a black vinyl travel bag with "Honda" embossed on the side. I smiled and thanked him.

"It is for your first business trip in Japan," he said, smiling back. I could already pictured myself carrying the bag and wearing my cream-colored suit. Then he added, "It is probably best not to show it to the other secretaries."

The trip was exactly the kind of experience I wanted, but I feared I might alienate myself from the others, and Mr. Higuchi knew this too. At the morning meeting the next day he made a cursory announcement that I would be out of the office on Friday to attend the executives at the convention. I held my breath. My face registered no sign of enthusiasm or even recognition, and I waited for Ms. Mori to make a comment, but the room was silent. No one said a thing.

On Friday morning I boarded the bullet train in Tokyo Station and traveled west to Suzuka. The train took less than three hours to travel 560 miles. From the Suzuka train station I had been instructed to take a bus, or a taxi if necessary, to the factory. I felt a little apprehensive about finding the right bus and was still debating what to do as I walked toward the station exit carrying my black bag. At the bottom of the stairway I saw a polished black Honda and a uniformed driver wearing white gloves standing next to the opened passenger door.

"*Konnichiwa,*" the driver greeted me, as though he knew exactly who I was. He reached for my bag and said, "Please get in."

The driver delivered me to the front entrance of the

factory, where a Honda associate, dressed in a white production uniform, welcomed me. Such treatment would be expected for the executives, but not for a secretary. I wondered if they had me confused with someone else.

The man introduced himself as a member of the General Affairs Department and showed me to the visitor's room, where I sat down on a blue Naugahyde chair with a white lace cover. A blown-glass ashtray sat next to a display of cigarettes on the coffee table in front of me. It looked like the decor hadn't been changed since the 1950s. On the walls hung fuzzy aerial photos of the factory and a color-coded diagram of the plant floor.

While I chatted with the General Affairs man, a young woman wearing the same white uniform came in and served us orange juice. The man wanted to know all about the directors and others from the tenth floor. I realized then the reason for my special treatment. Even though I wasn't an executive, I represented the executive floor and, in his eyes, deserved the royal treatment.

It took the entire afternoon to tour the largest motorcycle factory in the world. With over eleven thousand employees and three manufacturing lines, the Suzuka factory was Honda's biggest production facility.

After the tour I went to the convention site near the factory. The site operated year-round as an amusement park and racetrack. Dinner was held in a huge hall filled with tables, chairs, and hordes of Honda associates from all over the world. I noticed a small group of foreigners and suspected, from their casual dress and the beards some of the men wore, that they had come from the United States. They were the first group of English speakers I had seen in months. I sat with the Americans through dinner and later attended the welcome party for all the foreign guests, feeling comfortably inconspicuous for the first time since I had arrived in Japan.

I had been instructed to report first thing Saturday morning to a certain building to meet Tom. This building had rustic, A-frame construction and was about the size of a large two-car garage. In the front room, tables and chairs had been set up as a waiting area where the directors could leave their things and have a cup of tea. It was still early, and the room was deserted.

I peered into the room next door. It looked like a combination of an election campaign headquarters and command central for a major military offensive. Pinned on the walls were detailed maps and diagrams outlining convention activities and locations. Extra telephones had been hooked up. All the wires and cords were bound together and taped to the floor. Scribbled notes filled a large chalkboard, and meticulous lists and graphs were spread out on the tables. Ten bleary-eyed men walked around gulping coffee as they jabbered on their walkie-talkies, each wearing a red-and-white arm band that identified him as part of the Convention Organization Team.

I didn't see Tom and no one seemed to notice me, so I left my black bag in the waiting room and went to observe the presentations. Later in the morning I met up with Tom and asked him if I could do anything to assist him. He shook his head and told me that he was just waiting until the president gave his speech at the end of the day.

"This evening, instead of returning to Tokyo on the train, President Kume and I will return by helicopter. Since you and I are supposed to return together, I thought maybe you would like to join us?"

"That would be great," I said.

Tom told me that we would depart immediately following the speech. He asked where my things were and I told him that I had left my overnight bag in the waiting room at command central. He said he would arrange to have someone bring it to the president's private waiting room.

After lunch, President Kume gave his speech to a crowd of two thousand people in the outdoor grandstands at the race track. He spoke in Japanese about the importance of quality circle activities and general Honda worldwide news. An interpreter read an English summary of his speech, but I was so distracted with anticipation of riding in the helicopter that I only listened to about half of what he said.

After the speech I followed Tom and the president to the waiting room to collect our things. I looked around but couldn't find my black bag. Apparently, no one had brought it. Tom told me to go get it myself, and to hurry. I ran back to command central and searched all over for the bag. I couldn't find it and started to panic.

One of the Convention Organization Team members was standing in the waiting room. He saw my expression and asked what had happened. After I explained the situation he got on his walkie-talkie and instantly initiated a mass search throughout the entire park. I couldn't understand much of what was being said, but I did recognize one phrase being repeated through the static: "Ms. Laura's black bag."

A few minutes later someone located the bag and ordered it to be delivered directly to the heliport. I ran back to the waiting room.

With relief, I found both Tom and the president

there. I nodded calmly to Tom, indicating that everything was under control. The three of us got in the black Honda that had picked me up the day before and drove a short distance to the heliport. As we prepared to board the helicopter, another car drove up and delivered my black bag.

We climbed into the helicopter, where two pilots sat in front, and took off immediately. On the ascent we could see the grandstands and racetrack where the president had just given his speech. I could see the entire amusement park, the factory, and all the surrounding areas. I hadn't realized how close we were to the ocean, but I could see the beach right below me. In the distance we spotted a cargo ship that had the HONDA logo painted in big white letters on the side. On the sea, on land, and in the sky: for a moment I was enraptured with awe at the comprehensive power of this organization and the man sitting right next to me who controlled it.

Mr. Kume had been president for four years. With fleshy jowls and a solid physique, he looked like a heavy-set linebacker. When he spoke, he used short, gruff tones. His stoic appearance matched my observation of him in the office. I had never heard him utter more than a sentence or two at a time.

He sat next to me smoking quietly. I was so close I could have plucked the cigarette right from his mouth. I found myself wishing I had listened more carefully to his speech so I could make an intelligent remark. Tom complimented the president, and they talked about the speech for a minute.

I wondered how my colleagues would have handled this situation. In the office only Ms. Shoji and Ms. Ogi seemed to have any composure around the executives. As soon as any male authority figure came into the proximity of the women in the secretariat, most of them were transformed into high-strung nervous nellies who treated everything with a high-pitched urgency. They acted as though they were simultaneously terrified and impressed with the executives. Like yippy Chihuahuas, the women ran around the office in tiny, high-heeled steps and didn't breath normally until the executives left.

Around any kind of celebrity the women were reduced to giggling fools. When Aryton Senna, the famous Brazilian Formula 1 race-car driver, visited the tenth floor, my colleagues acted like goofy children. We kept a loaded camera on hand for such occasions, so someone asked him to have his picture taken with us. The women giggled and scurried behind one another and hid their faces in their hands. No one was bold enough to greet him or look him in the eye. I was embarrassed for all of them, so I said hello and shook his hand.

I couldn't imagine what my colleagues would think of me here with President Kume and Tom, both of whom were now dozing. I looked out the window and watched the ocean waves crashing against the beach.

* * *

After about an hour of flying up the coast toward Tokyo, the weather became a little cloudy and gray, but I wasn't particularly worried. One of the benefits of traveling with important cargo like the president of Honda was that safety would be the first thing on the pilot's mind.

A light rain started to fall, and the sky darkened. Within minutes the wind was blowing hard and the weather quickly got worse. Tom and President Kume woke up. We could feel every bump and wind gust. The president started smoking furiously; as soon as he finished off one cigarette, he lit up another. I began to feel a little sick to my stomach from both the smoke and the turbulence.

The pilots were talking rapidly into their radios; finally one of them turned and said politely, "Excuse me. I'm so sorry. We are going to have to make an unscheduled landing." By then the helicopter was really rocking, and I thought to myself, "Don't apologize, just do it!"

We started to descend into darkness. I couldn't tell how far above the ground we were, or if we were still over the ocean. Suddenly the pilot opened his door, and wind shrieked in through the crack. "What is he doing?" I wanted to shout. I had no sense of where we were. Then I realized that the pilot had opened his door in order to see the ground. Moments later we landed.

The helicopter sat in an unlit grassy field out in the middle of nowhere. A flashlight appeared, and someone approached the helicopter. It was as though they had been expecting us. I followed Tom and the president and stepped outside. I was so thrilled to be on the ground that I didn't mind the cold, pelting rain. The person with the flashlight quickly escorted us through the darkness. I felt completely disoriented and wanted to ask if anyone knew where we were.

Suddenly, up ahead, I saw bright lights. I followed the group into a building. It was a factory. Inside we were greeted by the very surprised plant manager of Seiki Giken, one of the companies that supply parts to Honda. Even though it was 6:00 P.M. on a Saturday, a contingent of employees sat working at their desks. The plant manager took us to a guest room for tea.

"I guess you never know when the president will drop in for a visit," joked Tom.

"Yes. I guess we should always be prepared for a storm," replied the plant manager. "We had requested a visit from President Kume, but didn't realize he would respond so promptly," he joked again.

Relief was still palpable, and we all laughed heartily at these stupid jokes. After resting and drinking hot tea, the plant manager asked the president if he would be willing to take a factory tour. Despite his long day and the harrowing helicopter ride, President Kume agreed.

An hour later the plant manager handed Tom the keys to a Honda, and the three of us drove back to Tokyo. While Tom drove, President Kume and I talked. I asked him about his hometown and his travels to the Ohio factory. When I told him that I had worked on the line there, he seemed surprised. I joked that the cars I helped make might be defective, and he promised to let me know in advance if there was ever a recall. He asked me about my hobbies, my family, and where I lived in Tokyo. He even invited me to play golf sometime.

Tom told me later that he had never seen the president so talkative. I suspected that part of his unusual gregariousness was plain euphoria. But the other part was that I could just talk with him. I didn't let his importance overwhelm or silence me because I was genuinely interested in knowing more about him.

When we arrived at the president's home it was after 10:00 P.M. Tom got out of the car to escort President Kume to his door. When he came back he showed me a ¥10,000 yen note (about $70 at the time) that President Kume had given him to treat us to dinner because it was so late.

Monday morning I went to work as usual. I expected having to say something about the trip. The general manager gave me a cue during the morning meeting by saying, "Rora-san, please give a brief report about the convention." I looked around the room at Ms. Ishii and my colleagues sitting quietly at their desks in matching blue uniforms.

Still fresh from the excitement of the adventure, I wanted to leap up onto the desk and describe the experience in vivid detail—riding the bullet train, the private chauffeur, the tour of the factory, misplacing the black bag, and the life-threatening helicopter ride ending in another factory tour and having my dinner paid for by the president himself.

But instead, without altering my expression, I glanced up and reported in Japanese, "The convention proceeded smoothly and the directors experienced no major problems. It was a very regular event." Things were starting to make sense to me. I was finally getting it right.

Alone

6 | LATE ONE AFTERNOON THE CHAIRMAN walked into the office wearing a formal black suit of the type usually worn to weddings or funerals. He was one of the few executives who had a commanding presence, perhaps because he was nearly six feet tall and rather aloof. I rarely heard him speak except to give monosyllabic directions to Ms. Mori in what struck me as a surprisingly feminine tone. The soft sounds, incongruent with his stern features, and the fact that he was Ms. Mori's territory, gave me every reason to avoid him.

He paused in front of the reception desk where I stood trying to avoid his gaze. Ms. Mori wasn't at her desk, which seemed to annoy him. He motioned to me, and I approached him hesitantly. He reached into his pocket, took out a small decorative envelope the size of a packet of sugar, and motioned for me to cup my hands together. Into my palms he poured a tiny mound of white crystals and then turned his back to me, issuing a one-syllable command I didn't understand. Was I supposed to eat this while he looked away? He glanced back at me and made a tossing gesture with his arm. I wasn't sure I understood him, but I took a chance and tossed my cupped hands toward his back. The crystals scattered over his black suit coat and fell silently to the floor. He turned around and briskly brushed his arms. The corners of his mouth curled up slightly, and for the first time I saw him smile. He nodded his head with approval and left the room.

Ms. Ogi was standing nearby and had witnessed the entire event. She came over and told me that the chairman had been to a funeral and that, according to Buddhist custom, each guest received a packet of salt with which to purify himself. The purification had to be done by another person as soon as the guest returned from the funeral, whether at home or at work. "You just purified the chairman," she said, laughing. "Not many people can say that."

* * *

Work was constantly challenging, and for several months I felt a strong sense of accomplishment from learning all the directors' code names and memorizing the characters for their full names. I felt comfortable enough speaking on the phone that I could take full messages from callers rather than just asking them to call back later.

Working with Mr. Chino continued to be enjoyable. I tried to converse with him more and more in Japanese, and slowly I got to know him. His wife was finishing her Ph.D. in California and teaching classes in Shakespearean literature. His daughter, who was about my age, was in law school in America but he hoped that one day she would practice in Japan. He treated me exceptionally well, and despite my disdain for some of the secretarial tasks, I found myself working harder just to please him. I wanted to be the best secretary that he had ever had—better than Ms. Mori.

When I asked him if there was anything I could do to be a better secretary, he mentioned that it would be nice if I could clear his morning tea dishes from his desk more promptly. I felt embarrassed that I hadn't noticed and privately chastised myself for forcing him to look at a cold, dirty tea cup all morning while he was trying to work. Cleaning his tea dishes became a measure of my success, and for weeks after his comment I would hover in the entrance of the executive office trying to detect the precise moment he was done.

My value system had shifted significantly. Sometimes cleaning dishes really did seem like the most important thing I did. There were, however, unpredictable moments of clarity that arose out of my frustration with the layers of meaninglessness of my work. In these moments I would act out in small, insignificant gestures of defiance, as if to launch an individual rebellion.

One day I purposely didn't button the vest to my uniform. Other women in headquarters wore their vests open or even left them hanging on their chairs. But there was an unwritten rule on the tenth floor that we wore them buttoned.

I went about my morning routine half-aware that this was a test to see who would try to correct me and what they would say. Before noon Ms. Mori and one other woman had commented on the open vest, encouraging me to button up because I would look like I was doing a better job.

Another day Mr. Chino gave me a letter to mail. He had already addressed the envelope and sealed it shut. All I had to do was affix a stamp and put it in the outgoing mail basket. The mail was picked up six times a day by women from the mail room pushing two-tiered black metal carts. Every time one of the unassuming mail-ladies rolled her cart into an elevator she would bow and apologize for the inconvenience. When she arrived on our floor her voice rang out apologizing for the interruption before taking the mail.

When Mr. Chino handed me the envelope I knew a mail-lady would be coming soon, so I got a stamp from the domestic stamp drawer and took it to my desk. I licked the stamp and was about to affix it when an impulse ran through my fingers and I placed the stamp at an angle—not straight against the edge of the envelope, but tilted so that a small triangle of the envelope appeared in the upper right corner. I placed the envelope in the out basket and went back to work.

A little while later the mail-lady announced her arrival, but by then I was distracted with something else. I had already forgotten about the letter until I looked up to see the mail-lady standing right next to my desk.

"I'm so sorry," she said, and held out Mr. Chino's letter. I gave her a blank look as if to say, "What?"

She pointed to the stamp. "It's crooked," she said.

I almost laughed out loud, but her earnestness stopped me. She waited for me to do something while I wondered how she knew the letter was my responsibility. She stood by with patient attention as I got a new stamp and delicately scraped off the old one. Even though I had suspected that I would get caught, I acted as though I felt unjustly accused. Before I licked the new stamp, I took out a ruler and lined it up with the edge of the envelope to guide the placement. If she was offended by my sarcasm she didn't show it. On the contrary, she appeared satisfied, took the letter, and left with a bow.

It was rare that I took on Ms. Mori directly; I usually kept to my quiet acts of imperceptible rebellion. But without much thought, I found myself correcting her in front of the entire office one morning.

The Administration Department seemed to be constantly promoting some new company propaganda with colorful flyers and posters. One week we were encouraged to be less wasteful, and another week we'd be asked to promote traffic safety. Tom usually explained the campaigns to me, after which I would promptly ignore them. It was hard enough for me to abide by the standard rules, so I rationalized that I didn't need to concern myself with all the extra stuff.

One week a new poster on our bulletin board attracted my attention. The white poster showed a dialogue bubble, like the ones used in comic strips, filled with common Japanese names like Tanaka, Furokawa, and Kuroda. Tom explained that this campaign was called *"San-tsuke undō,"* or "using the title *san,*" and happened to be the chairman's personal project. The idea was to encourage employees to start referring to their superiors by their last names adding the suffix *san* rather than calling them by their titles like *buchō,* manager, or *shachō,* president. The chairman believed that eliminating the titles would encourage a more egalitarian atmosphere in the office.

"So instead of calling our manager *buchō,* we should call him Yamada-san?" I asked. Even saying it sounded weird because only the executives called our boss Yamada-san.

"Yes," Tom nodded, although he seemed a bit uncertain. Tom's job as the president's gofer required him to constantly flatter the executives and other managers. His use of calling people by their titles was so ingrained that I wondered if he'd ever really be able to give up this effective language tool and call the president Kume-san.

I already referred to Mr. Chino as Chino-san rather than Chino-senmu, meaning Senior Managing Director Chino. Sometimes Ms. Ogi and Ms. Shoji and I made fun of the directors' titles by changing the words used to describe them. My favorite was substituting *senbei* for *senmu*, which made his title Rice Cracker Chino.

The idea of calling everyone *san* immediately appealed to me as a way to lessen authority within the hierarchy, and I decided to follow the campaign religiously. I referred to the president as Kume-san and once even said Honda-san, referring to the man whom everyone called Saikō Komon, the supreme advisor. I noticed that Ms. Mori ignored the white poster which hung limply on the bulletin board like an empty threat.

One morning as she began the group meeting with her usual phrase, "Today Chairman Okubo . . . ," I raised my hand and interrupted by asking our boss if we were supposed to be referring to the directors using *san*. Ms. Mori frowned. Mr. Yamada was startled, but he couldn't ignore my question. I looked at the poster, which seemed suddenly to have claimed a higher place on the wall. "It's just a question I had," I said innocently. "I mean, I thought it was the chairman himself who wanted us all to do that."

Mr. Yamada ground out his cigarette and looked

puzzled. The others waited quietly for his response. "Well," he chuckled uncomfortably, "I suppose you're right." He nodded for Ms. Mori to continue. Her face was red, and I thought she might refuse. But instead she started over, saying, "Today Okubo-san will . . . "

I realized that my attitude was petty, but sometimes I couldn't resist these momentary gestures of autonomy even though they didn't help. My attempts to be different only emphasized the real problem—I was lonely. But admitting this to myself would have been much more painful then dealing with these episodes of pettiness and rebellion. I yearned to have a boyfriend, but the only men I met worked at Honda and didn't appeal to me. They were workaholic underlings who acted awkward around all women, especially foreign ones. A few times I went out to clubs, but it never seemed like a good place to meet a man.

One Friday night after attending an executive secretariat dinner at a Chinese restaurant, I decided to take a detour through Roppongi on my way home. Roppongi was the hip area of town with lots of bars and dance clubs. It was also the place known as a hangout for foreigners. I felt tired from speaking Japanese all week, exhausted from the obligatory office dinner, and I wanted some American companionship.

I went to a club that was packed with young people; only one quarter of the crowd was Japanese. Standing at the bar and still wearing my coat, I ordered a beer and looked around. Young foreign models dressed in tight black clothing sat in exclusive groups smoking and drinking and laughing. Older-looking foreign businessmen flirted with young Japanese women who smiled and took dainty sips from their drinks. I didn't see any young professional people, men or women, who looked like me. I felt as out of place in this scene as I had earlier in the evening with my colleagues at dinner. I left without finishing my beer and went home.

Another time I met a twenty-year-old guy from Kansas in a bar. From his fuzzy blonde crewcut I knew immediately that he was in the military and stationed at one of the bases near Tokyo. We danced in the bar and he tried to kiss me. The next night we went to a movie. He tried to grope me and pressured me to go to his hotel room. Even though I didn't like him much, his touch in the dark theater made me tremble with desire. I refused to go home with him, but he continued to pursue me after he'd returned to the base. He wrote me letters about driving tanks in undisclosed locations and asked when he could see me again. When I broke our next date, he and his drunk buddies called up and left disgusting threats on my answering machine.

One Saturday afternoon while I was out running errands, I walked into a furniture store and saw a huge Papa-san chair that looked large enough to hold my entire body. I had always wanted one of these bowl-like bamboo chairs—perfect for cuddling up in to read, I thought. Although I admired it I knew that the chair itself would take up half of the tatami room. I wouldn't have room enough for it and my futon or the tea table. A saleswoman saw me admiring the chair and asked if I needed any help. For some reason her request made me feel lonely, and without thinking I said to her, "Oh, I'm just looking at it now. I'll have to talk it over with my husband." I felt a moment of comfort when she nodded her head, believing my lie. I couldn't even admit the truth of my loneliness to a stranger.

Finding Myself
on the Map

7 I WAS ON MY HANDS AND KNEES ON THE floor of my apartment looking at a map of Tokyo. The city was sprawling and colorful and chaotic, marked with black characters of varying sizes, most of which were meaningless to me. I scanned the uncertainty bound by lines and shapes, searching for something familiar, a recognizable starting place. There were thick black and white train lines snaking across the page and wide white paths signifying major roads. I pinpointed the two simple characters for Meguro—the name of the ward in which I lived. The entire ward was contained in a thin red line. I was some-where inside this line.

Within the red line there was a large green section labeled with a string of characters. I could read only the characters for park. The area was so large compared to the rest of the neighborhood I knew it must be Komazawa, the park where I went jogging and the place that had served as a secondary athletic facility during the 1964 Olympics in Tokyo.

From the park I traced a four-lane road that led toward my apartment. It was the biggest road in the ward—the one that I crossed over to get to the Daei Department Store and to the main post office. Although I had crossed this road many times, I didn't know its name. Most of the streets were poorly marked, and I didn't bother to memorize the names. Signs weren't my markers. I knew my path by sight. A low concrete wall lined with bonsai trees or an oddly shaped corner told me when to make a turn. Sometimes my signals were as elusive as a flowering plant.

When I was a new college exchange student, I relied on colors and repeated patterns to get around Tokyo. To get from school to my host family's apartment in the suburbs I took a yellow train that had a red express sign in the window and a four-character name displaying its destination. The yellow train deposited me at the Hanakoganei Station, where I got on a bus.

The bus stop was veiled in obscurity. There were complex lists of routes and timetables that I could not decode. I knew the number of my bus but not the route. When the bus turned left at the corner with the Denny's restaurant on it, I counted three stops and got off. It was months before I understood the sing-song voice of the automated announcer who said, as we approached my stop, "The next stop will be Takiyama Apartments, third street."

Takiyama means "mountain waterfall," and this was the name of the massive apartment complex of more than two dozen towering buildings, all made of salmon-colored concrete. Huge black numbers were painted on the side of each building, but unless you looked up to examine the number it was almost impossible to distinguish among the buildings. The stairwells, mailboxes, and bike racks in each building were arranged in exactly the same pattern.

One night after school, I had come home in the rain huddled under my umbrella. I got off the bus and followed my usual path through the playground. I was anxious to get inside and put on dry clothes. My host mother would have saved my dinner for me, each part of the meal in a separate bowl, now covered in plastic wrap, with little drops of condensation forming on the underside from the trapped heat.

I hoped for one of my favorites, marinated mackerel in a heavy soy-flavored sauce. The oily white fish would be tangy and sweet. Rice would be warming in the rice cooker. I liked getting the last bits that turned a little brown on the edges from being in the rice cooker all day. She'd also have a vegetable dish, or maybe tofu lightly fried with a delicate crust of flour and ginger in soy sauce.

I climbed the four flights to our landing and left my umbrella outside with the others leaning against the concrete wall. I pulled open the stainless steel doorknob —unlocked as usual. The foyer was dark, but a light shone through the lace curtain which hung from the doorway of the dining room. I started to slip off my shoes and was just about to call out the usual greeting, "*Tadaima*, I'm home," when I noticed that the shoe shelves that held all of our off-season shoes were gone. Then I noticed that the hall rug had been changed. There was a rustling sound of someone in the kitchen, and suddenly I realized that I was in the wrong apartment. I stuffed my foot back into my shoe and retreated, grabbing my umbrella and running down the stairs.

Outside the building I saw that I had miscalculated my ascent by one salmon-colored entryway.

Looking at the map spread across my apartment floor, I felt the excitement of an adventure. It wasn't just curiosity that accounted for my interest in placing myself on the map. I had a plan; I had a yellow highlighter. This journey couldn't be trusted to uncertain guesses and elusive clues. This time I was claiming a path.

The day was April 27, the day of my twenty-third birthday, and it wasn't a coincidence that I was charting a course for myself. My birthday was a time for reevaluation, a time to consider my life. In college I'd started making lists of goals and achievements that I vowed to accomplish by the next birthday. I had goals like getting straight A's, a boyfriend from Beta House, and losing twenty pounds. The goals inspired me and gave me a sense of purpose. Somehow I believed that any problems could be solved if I simply showed the resolve to reach my goals.

This year I promised myself that I would learn to read no less than two thousand characters, trek the Himalayas, and lose twenty pounds. As in college, I believed that accomplishing these feats would give me some peace of mind and erase the uneasiness that crept up sometimes, poking at me from the inside when I felt dull and unsatisfied.

I also decided this year that I would begin a new birthday ritual: I would attempt something that I felt afraid of, or try something that I had always wanted to do. Later in my life these feats would include sky diving and bungee jumping, but this year's goal was, in retrospect, equally terrifying—riding my bike from home to Honda headquarters.

To prepare for the journey I had taken short trips around the neighborhood. I had no idea how long it would take to get all the way to headquarters or what the roads would be like. Riding my bike along the curvy, unmarked roads of Tokyo seemed like riding into chaos.

I had planned for this morning. My uniform and shoes were in a backpack. I had emergency money, my identification card, and the office telephone number. I was prepared to abandon the plan at any time. If I got lost or had problems with the bike I would lock it up and take a cab to work. If it got too late, I would call in sick.

It was 7:00 A.M., nearly two hours before work began. I rolled up the right leg of my pink pants and put on my purple backpack. Before I left I checked the map once more and imagined the thick treaded tires of my red mountain bike following the transparent yellow line.

I pushed away from my apartment, coasting down the narrow road and wondering if this wasn't a mistake. It was so early that no one was on the street. I looked closely at my neighbors' gates, each with a white name plate displaying the family name in black characters. At the corner there was a triangular piece of earth, bordered by concrete, where a slim trunk stood. The green budded branches had opened and bloomed into beautiful magenta flowers.

Turning right, I saw Himonya park. It was much smaller than Komazawa, but big enough to contain a small pond with rowboats for rent and a tiny barn that housed a few chickens and ponies. On weekends children and their parents lined up for hours waiting to take a guided loop around a corral riding on the back of a brown-and-white spotted pony.

The road beyond the park paralleled the train line

and led to Gakugeidaigaku Station. I passed the tofu store, which was already open. The proprietor was cutting huge planks of tofu that swam in tubs of cold, clear water, his arms submerged past his elbows as he handled the white, quivering masses. Most of the other shops—the dry-cleaner's, photo store, and liquor shop—were still shut, dark behind their windows.

To get to the main road I had to turn away from the direction of the train. I checked the map again to make sure. It felt like an illogical move.

I found the main road easily; traffic was light, and the roads were clear. I pedaled along and felt somewhat certain that I was at least moving in the right direction. The road was bordered by grocery stores, convenience stores, clothing shops, and family-style restaurants. I had gone about ten minutes when I saw a shrine on the right behind a low concrete wall next to the road. There was a courtyard and a large building with a tall wooden roof. A *torii* gate made of red painted wood stood about ten feet high and peeked over the wall. If I could ever find my way back, this was a place I wanted to explore.

The road was flat and two lanes wide. To the left I looked out and saw my train in the distance. The silver body snaked along, moving closer to my path. When I caught a glimpse of people standing in the train I felt a jolt of self-satisfaction.

The road descended and I picked up speed. Ahead I saw a rising slope that I hadn't expected. I pedaled into the slope, downshifting to gain speed. The upward slope got steep quickly and I shifted back, trying to maintain momentum. My shirt was clinging to my back. I kept pumping, slowly, to the very top. Turning a corner I suddenly recognized the neighborhood, Daikanyama. It was one of my favorite places in Tokyo—full of boutiques and restaurants. I had taken the train here before, but getting here by bike gave me a whole new perspective. It was suddenly connected, not on a map but in my mind. I used to think of neighborhoods as connected only by subway lines and trains. The contours of Tokyo were starting to make sense.

I rode through Daikanyama, recognizing a clothing shop and a round building on a corner that looked like a fashion house in Beverly Hills. There were coffee shops and a health-food store that looked worth exploring. I kept pedaling, elated at my discoveries and making mental notes of places to which I wanted to return. From an overpass, I looked down and saw rows of anonymous train tracks leading to Shibuya Station, the halfway point.

There was another hill ahead of me, but it was less steep than the first. I pedaled up, riding past small apartment buildings and shops. The stylized architecture told me that Aoyama was close. The road dead-ended into a building called Children's Palace, a play-museum which had a surrealist sculpture with smiling stumps that protruded crazily from a tiled, stalk-like trunk. A wrought-iron fence on the right enclosed the Aoyama University campus.

I looked up and saw a street sign that read "Aoyama Boulevard." I stopped to check the map. Shibuya was to the west, and it looked like the Aoyama intersection was east. All I had to do was turn right and keep pedaling. It was only 7:25 A.M. I kept riding.

On the left of the six-lane road I saw the international grocery store where I had gone to buy taco supplies for the Halloween party. Italian and French restaurants dotted both sides of the street. There were bank lobbies fronted with glass, small galleries, and a Haagen-Dazs ice cream store.

I approached a big intersection and recognized two large stone lanterns that stood on the corner marking Omotesando, a large, tree-lined street off Aoyama Boulevard famous for its shops and cafés. I had seen the lanterns from another angle, and suddenly I made another connection, as though snapping in a critical puzzle piece that enables one to see the whole picture. I stopped my bike at the corner and looked down Omotesando Avenue. It was divided by a narrow island of shrubs and trees, an unusual feature for a Tokyo street. My parents used to attend Tokyo Union Church, which was just down this street in the Harajuku area, where traffic was blocked off every Sunday for shoppers, pedestrians, and street performers.

It seemed amazing that I was finally putting all these places into perspective. Simply renaming them in my mind and making connections gave me a feeling of ownership—the sense that I belonged.

Anderson's Bakery was near the corner where I stopped. The sidewalk in front of the bakery was wet from being hosed down. Trays of fresh pastries filled the front windows, and little white lights outlined the red painted doorway. I had plenty of time, so I decided to treat myself and buy something for breakfast. Inside, the smell of fresh bread filled me with warmth.

A young Japanese girl wearing a red-and-white striped apron and a matching hat carried a wicker basket full of loaves of French bread. I was tempted to buy one just to fulfill the Parisian fantasy of riding my bike with a loaf of bread sticking out of my backpack. Instead I bought two freshly baked wheat buns and packed them away for later.

Traffic on the street was getting busy, but I pedaled with confidence. Headquarters couldn't be far now. Ahead I recognized the main Aoyama intersection, where I usually emerged from the subway station. I saw the Ezokko noodle shop where Ms. Ogi, Ms. Shoji, and I often went for lunch. Then I saw the Honda building on the right; clean show cars were parked outside on the terrace and a red and blue banner flew from the building. I'd made it. It was still before 8:00 A.M. I had conquered the impossible map. For a moment I felt like Tokyo belonged to me. I stood up on my pedals and coasted, feeling as though I could fly.

*   *   *

One Saturday morning I rode up a steep hill in unseasonably warm weather. When I switched gears to ease the pedaling I heard a sharp clunk and felt the sickening pull of my chain getting locked up again. I got off the bike and stuck my fingers between the greasy black gears and tried to pry out the chain. It was jammed tight. I pulled and leaned back using all my strength, but my hands just got darker and grittier. My cheap mountain bike worked fine on flat roads when I didn't change gears, but riding around crowded Tokyo made that impossible.

I took the bike to the Kalavinka bike shop, a place I had discovered by chance near the main post office. The shop's corrugated steel walls made it look like an old garage. New and used bikes were parked in a row out in front nearly blocking the narrow sidewalk. A worn yellow kayak hung over the doorway, and two large windows on either side of the door were covered with colorful stickers advertising European bike parts.

The inside of the shop was smaller than a garage and had space for one bike at a time. To get inside, a bike had to be rolled in at an angle. On the floor were stacks of catalogs showing merchandise that the shop had no room to display. Smaller equipment—helmets, riding gloves, and water bottles—cluttered the shelves and floor space. Pictures of bike races and posters covered the walls. A new bicycle frame hung from a hook on the ceiling next to a small electric fan. The place felt more like a clubhouse than a store.

I had met the owner, Mr. Tanabe, once before, and he recognized me when I walked in. "So, have you finally decided to buy a new bike?" he joked. He had a smooth, soft voice and an easy smile. "I'm thinking about it," I said. He gave me a stack of catalogs to look through. "I'm sorry I don't have any bikes here," he said, gesturing to the limited space. "But I can order from the catalog and it will be here in two weeks."

I took a seat on one of three folding chairs and looked at the catalogs. Mr. Tanabe went back into his workshop. The space would have been better suited for a kitchen. There was room for only one person to stand between two workbenches.

The door of the shop slid open, and two boys dressed in full riding gear said, "*Tadaima.*"

"How was it?" Mr. Tanabe asked. The boys reported details of a ride they had just finished, telling him their average riding time and fastest speeds. Mr. Tanabe gave them some advice and asked about the bikes that were propped up just outside the door. Each frame was painted in an unusual color—one lime-green and the other light blue, with matching handlebar tape. They didn't look like they came from a catalog. The boys finished their discussion and left. I asked Mr. Tanabe who they were.

"Oh, they're just neighborhood kids who like to ride. Several groups who use my shop as home base."

I told him I would be interested in joining a riding club.

"Then there is someone I think you should meet," he said, and picked up the phone.

About ten minutes later the door slid open again and a young man walked into the shop. He was tall and thin and bowed his head to Mr. Tanabe. "*Konnichiwa*," he said. He looked at me and smiled. He wore black-rimmed glasses and had a long, thin face. "My name is Masakazu Iino; please call me Masa," he said in English, and stuck out his lanky arm to shake my hand. I introduced myself and we talked. Masa told me that he rode with a club, and that I could join any time. The group rode on weekends around the Tokyo area. Masa said he had been riding for about four years. I told him that I wasn't very experienced, but that I was thinking about getting a new bike.

"Mr. Tanabe builds very fine bicycles, but they may be too advanced for you right now," Masa said. "He has a special technique that has won awards. At one time Mr. Tanabe was a strong racer."

Mr. Tanabe shook his head as if to say it wasn't true.

"Oh, yes. Years ago he went to Canada to represent Japan in the International Bicycle Championship." Masa pointed to a trophy on a counter that was almost hidden between an old cash register and some oil cans. Behind it on the wall was a photo of a young Mr. Tanabe in a bicycle race.

Masa searched through some magazines on the floor and opened one to show me a picture of a Kalavinka bike. "See," Masa said, pointing; "Mr. Tanabe's Kalavinka bike is very popular." Masa took me out front and showed me his bike. It was an original Kalavinka. "This is Mr. Tanabe's label, " Masa said, showing me a small metal disk welded to the frame. There was a picture of a creature with a man's head and a bird's body. "Kalavinka is the Sanskrit word that combines the intelligence of a man and the strength of a bird to form a symbol of beauty," Masa explained.

He told me that his wife Tokiko liked to ride, that she was an artist, and that he would like me to meet her. We exchanged phone numbers, and Masa drew me a map to his house.

Masa and his wife lived in Masa's parents' house in an old section of Tokyo about ten minutes from my apartment by bike. When I turned off the main road to get to their house, I found narrow streets bordered by blocks of two-story buildings. Old stucco walls edged up right next to the road. The continuous bank of buildings insulated the quiet, narrow road. Above a few doorways were neon signs that marked them as small hostess bars or mahjong parlors. As I rode by, I could hear the muffled voices of people drinking and the clink of chips on the mahjong board.

A young man shuffled by me in plastic sandals carrying a plastic bucket and a towel on his way to the *sentō* public bath. It wasn't hard to imagine that some apartments still didn't have their own bathtubs. This neighborhood seemed nestled in another time.

Masa's house was large by local standards. He and Tokiko shared the second floor, which had a roomy sixteen-mat tatami room and a remodeled area with hard-wood floors and skylights. Tokiko painted in a small room across from an even smaller kitchen. A new bath-room was down the hall. They rarely used the kitchen and usually ate downstairs with Masa's mother and father.

That night we talked and got to know each other. Masa was twenty-nine and worked with his father doing small-scale engineering production from their workshop located on one side of the house. After Masa graduated from engineering school, he had joined a large machin-ing company outside Tokyo and worked as a company employee for two years. "The experience was good," he said, "but I didn't like the living conditions. I lived in a dorm for single male workers and cooked my own food. I didn't have any personal time because I was always working. There was no time to enjoy life." He decided after two years to come home and work with his father.

Tokiko was twenty-six and worked as an assistant to a sculptor and did her own painting. She had grown up in Kamakura, a beautiful seaside city about two hours south of Tokyo. After art school she had gotten the job with the sculptor, which seemed to fit her. I could never imag-ine her in an office-lady uniform serving tea.

Tokiko looked different from the OLs I knew at work. Her hair was cut very short and shaved close to her head on the sides and back. She wore jeans, polished silver jewelry, and an L.L. Bean sweater ordered from a U.S. catalog. She wore no makeup or lipstick and didn't even smile much. She had a strong, self-possessed attitude, almost to the point of being distant. But in place of the chirpy sweetness that so many women in Japan exuded, Tokiko had a sincerity that was rare.

She collected antique toys and miniature frog figures.

One of her favorite artists was Paul Klee. When she showed me some of her paintings I noticed a similarity in their work. She used watercolors and painted box-shaped collages with smudged colors, yellow running into purple, and waving metallic lines separated by textured white pockets.

Masa and Tokiko had recently been married in Oregon, where Tokiko's aunt was married to an American minister. Tokiko told me that when she and Masa had been dating, he once ran to her house to visit—an eighty-mile trip. I also learned that when he had proposed to her, instead of giving her an engagement ring he gave her a custom-made Kalavinka bicycle.

We talked about sports. Masa wanted to know what kind of bicycle trips I had taken. He encouraged me to join a biking club but said that he was recovering from a broken collarbone after a fall in a bike race so he wouldn't be able to go on any big rides soon.

Their sense of adventure and unaffected ways appealed to my desire to break out of the corporate mold. I wanted, and needed, friends like them, which explains why our friendship grew so quickly.

Soon I was calling them almost every weekend, sometimes just to check in and see what was going on. Many weekend nights started with the ten-minute bike ride from my apartment to their house. Masa was forever introducing me to his friends—the hair stylist, the swimmer, more bicyclists. When he wasn't orchestrating introductions he was planning our next adventure.

One weekend we drove five hundred miles to Aichi Prefecture to cheer on one of Masa's friends who was participating in a triathlon. We took our bicycles and followed the race. Another weekend everyone went to see Tokiko's paintings in a gallery in the Ginza area of Tokyo.

I found myself with Tokiko and Masa one Saturday at 3:00 A.M. having a late-night snack of fried chicken cutlets and hot chocolate in a Denny's restaurant. We were on our way home from watching Masa play in an ice hockey game. His college team played a couple of times a month in an alumni league. They played on various rinks around Tokyo during non-peak hours, which meant that the games didn't even start until midnight.

We talked about an autumn bicycle trip that Masa wanted to plan.

"I'm afraid I won't be able to keep up," I told him.

"Don't be so worried. How often do you ride your bicycle to work?" he asked.

"Almost every day."

"See, you're building your endurance. That's just what I did to prepare for running a marathon. Just start slow but keep your goal in mind. You can do anything."

Talking to Masa was like talking to a feel-good guru. He made me feel as though anything was possible.

"Image it," he said in English.

"Image it?" I asked.

"See the image of yourself doing it. It doesn't matter what it is. I used imaging to help me run and cycle. Tokiko thinks about her art this way. One of her goals is to some day have an exhibition of her work in New York. I told her to picture herself in a gallery in Soho. You've got to see yourself doing your goal."

* * *

I was regularly commuting to work on my bicycle. The main roads were so familiar that I had stopped carrying the map. I had even started experimenting with taking shortcuts, doing what I could to make the ride more enjoyable.

On my way home from work one night I decided to stop and investigate the shrine that I had seen peeking over the concrete wall on my first bicycle ride to work. From a side road I found a driveway that led into the courtyard. It was still and dark. I leaned my bicycle against a stone bench. There was a faint scent of incense. The cherry blossoms had come and gone, but their fleeting visit had sweetened the spring air. I followed a concrete path that led to a row of red *torii* gates. Each *torii* looked like a symbolic door with no house attached— just two stilt-like legs sticking up from the ground with a single beam across the top. If I jumped really high I thought I might be able to grab the beam, but I didn't think it could hold me. Half a dozen *torii* were lined up, each a foot away from the other, forming a kind of tunnel—a gateway of endless doors.

Near the steps leading up to the shrine, I saw a sign announcing daily meditation meetings. The dark wooden doors were open, but I could only see the faint outline of some statue or figure inside. I sat on the steps and looked at the sky. The moon was out. I slowed my breathing and let my body relax. The air felt warm and soft as I breathed in the mellow, burning aroma.

I was amazed that a place like this could have seemed so mysterious and unreachable when I had first seen it. Now I was resting here. I felt connected to Japan in a way I'd never felt before. I was recognizing and naming the contours of my life in this foreign place, finally making gestures toward ownership, not borrowed or visited, but making it my own.

The Maverick

8 THE FIRST TIME I MET MR. HONDA WAS FOR a social call in his office in the advisors' building near Tokyo Station. The building—Honda Motor's first headquarters—was only a fraction of the size of the Aoyama location. It was now a place to which top-level executives retired. Mr. Honda became a *saikō komon*, or supreme advisor, when he retired from the company. Since the death of his partner Takeo Fujisawa, Mr. Honda was the only supreme advisor and the only person in the company to have his own office.

On the wall outside his office were pictures of him with various dignitaries—Mr. Honda shaking hands with Princess Diana; Mr. Honda with his arm around Marc Chagall, his favorite painter; Mr. Honda showing a car to the Emperor of Japan. He was active and smiling in all the photos, looking more like a cheerful buddy than a supreme advisor.

I met Mr. Honda's personal assistant in the entryway to the office. He introduced himself as Mr. Sumikawa.

He had a youthful look with jet-black hair carefully slicked into place. Trim and tan, he reminded me of an Asian Clark Kent. Mr. Sumikawa told me that Mr. Honda couldn't see me just yet but that I could wait in the visitors' room. He showed me to the room down the hall, explaining that he would come to get me when Mr. Honda was available.

The visitors' room looked like an elegant living room with its large yellow leather sofa and matching leather coffee table with a glass center. I took a seat and waited. One of the secretaries from the advisors' group, a woman I recognized, came in.

"Would you like some coffee?" she asked me.

"Oh, no, I'm fine."

She edged into the room a little more. "So what do you think of the advisors' office?" she asked. "It's much more boring and quiet than the headquarters, isn't it?"

"Well, it certainly is quiet," I agreed. "But the rooms are much nicer."

She chuckled and said in a conspiratorial tone, "Do you know the story about this sofa?"

I shook my head.

"Well," she said, glancing toward the closed door, "this is a rather famous piece of furniture. You see, it's made from an elephant."

"An elephant?"

"Yes. It's elephant leather. It was an extravagant purchase. And see this coffee table? You can fill the glass with water and fish and make it into an aquarium." She grimaced. "Isn't that kind of distasteful? How would you like to watch fish swimming around while you sit on the hide of a sickly, yellow elephant? It's difficult to clean the aquarium, so we rarely use it."

I nodded in agreement.

Mr. Sumikawa knocked on the door and announced that Mr. Honda was free now. I stood up from the yellow sofa wondering how it had ended up here.

Mr. Sumikawa led me back to the office and I glanced at the row of pictures as we passed. Even though Mr. Honda no longer had an official connection with the company, his influence was immeasurable. There was a special telephone in the secretariat reserved for only a few callers; Mr. Honda was one of them. That phone never rang more than once before someone ran to answer it. If Mr. Honda wanted to speak with a specific executive, instead of taking the call in the executive office, the executive scurried out to the phone. Sitting among the secretaries, he would sit close to the phone, unconsciously bowing his head as he spoke.

Mr. Honda made impromptu visits to the headquarters, sometimes to see a car in the showroom or for a social meeting. Usually we would be tipped off by a call from the advisors' office that the supreme advisor was on his way over. Word spread immediately, and the entire headquarters would go into a flurry of preparation, each department readying itself for the unlikely chance that he might stop by. When Mr. Honda visited the factories they were scrubbed clean and repainted. All of the employees, from the assembly-line workers to the chairman, appeared to sincerely respect Mr. Honda and seemed to want to show that they were taking care of the company and the jobs that he had created for them.

He had started the company with a good idea and a supply of surplus engines from the war, which he affixed to bicycles. At a time when transportation was scarce, this fuel-efficient, engine-powered bicycle was very popular. This led to a successful motorcycle manufacturing business.

Although he never had a formal education in engineering, Mr. Honda had always loved engines. I had read in books that as a boy he would get so excited about seeing a car drive through his small farming town that he would lean close to the ground after the vehicle had passed to smell the oil that had dripped on the dirt. When he was a teenager, he got a job as a mechanic and began a lifelong engineering career that would lead him to start his own piston factory. This led to motorcycles and eventually to mass production of automobiles against the wishes of the Japanese government.

In the postwar period, the Japanese government tried to maintain very tight control over mass production of machinery because of the delicate balance of supply and demand for resources. Toyota and Nissan, both prewar manufacturers, were already making cars in 1961 when Mr. Honda wanted to expand his successful motorcycle business into automobiles. The Ministry of International Trade and Industry discouraged him, saying that he would not get the necessary support. Despite the warnings, Mr. Honda told the government he didn't need their help, that Japan was a free country and he was going to make cars. It was this act, above many others, that earned him the nickname "the Maverick."

There were other stories—now corporate legends—about Mr. Honda's eccentricity. There was the time in the early years after the war, before indoor plumbing, when an important guest had gone to Mr. Honda's home for a party. The guest drank too much, got sick, and dropped his dentures into the septic tank of the outhouse. Mr. Honda insisted on retrieving the lost teeth himself, and later put the dentures in his own mouth to prove that they were clean.

I felt nervous about meeting the supreme advisor. I saw how Mr. Chino bowed to him even over the phone, and how the secretaries were practically hysterical in planning anything that included him. I would definitely introduce myself in Japanese, I decided. But should I bow or shake his hand? What if he didn't understand me? I had to remember to hold my hands together at my knees when I bowed, not down at my sides like a man. He might think I was rude. Or maybe he was just old-fashioned.

Mr. Sumikawa opened the door to the office and walked in. Mr. Honda was sitting behind his desk. He stood up.

"This is the new employee from the secretariat, Ms. Rora. She has come from Honda North America and will be working with us for a while," Mr. Sumikawa said with the ease of a man who had initiated thousands of introductions in his career.

"*Hajimemashite. Dōzo yoroshiku onegaishimasu,*" I tittered and bowed.

Mr. Honda walked around his desk and extended his hand. I offered mine. He gave it a hearty shake and smiled an endearing smile. "Herro Rora," he said in English. I tried to think of something else to say, but there wasn't time. Mr. Sumikawa said something about Mr. Honda's next appointment and expertly ushered me out the door.

The next time I met Mr. Honda I was standing in his backyard near a stream filled with fish that I was trying to catch. A few weeks earlier Mr. Sumikawa had told me that every spring Mr. Honda hosted an Ayu Fishing

Party. The *ayu* were a particular type of fresh-water fish common to Mr. Honda's hometown of Hamamatsu.

"Mr. Honda invites many guests, including foreigners," Mr. Sumikawa had explained.

I had never been to a fishing party, and I felt flattered just thinking about attending the private affair hosted by Mr. Honda and his wife. I immediately began to consider what I would wear and how I would explain my invitation to my envious colleagues.

"I was hoping you could come to the party and take coats from the foreign guests," Mr. Sumikawa said.

"Take coats?" I said, my glamorous image of dining with dignitaries deflating rapidly. "Of course I can help."

Mr. Honda lived in a suburb outside Tokyo. The fenced-in backyard was the size of an extra-long tennis court, and a narrow stream, bordered by large moss-covered rocks, ran near the back fence. Lush bushes and flowering plants masked the edges of the yard, making it look like a miniature forest. I stood at the edge of the stream with several men from the General Affairs Department who were wearing casual golf shirts and slacks. Each of us had a bamboo fishing pole.

I could see swarms of fish covering the shallow stream bed.

"You don't have to be a good fisherman to catch these fish," Mr. Sumikawa said to me, grabbing a pole. "There are more than five hundred *ayu* in there and they haven't eaten recently. You could probably catch one just by announcing that there is fish food here on the bank."

Mr. Sumikawa reached into a bucket and grabbed a glob of a brown, gritty substance he called *esa*. He tossed it into the water, and instantly a mob of fish swarmed around, slapping and flipping over one another, trying to snatch a bite. Without baiting the hook he lowered it into the mass. Within seconds there was a tug, and he pulled out a squirming, silver-gray fish. The fish, no bigger than his hand, tried desperately to escape, but Mr. Sumikawa kept a firm grasp on the slick body while he removed the bloody hook. He showed me a basket of chopstick-sized metal skewers. With one smooth stab he speared the whole fish as though it were a hot dog and placed it on the grill.

On the opposite side of the stream were a group of white-haired men in coveralls who looked as though they'd been transferred directly from the assembly line. They were taking leafy branches out of small plastic cages and placing them in the bushes near the back fence. "Those are mulberry leaves," Mr. Sumikawa said. "You can't see them, but there are fireflies on those branches. Later, when it gets dark, the fireflies will provide a light-show for everyone."

Under a canopy set up near the house, several other old men in white coveralls set up tables and chairs—enough for seventy people. Along the wall of the house stood a bar and several counters for food. Behind one counter a sushi chef, wearing a traditional white cotton apron and hat, used both hands to mix heaps of vinegared rice in a large wooden tub.

Mr. Sumikawa took me inside the house to explain my duties. The front door opened into a spacious tiled foyer. We both took off our shoes before stepping onto a thick sheet of plastic that had been placed over the carpet. He showed me more than one hundred numbered clips lined up on the floor. "These clips will be attached to each pair of shoes, and a corresponding tag will be given to each guest," he explained. "Just like a coat-check for your shoes." He told me that someone else would be in charge of taking the guests' shoes, but that I should be ready to help and remind any foreign guests who might forget.

We skated in our stocking feet over the stiff plastic through the living room. Most of the furniture had been pushed to the sides, and a paper screen closed off half the room. Mr. Sumikawa opened a sliding glass door that led into the backyard. Directly below the doorway were more than one hundred tan plastic sandals lined up in perfect pairs.

Mr. Sumikawa took me into the kitchen. "There is someone you might like to meet," he said.

The large kitchen had a full-sized refrigerator and a cooking area behind an L-shaped counter. On one side of the counter was a round table with four chairs. A sliding glass door took up the back wall of the kitchen and opened into the backyard.

Three women in Japanese-print aprons were work-ing. Two of them looked like teenagers and the other was significantly older. She was giving directions to the girls in a strong, yet courteous manner.

"We need to take the rose outside soon," she said. "Here, let's put that in the refrigerator." To each of her requests the girls responded politely with, "Yes, I under-stand."

Mr. Sumikawa approached the gray-headed woman, who recognized him and bowed her head.

Mr. Sumikawa bowed back and turned to me. "Rora-san, I'd like you to meet Mrs. Honda."

I was stunned. I'd thought she was a maid.

"*Konnichiwa*," she said.

"*Domō, hajimemashite*," I managed to squeak. Mr.

Sumikawa gave her my brief employment history and then left me to chat. Mrs. Honda motioned for me to sit on a stool facing the counter. I felt awkward, as though I should be working, but she insisted that I sit.

In reading about Mr. Honda, I had learned about Mrs. Honda, daughter of a farm-machinery salesman in Shizuoka Prefecture near Mr. Honda's hometown. They had met through a traditional *omiai* arranged marriage meeting and had married when she was twenty-one and Mr. Honda was thirty.

"Mr. Honda will be here for his snack soon," she said to the young women who were busily cleaning up. She started to prepare tea.

I had heard stories about her efforts in the early years of Honda Motor Company. On long winter nights when Mr. Honda and his business partner Takeo Fujisawa stayed up planning the future of the company, she made noodles in hot broth and brought them to the factory where the men sat trying to keep warm under a charcoal-heated table. She had encountered many struggles herself. One of her four children had died suddenly at the age of 24 of diabetes. He had passed out on the street but was mistaken for a drunk and didn't receive proper care until it was too late.

Mr. Honda suddenly bounded into the room wearing a bright blue-and-white Hawaiian shirt and asked if his snack was ready.

"In a minute," Mrs. Honda replied.

He sat down at the table and turned on the television with the remote control, looking chipper for an eighty-two-year-old. When the tea was ready Mrs. Honda served it to him with a sugar donut. When she came back to the counter, she asked me if I wanted some tea.

I felt nervous about intruding on Mr. Honda's snack time, but I nodded. She poured two cups of tea and produced a plate of peanut rice crackers. To my relief she said, "Let's not bother him," and indicated that we should stay at the counter.

A little while later Mrs. Honda's daughter-in-law burst into the kitchen carrying a hair dryer and announced that it was time to get ready for the party. Mrs. Honda told me to finish my tea and graciously excused herself from the counter. I watched her daughter-in-law unfold a privacy screen right there in the kitchen. She pulled a chair behind the screen and they both disappeared. The whir of the hair dryer drowned out the television, but by then someone had come in to talk with Mr. Honda, and they sat at the table seemingly unfazed by the commotion.

Party guests began arriving at 5:00 P.M., many in chauffeured cars with miniature embassy flags mounted on the hoods. I took my place standing on the front landing. In stocking feet and clasping my hands in front of my body I bowed and welcomed the guests. People of so many nationalities came to the door that I wasn't quite sure what language to use. I opted for Japanese and repeated "*Konnichiwa*" as the guests walked in.

The weather was warm, so my job as coat-taker left me with a lot of time. I focused my attention on shoes and decided that I could almost predict the guests' nationality by the way they handled their shoes. Japanese guests instinctively paused, slipped off their loafer-style shoes, and then easily ascended the low step to the landing. Non-Japanese guests would stop for an awkward moment to look for clues, as if saying, "Is this one of those take-off-your-shoes events or not?" With an indication from me they got the message and struggled with complicated laces or straps. A few, breaching etiquette, sat down on the landing to untie their shoes.

An hour later the party was in full swing and about seventy people were gathered in the backyard. An elegant Japanese woman wearing a string of pearls stood nervously at the edge of the stream as though she feared falling in. One of the General Affairs employees helped her with the pole and gave her elaborate instructions. Dangling the pole away from her body like a dirty mop, she carefully dropped the hook into the water. A moment later, when a famished *ayu* grabbed her line, she shrieked with excitement as the employee helped her secure her meal.

The fragrance of oleaster scented the summer air. Red and white paper lanterns hung from the canopy and illuminated the tables, casting light on the happy faces. I walked around the meticulously manicured lawn and listened to people talking in Japanese, English, and French. The closely cropped grass felt like the cushy green of a golf course. Near the grills, I caught the fresh aroma of roasted *ayu*.

The general hum of laughter and talking filled the yard. All kinds of food and drink were available, but, like the other helpers, I remained on the periphery. Mr. Sumikawa darted about like a minnow from group to group, laughing and talking.

Dessert arrived toward the end of the evening—the rice-cake pounding ritual. One of the sushi chefs, now dressed in a blue apron and wearing a white cloth tied around his head, came out into the middle of the party with a knee-high wooden mortar, a wooden mallet the size of a baseball bat, and a large bowl of steaming rice.

A cloud of steam rose into the chef's face as he placed the freshly cooked rice into the mortar.

Holding the mallet with both hands, the chef pounded the rice. Between each swing his assistant quickly mixed the rice by hand. The process was like a dance. The two moved in precise, rhythmic motions: swing-pound-mix, swing-pound-mix, turning the mound of rice into a glutinous ball the size of a loaf of bread.

After the chef and his assistant had done most of the work, the guests were invited to take turns beating their dessert with the mallet. The brave sushi chef reached his arms under the unwieldy mallet swings, risking serious injury. While everyone watched the excitement from their chairs, only Mr. Honda stood up next to the mortar, laughing and clapping his hands to the rhythm. He shouted encouraging words to his guests and almost jumped into the air every time the mallet seemed to waver out of control. After the rice was pulverized, small pieces were pulled away like taffy and covered with flavored toppings like sweet bean paste, grated radish, and salty ground sesame seeds.

In the darkness of late evening, the flickering fireflies appeared from across the stream. They glittered like a Christmas light-show. A woman from the Chinese embassy squealed because she had never seen a firefly before. Finally, around midnight, the guests began to gather their shoes. As I handed out small plastic cages stuffed with mulberry leaves and fireflies, the guests waved and thanked their hosts. Mr. and Mrs. Honda stood, in matching plastic slippers, bowing together in the backyard.

*   *   *

A few weeks after the fishing party, a memo circulat-ed through the office encouraging employees to form quality circles—small groups who problem-solved in their own work areas. The objective was to select a spe-cific problem and create a solution that would improve safety or quality, reduce costs, or improve the work envi-ronment. From my experience attending the convention I knew that some quality-circle groups had saved the company millions of dollars with their ideas. But not all ideas were related directly to manufacturing. I remem-bered one group whose goal it had been to create smoke-free office space, an accomplishment almost unheard of in corporate Japan. The memo announced that a com-petition would be held at headquarters at the end of the summer; the eventual winners would attend the interna-tional convention in the fall.

I paged through the quality-circle handbook. It illus-trated step-by-step instructions on circle activity, start-ing with brainstorming about the immediate work envi-ronment. "The people in your specific work group are best qualified to create solutions in your own work envi-ronment. Think about changes you would like to make—how to improve safety and quality or how to save time and materials."

I looked around my office. It was the same as always—the general manager smoking at his desk and buried in a stack of papers, Ms. Ogi making a phone call, Ms. Mori wrinkling her nose at a memo. Tom was unwrapping a carved-wood fish that a visitor from Thailand had brought. It was hard to look critically at something that had become so familiar.

"Think about changes you would like to make." I re-read the instructions and thought about Masa's advice to "image it," to picture in my mind the goal I wanted to achieve.

An idea popped into my head—the uniforms. Of course! Would it be possible to get rid of the women's uniforms through a quality circle? I tried to picture the secretaries doing their work without polyester blue vests and skirts. I liked what I saw, and the image inspired me. Maybe it was possible; maybe I could change the uniform rule at Honda.

I carefully designed a sign-up sheet in Japanese. It said, "Quality Circle to Abolish Uniforms. Anyone interested in participating in this group, please sign your name to the list." I fed the document into the flow of circulating memos, but when the document came back to me there was only one name on the list—my own.

I felt discouraged but not entirely surprised by the group's response. I guessed from experience that either everyone or no one would have participated, and since it was an admittedly controversial topic, they all opted out.

But I didn't want to give up. The chance to make a change in the system was too important, and now, thanks to Masa, the image was stuck in my mind. Just because my immediate work group didn't rally around the idea didn't mean that others wouldn't. I had a feeling that other women in the company, women who had less traditional jobs, would be more likely to join my cause.

The idea was radical, but I could use the quality circle to disguise my plan. And there was something else I had going for me—the maverick tradition. Somehow I felt Mr. Honda would approve of my thinking precisely because it went against convention.

One day at lunch I cornered Ms. Uno from Personnel, knowing that she was one of the few professional women in the company. When I told her about my idea she seemed interested but unwilling to commit herself. She gave me the names of several women in the Overseas Sales Department that I should talk to and said that she would think about it. These women, like Ms. Uno, had been hired for their specific skills in foreign languages and worked in positions nearly equal to their male colleagues. During my breaks I snuck around the headquarters searching for kindred spirits. I felt like an undercover agent setting up an underground rebellion. When I explained my ideas to the target members, they all agreed it was a worthy idea. One woman said, "I have often met foreign colleagues when they come to Tokyo after I have corresponded with them for months or even years. When we finally meet, they are always surprised to see me in a uniform, and I feel embarrassed."

No one wanted to commit to being in the circle unless someone else did first, so I was forced to be slightly surreptitious. I told each person that the others had already agreed to join, which by the end was true. I had approached men and women in the company, but no Japanese men would consider joining. A French-Japanese man from African Sales agreed to join us, as did one American man who worked in the Parts Department. With Ms. Uno and two other women, our six-person group had a solid base.

Our first meeting was held at 7:00 A.M. in the company cafeteria to discuss our strategy. We decided to investigate the costs involved in supplying uniforms, corporate policy on the matter, and what other companies like Toyota and Nissan were doing. We also developed a questionnaire to distribute among employees to get their views.

We decided to distribute the questionnaire on a single day. On the morning of the survey, we arrived early and positioned ourselves strategically around the headquarters building like a group of ninja warriors ready to attack. Standing in front of the women's twelfth-floor locker room, I planned to approach anyone who tried to go through the door. As I passed out the questionnaire, some women seemed afraid, as though I were administering a mandatory English test. Once they saw the questions written entirely in Japanese, they relaxed and obediently filled it out.

I feared that our results would reflect only lower-level employee opinions because many of the managers arrived after the official work bell sounded. The solution, I decided, rested on the tenth floor, the office with the highest percentage of management personnel in the building.

I suspected that getting permission to distribute the questionnaire among the executives would take longer than trying to get the uniform policy changed, so I decided to take a risk. After checking to see which executives would be at headquarters that day, I put a questionnaire on each desk. My defense against potential criticism was that the questionnaire was all part of the quality-circle activity which management supported.

Mr. Chino gave me his completed questionnaire immediately, making the accurate observation that the way we phrased our questions would not give us conclusive results. Slowly, throughout the day, the other secretaries, all except Ms. Mori, and a few of the directors brought me more completed questionnaires.

For two months the quality circle met once or twice a week before work and shared the results of our research.

I was concerned that my language skills would be insufficient to lead the group, but after a few meetings I discovered that where my language skills left off, my enthusiasm took over. The group members didn't care about my vocabulary; they cared that I was there each day, listening and working to make a change.

My job was to research the actual rules for uniforms. For several hours I paged through four encyclopedic volumes of corporate policy in Japanese and made copies of anything referring to uniforms. At the next morning meeting, I reported the results over coffee and toast.

"There is no actual rule that states that only women are required to wear uniforms at headquarters. I found only one vague statement that read, 'Consequences exist for employees who do not follow the proper dress code.' I also interviewed several older employees who remembered that in the early days of Honda Motor Company men also had a blue uniform jacket. But about twenty years ago the uniform for men was eliminated."

"Why?" asked Ms. Uno.

"Well, my guess is that at about this time, because Honda started to do more overseas business, Japanese men went abroad and saw that European and American businessmen did not wear company uniforms, and it must have influenced them."

Honda was more popular overseas than in Japan. Although the company seemed very Japanese to me, Honda had a reputation in Japan for being a youthful, modern, international company—an image cultivated by most corporations, if not in practice, then at least in appearance.

Ms. Yamamoto, from European Sales, reported on uniform policies at other companies. "I called Nissan and spoke to a public-relations representative. Not surprisingly, Nissan has no uniform policy for men, and several years ago they made uniforms for women optional. They reasoned that uniforms did not encourage individuality and that abolishing uniforms would make the work atmosphere more pleasant. The most interesting point, however, was their belief that it was strange to have a women-only uniform policy. Since implementing their policy, they report that the office environment has become more pleasant and most women choose to wear their own clothing. They also did not hear the complaints about clothing costs that they had anticipated."

"Do you think many women at Honda would complain about clothing costs?" I asked.

"Since most women at Honda are unmarried and live at home, they spend much of their income on clothes anyway. Every morning on the subway you can see that most women dress up to go to work. I think cost is not a problem because they already have nice wardrobes," Ms. Yamamoto said, and others nodded in agreement. Then she told us about a famous cosmetic company. "Shiseido also abolished uniforms a few years ago. Their representative said people should be free to wear fashions they like and that freedom to choose contributes to a relaxed work atmosphere. Since they abolished uniforms, no major problems have been reported."

Ms. Uno reported on the financial view. "A uniform costs the company approximately ¥8,000. Each woman has two uniforms, so for three hundred women the total cost is ¥4,800,000. Locker rooms for changing also take up valuable space. The company rents several meeting rooms in the building next door because we don't have the space here at the headquarters. Applying the rental rate for the equivalent space currently used for locker rooms, the company spends an additional ¥10,000,000 a year." This meant that Honda was spending the equivalent of over US$150,000 a year to maintain the women-only uniform policy.

Reports flooded in with facts and statistics to support our argument. The results of the questionnaire, though not conclusive, also supported our position. The majority of the five hundred people we asked agreed that uniforms did not help women advance their careers and did not improve Honda's image.

We prepared our presentation for the circle competition, and after several dress rehearsals we were ready for the first round. Each group had approximately ten minutes to present its idea and findings to a panel of four managers, who decided which groups would move on to the next level of competition. The presentation took place in a small, dark conference room. There wasn't enough room inside for all the employees of the eight competing circles, so we took turns listening to the other groups. We waited in the hall, reviewing our speaking order and double-checking our stack of overhead transparencies.

When it was our turn, all six of us marched up to the front of the room. Arnaud, the French-Japanese man, opened our presentation with impressively polite Japanese and announced that our goal was to abolish women's uniforms. With well-timed precision, we took turns standing at the projector and explained our findings. We incorporated pie charts and graphs, a diagram of the women's uniform, and even a copy of Japan's Bill of Rights with the anti-discrimination clause in Article Fourteen.

The only items missing in our presentation were the results of implementing our solution. An important part of the quality-circle process was testing the proposed solution by measuring the results in order to prove its value. But our results were based totally on conjecture. We believed that abolishing uniforms would save the company money, increase morale, and improve Honda's corporate image, but it was impossible to prove. Without these statistics, chances of advancing were slim.

After all the groups were finished with their presentations, we gathered in the conference room. One of the managers stood up and complimented everyone's efforts. He then made comments to all the groups. Of ours, he said, "The project is very interesting, but the survey results are vague. Perhaps an opinion survey of what women think about wearing the uniform would be a more useful tool."

I held my breath. Did this mean we were out? We didn't qualify? He was still talking about the other groups. My palms were sweating, and I felt like screaming, "What does it mean? Do we get to go on?"

Finally he announced the names of two circles that would move on to the second round of competition. He read the name of another group and then ours.

The Art of
Negotiation

9 After the summer rainy season, I started riding my bike to work almost every day. The roads became so familiar that I could coordinate myself with the traffic signals. If I timed it right, I could coast full-speed down the small hill in Ebisu, reach the traffic light at the bottom just as it turned green, and use the momentum to propel myself up the big hill that led to Daikanyama.

My favorite part of the ride was the last stretch on Aoyama Boulevard. There were a few apartment buildings, but it was mainly urban Tokyo—wide, six-lane roads bordered by tall, modern buildings. Aoyama was chic, a place where you were more likely to see a woman in a mink coat than a bicyclist on her way to work. Sometimes I rode on the sidewalk to get a better look at the mannequins in boutique windows. I'd image that someday I'd wear those stylish fashions to work.

I was surprised, one day, when I saw a speed-walker coming my way on the wide sidewalk. His arms were held high and out to his sides like wings. He took short, powerful steps and swung his elbows with punctuated force. As he approached I saw that he was an older man with muscular thighs and a compact frame. He wore a sweatband around his head and had a white towel tucked into the neck of his sweatshirt. I nodded my head to him as he passed me, and he nodded back with a smile.

"Good morning," I said.

"'Morning," he said without turning around, and stuck his hand up in the air to wave.

The following day I saw the speed-walker near the same spot. He pumped his arms briskly, and I could see him smiling at me. As we got closer, I took my right hand off the bicycle handle and held it out with an open palm. He saw my hand just as we were about to pass and opened up his right hand. We slapped a high-five and kept on moving. After that day, every time we met we greeted each other like this, sometimes without saying a word.

*   *   *

The quality-circle group had only two weeks to prepare for the second round of competition. We decided to do an opinion survey of all the women at headquarters, so we developed a questionnaire that would give us an idea of what women really thought about eliminating uniforms.

Please mark with a check those issues that are important to you when considering the elimination of uniforms for women working at headquarters.

MERITS:

1. Ability to make a personal choice in clothing.

2. No need to spend time changing clothes before and after work.
3. No need to change clothes when visiting outside representatives.
4. Equality between men and women.

DEMERITS:

1. High cost of own clothing.
2. Must decide what to wear every day.
3. Cannot wear casual clothes to work.

Other comments

We handed out the questionnaires early one morning to nearly all of the two hundred women at headquarters, and by the end of the day we had collected 160 responses. The quality-circle group members met after work in the cafeteria; each of us carried a pile of completed questionnaires. I started a tally sheet and paged through my pile adding up the merits and demerits. The results were surprising.

The majority of women agreed that there were more benefits to eliminating the women-only uniforms. But the most popular reason for wanting to change the uniform rule was to save time changing in the morning. Only a small percentage of the women even mentioned equality as an issue they considered.

I was also shocked to read that some women wanted to keep the uniform. Several wrote lengthy responses saying they were worried about getting their own clothes dirty at work and about cost.

Ms. Uno explained that some women had never chosen what to wear. From junior high school to junior college, they had always worn uniforms. They didn't have good role models or many alternatives, so they felt uncomfortable with the idea of making a decision every day.

But I still didn't understand why so few women had marked equality as an important issue. To me it was the only one worth fighting for. "Most Japanese women just think differently about this," Ms. Yamamoto said. I wondered if I would ever understand.

The new questionnaires helped us see a wider range of opinions. With the new information, we decided to change our goal from "abolish uniforms" to "make uniforms optional." But even with the change, I didn't think we would be selected to go on to the final round of competition. We still didn't have any concrete results—and we never would unless the company changed the rule.

I felt much less excited going into the second round. The first round had given us the legitimacy that I had wanted, but now I wasn't sure how succeeding as a quality circle would make a difference in company policy.

We approached round two much like round one, with our pie charts and copy of Article Fourteen of the Bill of Rights. The managers listened attentively to our presentation. As before, a manager stood up at the end and evaluated each group. "Changing the uniform policy is an important topic," he told us. "You've shown that many employees want a change, so I think it would be useful for you to present your project to the Administration Department. There is a new committee for special projects that should find your information very interesting." He asked us to make an appointment to see this group, which became our consolation prize since we were not selected to move on in the competition.

The new Special Projects Committee at headquarters

consisted of seven management-level employees who worked on specific projects that affected the entire company. They made their recommendations directly to the executives.

When we met with them in a small conference room a week later, I was surprised to see that there was a woman in the group—and she wasn't serving tea. Her name was Ms. Kawamura, and I learned that she had worked at Honda for over twenty years. She was one of only five women in the company who had reached the level of assistant manager.

We gave our standard presentation and answered questions about our sources and what we thought might happen if the company actually changed the rule. I watched Ms. Kawamura quietly making notes. Like a myopic librarian, she wore large-framed glasses attached to a gold chain that hung around her neck. Throughout the discussion she asked questions in a direct yet gentle manner. I could tell from her questions that she thought the uniform policy needed to be changed.

At the end of the two-hour discussion the Special Projects Committee commended our work and thanked us for our time. When they told us that they would take on the project I felt like jumping into the air. Finally—something was going to be done! Our efforts had paid off, and I knew it would be only a matter of days before they recommended to the executives that the rule be changed.

A few days after our meeting with the committee there was still no announcement concerning the uniforms. A week went by, and then two weeks. I wondered what was going on. I would see Ms. Kawamura in the lunchroom and she always smiled pleasantly. Finally I got impatient, and one night I approached her after work.

"Good evening."

"Oh, Rora-san. How are you?" she said with the smoothness of a grade-school teacher.

"I'm sorry to bother you now. I know you must be busy."

"No, that's quite all right."

"Well, I'm sorry for being so direct, but I was just wondering what had happened with the uniform project. It's been over a month and we haven't heard anything."

She smiled fondly as if recalling a favorite pet. "Oh, yes," she said. "We are still in the investigation stage."

I believed she was telling me the truth, so I thanked her and left. But as the weeks and months passed, I made a point of stopping by regularly to see her. Each time I got the same answer—the investigation stage. I wondered what they could be investigating that we hadn't already researched. Finally, I could come to only one conclusion: that for whatever reason the project had been dropped, and Ms. Kawamura was simply being polite by avoiding the truth. It was clear that some things would never change.

Although my group didn't make it to the International Quality Circle Convention, I was invited by the Convention Planning Committee to come and co-host the international party. There would be a record number of international employees attending this year's convention, so the party on Friday evening, before the Saturday presentations, was going to be a main event.

When I took the bullet train to Suzuka this time I knew what I was doing and where I was going. Knowing what to expect at the convention gave me a new sense of confidence. I went to the gymnasium where the party would be held and met my co-host, Mr. Ozaki. *"Ōzaki desu. Yoroshiku,"* he said, introducing himself without the usual formalities. I liked him immediately.

Mr. Ozaki and I were the same height. He looked like he was in his early forties. Even though he was almost completely bald, his huge grin and twinkling eyes made him look like a little boy who was about to pull a prank.

He told me that he worked in the engine factory and that he'd been asked to do this kind of event before. I could see why. He was energetic and gregarious and comfortable with new people. When I told him that I was a little nervous about speaking into a microphone in front of several hundred guests he told me not to worry. "I'll take care of the Japanese; you take care of the English."

We spent the afternoon looking over a detailed script. The planning committee had carefully orchestrated each ten-minute interval of the two-hour event. With a microphone in one hand and a script in the other, Mr. Ozaki and I walked around on a raised pavilion set up in the center of the gymnasium and practiced our parts. Behind us was a stage set up with flags from fifteen nations, each represented by employees at the convention.

The main activity of the party would be a huge game of bingo. We practiced using the bingo cage with labeled ping pong balls inside. Mr. Ozaki turned the handle on the cage until a ball got caught in the holder. I retrieved the ball and called out the number and letter into the microphone in English; Mr. Ozaki repeated it in Japanese.

The prizes were Honda goods from the Formula 1

racing collection: sweatshirts, raincoats, T-shirts, umbrellas, caps, and bags, all marked with Marlboro, Camel, and other Honda-sponsor logos. The grand prizes were two bright-red canvas Honda jackets.

People started to arrive around 6:30 P.M. carrying cameras and dressed up in suits and ties; the women wore skirts and dresses. Some groups wore matching coats or sweatshirts. A few people wore their country's traditional clothing: Indonesian batik shirts, Japanese kimonos, or Indian capes. Mr. Ozaki and I wore the grand-prize jackets. We also wore matching red and white Marlboro Racing sweatshirts and jeans.

Madonna's music blasted over the loudspeaker as the guests milled around the gym and congregated around tables set up with food and beer. At 7:00 P.M. Mr. Ozaki and I climbed up on the raised pavilion in our matching red jackets. Bright lights and a video crew followed us wherever we moved. I felt like I was on television. Mr. Ozaki introduced himself and me in Japanese; then I did the same in English. Although we'd practiced with the microphones, it sounded funny to hear my voice echoing above the music and throughout the gymnasium full of people.

A young American man from Ohio had been asked to give the toast. He got up on stage and recited a rehearsed speech in Japanese. Mr. Ozaki and I stood by with cans of Kirin Dry beer and toasted each other as the whole room shouted "Cheers!" After the toast came a long series of greetings from each of the international groups. Some groups performed short songs in their native languages, but most shuffled onto the pavilion and listened while one designated member delivered a heavily accented phrase of Japanese read from a hand-held note. The inadequate public-address system further diluted the mutilated Japanese, but the crowd cheered and respond- ed to each group by calling out a primal-sounding "oooh weee." Mr. Ozaki and I joked, laughed, and acted silly, setting the precedent for the others. If people looked even a little foolish, the audience liked them all the more.

We ushered groups on and off the pavilion and asked people to say where they came from and to say their names in English. At first many of the participants seemed shy and embarrassed. I admired their efforts to speak Japanese into a microphone in front of a room full of strangers. As people drank more beer and more groups came on stage, the crowd loosened up and got into the spirit of the party.

The last greeting was to be given by the handful of executives who had come to the convention to listen to the next day's presentations. Eight of them had snuck into the auditorium after the party had already started. Now they were standing out of sight behind the pavilion in a dark-suited group. I noticed that each of them had a ridiculous paper flower made of white ribbon attached to his suit that was supposed to designate him as a special guest. But how would anyone know who they were if they were so distant and almost hiding?

I was relieved to see Mr. Ozaki persuading the execu- tive group to come up on stage so that the employees could at least see them before having to present their quality-circle ideas to them the next day. But as the exec- utives filed onto the pavilion looking like their formal photos from the corporate directory, I wondered if it wasn't a mistake. They looked intimidating and unfriendly. I had an urge to yell at them to loosen up and smile. "This is a party!" I wanted to remind them. Mr. Ozaki introduced the executives in Japanese by name. As he went down the row, I got an idea.

One of the executives was a man whom I knew because he had been the president of the Ohio factory. Because of a promotion, he had recently returned to Tokyo. He was a dynamic, popular president in Ohio, and all of the American associates in the audience recognized him. His name was Mr. Irimajiri, but everyone called him Mr. Iri.

I leaned over to Mr. Iri and told him my idea. All of the international guests had at least attempted in introduce themselves in Japanese, so, I wondered aloud, rather than having me translate the introductions, would he introduce himself in English?

When Mr. Ozaki was finished with the Japanese introductions, he looked at me to translate. Instead, I handed the microphone to Mr. Iri. He stepped forward and said, "Welcome to the Suzuka Quality Circle Convention. I'm so happy to see you all here. My name is Iri and I look forward to hearing your presentations tomorrow. Good luck." The crowd roared "oooh wee" and applauded wildly. Then instead of taking back the microphone, I asked the next executive in line, Mr. Iwai, to introduce himself in English. He was a large man with the most gregarious personality on the tenth floor. Mr. Iwai looked amused and took the microphone. "I am Iwai. Nickname is Gan," he said in a booming voice. I had no idea what Gan meant, but his attempt to speak English inspired great laughter among the executives and the crowd.

The microphone went down the line, each executive making a spontaneous, although sometimes tentative, self-introduction in English. I was surprised by the abilities of most of them—even tall, quiet Mr. Yamada, who gestured grandly as he grabbed the microphone and said, "Ladies and Gentleman," and laughed nervously as his colleagues guffawed. "Welcome to Suzuka. That's all."

Mr. Ozaki and I stood by watching the executives transform themselves from inscrutable bosses to likable people. The audience laughed along with the executives and applauded each time one spoke.

Just as the directors were preparing to leave the stage, Mr. Ozaki suggested that they sing the Honda fight song. I had never heard of such a thing, but I joined him in encouraging the directors, who were clearly caught off guard. Without giving them a chance to say no, Mr. Ozaki announced to the audience that the directors would perform. We handed over our microphones and got out of the way.

The directors were all laughing and smiling. I watched from behind when I saw the unbelievable—the directors put their arms around each others' shoulders. Suddenly they were singing and swaying together like fraternity brothers in a moment of inspired togetherness. Their transformation from a stiff group of corporate executives to a gang of fun-loving guys was unparalleled in my corporate experience.

On my way back to Tokyo the next day, I wrote my mother a letter describing the event. Being on stage with Mr. Ozaki and cajoling the executives into introducing themselves in English and singing together was something I had never imagined doing. I had recognized on stage that I had a kind of knack for getting people to do things that they wanted to do but were too shy or timid to try without encouragement. In Japan, no one wanted to be the nail that stuck up, but I didn't care. It had been the same with the quality-circle group. We'd discovered that the majority of the women at headquarters wanted to eliminate uniforms, but no one wanted to say so first. In the letter I wrote what I could say only to my mother—that I had been a smash. I felt great. I had found something that I could do well.

* * *

A significant, yet almost imperceptible change started happening around this time—I began to develop the art of negotiation. It wasn't something that I anticipated or prepared for; it just happened one weekend when I went to a small hot-spring resort with two American friends, Jonathan and Stephen, who were living in Japan.

The three of us went out for dinner late on a Saturday night and had some trouble finding a restaurant that was still open and not crowded. We finally found an empty single-room restaurant. The owners welcomed us enthusiastically. We told the man behind the counter that we wanted some good food. "You've come to the right place," he exclaimed. "I'll give you a good bargain."

We took three seats at the counter and started to talk with the husband-and-wife team. He did the cooking; she took care of the bills and followed his demands. The man made a big show of preparing the food and ordering his wife around. "Get me a pot." "Pick up those glasses." "Pour them some more beer."

While we ate a delicious succession of grilled meat, fish, and marinated vegetable dishes, he told us stories about running the restaurant. There was the time that a famous sumo wrestler came in and ate all the food. Another time a well-known actor had gotten drunk and passed out. We were happily stuffed and entertained by the end of the meal when the wife brought us the bill— a piece of paper with only the total written on it. We hadn't discussed price with the old man, but the bill was more than we had anticipated.

All three of us were shocked. My friends didn't think we could do anything about it now, and took out their wallets. I asked the wife if I could see the bill again. The old guy was hovering nearby. It was clear that he was concerned, but I didn't say anything to him immediately. I knew that wouldn't work. Instead, I looked at the bill and nodded my head thoughtfully. I continued to keep quiet, put on my coat, and sat back down again. Then the old man asked me about the bill.

"Is there something wrong?" he asked.

"Oh, it's nothing," I replied. Then I paused and advanced calmly. "Well, ummm. You know. So, well. I guess I kind of thought you were going to give us a deal. But, well. I understand." He nodded, acknowledging my gesture.

"So what do you think the price should be?" he said, retreating without being defensive. I nodded and put my hand on my chin.

"Well, I really don't know," I said, avoiding any posture of strength.

"No, really, what do you think?" he asked again, inviting me to compromise.

"Hmm. Well. Maybe I was thinking that the price would be about ¥4,000." It was two-thirds the price his wife had written down.

"All right," he said, "¥4,000 it is."

My friends were as impressed as I was excited. I was beginning to communicate in a language I couldn't learn in a textbook or by listening to tapes. The art of negotiation was something that I couldn't label or describe, but I knew that I had just done it successfully for the first time. The art wasn't saving the money. Anyone could have done that just by making a scene. The art was in successfully communicating in Japanese terms, not just Japanese language.

In college on the judo team I had learned the vocabulary of an extreme world where language was limited but concise: *ukemi*—fall, *maketa*—failure, *katta*—victory, *itai*—pain. These were the words I used to strike out into the daunting corporate world. On the first day in judo I'd practiced *ukemi*, over and over again until I'd learned to fall gracefully and without hurting myself.

I realized that over the past year I had been doing the same thing, only not in the dojo, but in the office. I had struggled with Ms. Mori and the rules at headquarters, but each time I fell I bruised less easily. Although we'd failed at changing the uniform rule, I had successfully organized the group. Being able to negotiate my way around—even on such a small scale as getting a bunch of middle-aged men to sing or lowering the price of a meal—gave me hope. Maybe one day I would be able to fall with grace.

As much as my negotiation skills pleased me, I didn't always choose to use them. There were times when I didn't have patience and took matters into my own hands.

I was in the stall in the ladies' bathroom one evening when I was startled by a sudden chorus of high-pitched melodies. I couldn't tell exactly where the music had come from, but then I heard it again. The tune was, "Oh when the saints go marching in," and I discovered the source. The music was coming from the roll of toilet paper that I had just touched. The rolling action apparently activated the electronic tunes located somewhere inside the roll holder.

I knew why the musical roll had been put in our bathroom. It was for the same reason that all the Japanese women I knew flushed the toilet twice—once to actually flush the toilet, and once before to camouflage any unladylike sounds. Some toilets in Japan had electronic buttons that activated nature sounds like waterfalls and rushing rivers. I thought it was all ridiculous—wasn't the sound of using the bathroom as natural as the sound of Niagara Falls?

For the next few days I listened for comments about the musical roller. Someone made a joke about it, and then someone else indicated that they found it annoying. No one knew where it had come from, or why there was only one, even though the bathroom had two stalls.

Using the comments as justification, I decided to do something about the musical roller. Consensus had no part in my plan. I waited until almost everyone had gone home and snuck into the bathroom. In the cabinet under the sink I found the old plastic roller. Because the music was activated by motion, delicacy was the key.

I disassembled the roll of toilet paper and removed the musical roller, holding it as gently as I would a beaker of liquid nitrogen. I was afraid that I might expose myself if the music started playing. While listening for sounds of anyone approaching the bathroom, I whisked the roller toward the cabinet but accidentally bumped it on the edge of the door. The roller started to play, "Oh when the saints go marching in," so I hastily buried the singing gadget under some old rags and closed the cabinet door. Even with the door closed I could hear the muffled music, so I stood guard until it finally reached the end of the stanza and fell silent.

The next day I waited to see if anyone would mention the disappearance of the music. I was prepared to initiate another switch if I had to, but no one said a thing.

Lessons on Mt. Fuji

10 THE BLAZING SUN BEAT DOWN AS I PEDALED up the incline. Mount Fuji towered overhead, an overwhelming opponent. This marked my first bike ride as a member of Team Tra-Montana, Masa's bike club. I had been surprised when I learned that our destination was to be one of the tallest mountains in Asia. The journey seemed feasible when we had all pushed off together wearing matching lemon-yellow jerseys. But now I was alone, pedaling solo on a hot August morning and climbing Mount Fuji seemed impossible.

Mount Fuji, the most famous natural symbol of Japan, stands 3,776 meters (12,388 feet) high. A trail of ten stations marks a path up the mountain and a twenty-four-kilometer paved road extends from the base to the fifth station at the midpoint. From the fifth station the only way up is with a sturdy pair of hiking boots. The paved road goes unnoticed by most Mt. Fuji trekkers, who usually take tour-buses to the fifth station and then begin climbing the rocky footpath. For Team Tra-

Montana, however, the twenty-four-kilometer uphill road represented a challenge in itself.

Masa still wasn't able to ride because of his healing collarbone, but he had introduced me to this all-male cycling club. The members seemed curious about me. As a relatively new cyclist, I naively believed my enthusiasm to make cycling friends would make up for the significant experience gap.

Team Tra-Montana consisted of seven men, ranging in age from the early twenties to the mid-fifties. They toured every Sunday even though, like many Japanese men, they worked six days a week. The club name, Tra-Montana, reflected the Japanese fascination with using English words to add an international flavor. Concocted by the non-English-speaking club members, it combined the idea of traversing—Tra, and mountains—Montana.

Preparation for traversing Mount Fuji had begun at 5:30 A.M. that Sunday in front of the Kalavinka bike shop. We packed our gear into three compact cars. The amount of gadgetry that my fellow team members carried amazed me: multi-sized bike packs, a plethora of wrenches, tubes, meters, and other mechanical tools. Meticulously packing the equipment, the members acted as if every little gadget had to have its own bag or compartment. My simple riding gear included a helmet, water bottle, and air pump, all haphazardly carried in an old backpack. I felt like a burger-flipping fry cook inadvertently thrown in among an entourage of gourmet chefs.

I lifted my new purple Panasonic racing-style bike onto the overhead rack of one of the cars. The bike's black, unmarked tires rotated slowly, and the spokes glittered like a Ferris wheel. The other bikes, all custom-made Kalavinkas, had a well-handled, familiar look like that of a beloved leather baseball mitt. Next to them, my mail-order bike looked like a cheap impostor.

With bikes secured overhead, we started on the three-hour drive from central Tokyo to Mount Fuji. By the time we reached the base of the mountain, the sun had warmed the clear summer air. At 9:30 A.M. we were ready to ride. Lined up on the side of the road single-file, in our yellow shirts, it was not hard to identify team Tra-Montana.

Standing in the bright sun, with a full water bottle and new riding gloves, I felt primed—ready to take on Mount Fuji. Being with the team gave me a feeling of confidence—as though wearing the same color T-shirt proved I was worthy of this adventure.

The first starting push had been together, but the space that quickly grew between me and the pack reflected my inexperience. I pedaled as fast as I could, but soon I couldn't even see the others. Riding my bike to work every day had been good exercise, but it hardly prepared me for a twenty-four- kilometer uphill ride.

Mount Fuji was daunting. The road went up and up—there was no coasting or pause. The sun pounded down; sweat liquefied the sunblock I had slathered all over my face. Streams of stinging chemicals flowed directly from my brow into my eyes, and my thighs became tight and heavy with each revolution of the pedals. I gripped my handlebars and tried desperately to keep together the lingering traces of momentum.

I had only been riding for about twenty minutes, but the constant uphill climb and the penetrating heat wilted my lofty ideas of conquering Fuji. I considered turning back. Then, unexpectedly, I sensed someone riding behind me. He was a member of the club whom I had met for the first time that morning. By far the oldest member, in his mid-fifties, he had thick, sturdy legs that looked as though they could power a steamroller. It was obvious that he was riding slowly for my benefit. Part of me was glad to see him, but another part wanted to tell him to go on and leave me to my self-pity.

Before I had a chance to tell him anything, sweat obscured my vision and forced me to stop. Tumbling off my bike, I reached for the water bottle and flooded my face with a spray of cool water. My riding partner also stopped and handed me a towel to wipe my eyes. I sat down on the pavement. His smooth, absolutely bald head hovered over me. He offered a little smile, but it wasn't very convincing. It seemed impossible, but even though we had been riding uphill for over twenty minutes he looked as fresh as a May tulip.

I tried to figure out a delicate escape from this hopeless situation. Hadn't one of my brand-new tires gone flat yet? Perhaps my brakes needed major mechanical attention. I was just about to suggest to my partner that he go on without me when he said in Japanese, "It is great at the fifth station. You are really going to like it." For a moment I felt confused. Did he truly think that the exhausted person sprawled out on the road in front of him could actually make it all the way to the fifth station? We weren't even halfway to Station One. "Ready?" he asked as he held my bike in a starting position. The rest and water helped me regain some energy, so I decided to get back on the bike. He gave me an effortless shove that sent me flying for a few blissful meters.

The two-laned road curved gently up and around the

mountainside, making it impossible to see what was ahead. Scraggly bushes and small trees covered the landscape. I saw no buildings, houses, or signs of civilization. The road was free of traffic except for the occasional gargantuan tour-bus that chugged by, belching clouds of noxious smoke into the air as it carried hoards of hikers to the halfway point.

We continued at our own pace, and, after what seemed like an eternity, I saw a sign in the distance that lifted my spirits and energized me with hope. Sticking out of the grass was a rustic wooden sign announcing that we had reached STATION ONE. At last, a marker of our progress! We'd been riding for forty-five minutes. I quickly calculated how long it should take to get to the fifth station, and, intellectually at least, it suddenly seemed within reach.

My cycling partner and I established a riding rhythm, stopping often for rest and water. Our progress seemed uncertain—almost imperceptible. Every time I thought of all the kilometers that lay ahead I felt like giving up, so I concentrated only on the pavement directly in front of my bike. Nearly an hour later we reached the second station and then the third.

The sun heated my dwindling water supply, and every muscle in my body felt strained. As we got closer to the fourth station, exhaustion began to erode my determination. We had been pedaling for more than three hours. I started thinking of compromise. How much different could the view from the fourth station be from that of the fifth? Just as I was about to declare my decision to turn around, my partner excitedly called out, "Listen! Listen to the call of the lark." Although he sounded sincere, I almost laughed out loud. "A lark?" I wondered—

bird-watching was the furthest thing from my mind! Trying to appease him, I continued to pedal and listened for the elusive lark. Before I knew it, I had momentarily forgotten about my decision to quit, and we reached the fourth station.

A while later two younger members of our group, exhibiting what I viewed as superhuman strength, passed us for the second time. The first time they had passed us on their way down the mountain, and now passed again on their way back up for the second climb! As they rode by, I received shouts of encouragement, but could only respond with a lethargic, discouraged bob of my head.

I pictured the other team members casually resting under a huge sign board that proclaimed, CONGRATULA-TIONS, YOU HAVE REACHED STATION FIVE. Beads of per-spiration had collected on their upper lips, forming translucent mustaches. They joked and passed around a water bottle. But maybe they were talking about me—and laughing. Insecurity poisoned my thoughts, and I concluded that either they had totally forgotten about me or they were sorry they had let me tag along, forcing them to wait.

I felt foolish for ever attempting this ride. Climbing Mount Fuji—ha! To save myself from any further embarrassment I decided to immediately call it quits. As if he could sense my intention, my partner again called out, "Look! Notice the white birch which is plentiful in this area." Again I was distracted as I pedaled and searched for the plentiful birch. The Mount Fuji Zen-like trivia continued, and my cycling guru and I rode on.

Around 2:30 P.M., we encountered the first indications of the fifth station. Multitudes of hikers carrying cam-eras milled about roadside shacks that sold steaming noodles in fish broth and plastic replicas of Mount Fuji on key chains. In the distance I saw the Station Five signboard and the members of team Tra-Montana resting underneath. I rode up feeling a bit embarrassed that it had taken me so long to get there, but the group cheered and welcomed me.

My partner and I sat down. Someone handed me a can of Japanese Gatorade. I gulped the cool liquid and listened as the others talked about the ride. It was then that I realized that I was accepted as part of the group. None of them cared whether or not I had a custom-made bike or well-worn gear. Riding at a slower speed did not disqualify me from participating, and neither gender nor nationality was a consideration. I didn't need to have anything extra or special. I didn't have to be just like them—being myself was enough. I had all that I needed.

* * *

"Mount Fuji again?" I thought to myself. I was sitting in the pantry thumbing through a slick brochure that showed handsome young adults cheerfully romping around an amusement park, sipping beverages in a pristine coffee shop, and lounging in manicured hotel rooms. The title across the top of the brochure said, "Having fun at Fuji Highland Resort." Ms. Ogi sat across from me looking at a fashion magazine and sipping her tea.

"So this is where we're going for our company trip?" I asked her.

"That's the plan. I've heard it's a really nice resort."

"Do you think we'll climb Mt. Fuji?" I asked hopefully.

"I don't think so," she said, chuckling. "The resort is located at the base of Mt. Fuji. There will be plenty of things to do there."

"Amusement park rides, bowling, swimming, shopping," I read aloud from the brochure. Going to an amusement park at the base of one of the most scenic places in Japan seemed strange to me. I thought of all the amusement parks in Ohio that were there precisely because we didn't have mountains or oceans nearby.

"I'm sure it will be fun," Ms. Ogi remarked. "Everyone is going."

A year had passed since I had become a member of the executive secretariat. I felt as though I had come a long way in being able to manage my work, understand Japanese, and get along with everyone. Except for Ms. Mori, I liked my colleagues.

Even my struggle with Ms. Mori had subsided significantly. I avoided her as much as possible, and as long as I took care of my responsibilities she usually stayed away. I could never predict when she might be in a sour mood and I always felt on edge around her, but we had learned to tolerate each other. I tried to keep in mind the things I admired: her strong dedication to a career and her high work standards. But that didn't mean I wanted to spend a weekend with her. I didn't like feeling obligated to go on the trip, especially since I knew that everyone else felt obligated too. Traveling with certain members of the group could be fun, but a weekend with all fifteen of my colleagues and bosses? It would require the most extreme display of my *tatemae* public self that I could imagine.

The group converged at the Fuji Highland Resort late Friday night. We went to a French restaurant located on the top floor of the hotel where waiters in black coats and ties served the meal course by course. The delicate china plates looked like pieces of artwork, arranged with sprinkles and leaves surrounding tiny, unidentifiable pieces of food. More courses arrived. The presentation was meticulous; it looked just as it had in the brochure. But after dinner was over I didn't feel as though I had eaten a whole meal.

I went down to the room I was sharing with Ms. Ogi and Ms. Shoji. It was like a big, puffy cloud. Everything was white, from the furniture to the walls. The fluffy bedspread, curtains, wallpaper, and pillows were decorated with tiny pink and green flowers. Rather than just looking cute, the room felt cozy. At the end of each bed was a thick white terry-cloth robe. I plopped down on the cushy covers and realized that I hadn't slept in a real bed in more than a year.

Ms. Ogi announced that a drinking party would soon start down in Tom's room. I knew I was expected to go, but my *honne* private self wanted a rest. I told her I wanted to take a quick bath and that I would meet them there. Ms. Ogi shrugged and headed toward the party.

I soaked in the tub and considered my resistance to the trip. Maybe I shouldn't have come at all. Although I did feel good about how I had progressed in my job, I wasn't happy as a secretary. The daily routine weighed on my limbs and slowed me down, making the days so monotonous that time seemed to move backward. I organized my day around trips to the pantry and counted the hours and minutes until it was time to finish for the day.

I recognized that most of my pleasures at work revolved around food—lunchtime, and eating chocolates in the pantry. I questioned my discontent, accusing myself of just being spoiled and lazy. Wasn't I lucky to have a job, to be supporting myself? When I talked about my job to people outside the company it sounded much more interesting than it really was. I felt guilty for even thinking this: but why did I have to be content with tedious work that put my brain to sleep? Why was I so hard to satisfy? What did I want?

I wasn't sure what I wanted, but I knew I didn't want to be an office lady. Being on this trip only emphasized it. If anything, being with everyone at Fuji Highland showed me how little I had in common with my work-mates. During dinner I had felt as though I were an impostor: pretending to have a good time, pretending that my job and my life were wonderful, pretending that I didn't want out of the tenth floor. Mr. Yoshida had said it would be a one-year assignment, but I hadn't heard from him. I couldn't bring myself to join the drinking party after my bath, so I snuggled into the comfy white robe and watched MTV in Japanese.

That night I had a vivid nightmare. I was walking around outside. An invisible string had been stretched horizontally across my path. I ran through the string and it cut me through the middle at my waist. From the outside the top half of my body still appeared to be attached to the lower half, but on the inside I knew I had been split in two. I ran around desperately trying to get someone to help. But no one understood me. No one could see that I was not whole.

In the morning we all ate breakfast together and small groups split up to go swimming or to the amusement park. I had brought my bathing suit but decided that I felt too tired to do anything, so I returned to the room and took a nap. When I got to my floating cloud I fell fast asleep and didn't wake up until noon. Sleep had never felt so good, as though I were swallowing huge gulps of comfort.

I met up with everyone for lunch. Again there were plans for afternoon activities. I took a brief walk with Ms. Ogi and a few others around the resort. We could see beautiful Mt. Fuji clearly. I wished the Tra-Montana bike club would suddenly come riding up and take me away.

After our walk I went back to the room and again sleep came quickly. When I woke I again felt a deep sense of comfort. Ms. Ogi asked me if I was OK. I couldn't explain my sleeping except to say that I must have been more tired than I had realized.

When we got ready to leave the resort everyone gathered on the steps for a group picture. Standing in formation with the other secretaries I was aware of making a small hand gesture when the picture was taken. I held my thumb and forefinger as if making the "OK" sign, but I held it down at my side. It was almost unconscious, but I'd done it before when my picture was taken and my *honne* didn't match my *tatemae*. It was just a small thing, a signal to myself that when I held my hand in this certain way I wasn't totally conforming to the public self. I was holding on to a small part of myself that couldn't pretend this was fun. Although I had come to understand the rules of conformity and negotiation, I didn't wholly accept them.

I wondered what I would do with a picture of all of us smiling on the steps of the Fuji Highland Resort and what memories it would inspire. My main thought at the moment was that something needed to change.

A few weeks later Mr. Higuchi brought news of my job transfer. He told me that he'd been working on finding a replacement and that I would start my new assignment in the Public Relations Department after the new year. I started to clean out my desk right away.

Transition

11

THE TEN-DAY WINTER VACATION ENDED ON a Wednesday. I spent the first couple of days of the new year finishing my secretarial work and shuttling my things from the tenth floor to my new desk on the seventh floor. Moving from the secretariat to Public Relations was like going from the contained quietness of a reptile pavilion to the unpredictable ruckus of a monkey house. People actually called out to one another across the room, an action that surely would have interrupted the restrained harmony of the tenth floor.

Over one hundred people worked on the seventh floor, which housed three main departments: the department responsible for company events called General Affairs, Public Relations, and Administration. Clusters of white formica desks and rows of beige metal cabinets gave only vague indications of departmental territory. As in an open-air market, only informal boundaries existed. By standing in just the right spot, I could be in two different departments at the same time.

The Public Relations Department could be distinguished by the stacks of newspapers and loose documents that towered on the desktops. Loosely scrolled posters leaned against each other in corners, and old motorcycle magazines were strewn on tables along with old paper coffee cups and overflowing ashtrays. There were no secretary-mothers in this office.

Although I felt an urge to wipe all the desktops with a white terry-cloth cleaning rag, the clutter and constant motion of the open office somehow gave me a feeling of well-being. There was more space here, space that allowed me to wear my uniform vest unbuttoned or drink coffee at my desk if I wanted to.

When my new boss, Mr. Amamiya, sat down to discuss my assignment he had to shove a pile of magazines and dirty ashtrays out of the way.

"Here," he chuckled. "We finally have some space." He was a middle-aged, junior-level manager with a squarish face and heavy cheeks. He was also one of the most likable people in the building. Two of the things I liked best about him were his hearty laugh and that he was at ease around me. He looked me in the eye when we spoke and seemed to take me seriously.

"Perhaps this office is quite different from the tenth floor," he said and looked around the room. "You may find it difficult to get used to."

"Oh no," I assured him. "I already like it here very much."

How could I tell him that just being away from Ms. Mori and my tea-pouring responsibilities was enough for now.

"Good," he said. "We are glad to have you join us. Our job is to communicate with the public, and our public is international. It is important for us to bridge the gap between Japan and America, but not many of the employees here speak English. You can help us, just like Bret Anderson."

I had known Bret from the beginning of my assignment, but this was the first time for us to work together. He was one of the first Americans to be employed by Honda Motor Company in Japan and had started work at headquarters a few months before I arrived.

"Since you will be here for only three months I want you to have exposure to many areas of public relations," Mr. Amamiya continued. "This will include domestic and international events for cars, motorcycles, and power products."

He introduced me to the people I would be working with: Yoneta, Shiobara, Kawakami, Horiguchi, Kato, and Kobayashi. Their names all ran together, so my first task was to make a list of everyone's name and what each person did.

By Friday I had finished up all my work in the secretariat, so Saturday would be my first full day in Public Relations. We didn't usually work on the weekend, but since we'd just had a long, corporate-wide vacation, the company scheduled a make-up day. I expected that Saturday would be kind of exciting for me, but I didn't know that the date would forever have significance in Japanese history.

When my alarm rang at 6:00 that morning, I got up and turned on the television. Every channel showed the same footage of shiny, black government cars driving urgently to the Imperial Palace. The coverage didn't surprise me. Ever since eighty-eight-year-old Emperor Hirohito had fallen ill in early September, there had been detailed reports on his physical condition on a daily and sometimes hourly basis. Grave-faced newscasters reported his vital signs, often as the first story of the broadcast. Hundreds of reporters across the country had dedicated themselves to following his condition. Camera crews from every news station had been camped outside the stone wall of the Imperial Palace for the last five months. They took photos of anything that passed through the imperial gates, from delivery trucks to the Prime Minister, searching for a sign that the Emperor's condition might have changed. By now, official-looking cars racing in and out of the palace driveway hardly seemed like news.

When I got to work I went down to the basement locker room that I had begun using when I started riding my bike to work because it had a shower. There was only one other woman in the building who used that locker room. She didn't ride the subway to work; she rode her motorcycle. Usually when I walked in the radio would be blasting and the tiny room would be cloudy with her cigarette smoke. She was kind of an enigma in the company and acted rather aloof, so we didn't talk much while we changed from our riding outfits into our uniforms. We took turns standing in front of the single mirror where I'd watch her balance a smoldering cigarette on the ledge of the sink long enough to spike her cropped hair with mousse.

I opened the locker room door that Saturday and noticed that the air was clear. The radio was on, but instead of music I heard the news in Japanese. I walked in and saw my radical locker room partner slouched on the floor against the wall. She was still wearing her leather riding pants. Her knees were drawn up and her head was tilted toward the old radio listening to the announcer, who spoke much too quickly for me to understand. But I could tell from her sorrowful expression that something big had happened. She slowly turned her head in my direction and gazed at me. "His Majesty the Emperor has passed away."

Without changing into my uniform I went directly to the Public Relations Department to get more information. Five men were gathered around the only television on the floor, anxiously listening to the reports. I could understand only bits of the very formal speech used by the announcer.

I was actually more curious about the event than upset by it. I wondered how the country and the company would respond. Employees arrived and clocked in without knowing what had happened because the first announcement had been made during prime commuting hours. People spoke in whispers and with expressions of disbelief.

At 8:40, instead of the chirpy morning exercise music, a gruff male voice came over the public-address system. "This is a Security Department announcement. This is a Security Department announcement," he said. "At 7:05 A.M. His Majesty the Emperor passed away. Please face the Imperial Palace for a moment of silence." All the lights in the building went out, and everyone on the floor turned toward one corner of the room and bowed their heads. It was as though a huge pause button had suddenly been pushed.

I stood with my head bowed in the darkened room. Phones rang unanswered while my colleagues remained motionless around me. I wondered about their thoughts.

Were they experiencing some kind of collective spiritual pain that I could not understand?

The Public Relations Department buzzed all morning with confusion and uncertainty. This was the first death of an Emperor in the postwar period, and nobody knew what to expect. It was announced that we would stay at work, but all activity revolved around the Emperor's death. Mr. Honda came to headquarters to be interviewed on television, and the company issued a public statement. There was discussion about canceling the annual New Year's press conference three days away.

One of the big questions people talked about was the name of the new era. Since 1926, when Emperor Hirohito had ascended the throne, it had been the Showa Era, Showa meaning "bright peace." 1989 was known in Japan as the sixty-fourth year of Showa. People speculated on what the new name would be, but no one really knew. That information could have made someone rich. Printing shops had been on alert ever since the Emperor had become ill—just waiting for the name so they could start printing all the new documents that would be needed, from bank statements to birth certificates and insurance forms.

When the announcement was broadcast on television that afternoon, everyone gathered around the set. I envisioned printing companies poised with anticipation with the presses ready to go.

A dour-looking member of the cabinet appeared on screen holding a large white flash card face down on the desk in front of him. In a moment of historical drama, he picked up the card with two hands and revealed two characters written in thick, black strokes. 平成 *Heisei*, he said, pronouncing the new name. *Heisei*—the era of everlasting peace.

* * *

Every Monday morning we had a Public Relations Department meeting in the press room, a small but private room on the second floor where journalists could conduct interviews. There were several neat, comfortable sitting areas, and a nicely organized video and book library. On one shelf sat a row of sparkling plaques and awards that Honda had received over the years. The press room was the antithesis of our own department and the only place with a table that could accommodate all twenty-five of us.

During the meeting Mr. Amamiya would review the week's activities and discuss upcoming projects. I listened to the wide array of exciting events: someone would go to France to cover a motorcycle race from Paris to Dakar, the British Broadcasting Corporation would visit headquarters, and there would be a press event at a downtown hotel to show a new car.

Mr. Amamiya was vigilant about making sure I was included as an observer in many of the local events. I went to the Japanese Press Club, which turned out to be even more cluttered and disorderly than our office, and traveled to factories with VIP guests and journalists.

The daily activities in public relations were far more interesting than keeping track of the tea-serving schedule in the secretariat, but I still longed for some significant work. The only real responsibility I had was the job of reviewing the Japanese newspapers and clipping out relevant articles to send to the overseas offices. I was much less proficient in reading Japanese than in speaking it, so I clipped any article that had either the kanji character for car 車, or those for Honda 本田.

Being on the seventh floor made me feel less isolated from the handful of other foreigners who were sprinkled throughout the building. Since everyone worked in different departments, we got into the habit of having breakfast together on the sixth floor before work.

All of the breakfast club members—Bret, Rod, Bill, Arnaud, and Eric—were bilingual and had some previous connection to Japan. Bret and Rod had both lived and worked in Japan as Mormon missionaries, Bill was married to a Japanese who had been his college sweetheart, Arnaud's mother was Japanese, and Eric had worked in Tokyo during his graduate school years. We gathered every morning to talk over the company breakfast: cold toast, a hard boiled egg, cabbage salad, and coffee.

Since I couldn't enjoy my own wardrobe at work, I made a point every morning of evaluating the men's clothing. Bret could always be counted on for a fashionable ensemble, often incorporating daring geometric patterns and primary colors, while at all times maintaining his all-American, clean-cut look. Eric, on the other hand, had a European flair that I suspected was a result of his experience living in Germany for several years. He was perhaps the only person in the entire company, and possibly in all of Tokyo, who could get away with wearing a genuine bow tie and a mustache. Then there were Bill, Rod, and Arnaud, the most conservative ones, who wore plain white dress shirts and unassuming ties. Bill's idea of getting really crazy was wearing a pale pink dress shirt to work on a Friday.

Our common bond was complaining about Japan, its national customs, corporate policies, and idiosyncrasies.

We competed with each other to see who could find the strangest misuse of the English language, such as the name of a bar that was called "Wet Dreams." The men complained about always having cold feet when they slept because the futon were too short for them, and every other week it seemed that one of them had a bruise on his head from hitting a low doorjamb.

We commiserated about working on the weekends or on American holidays. Sometimes we mimicked our least favorite associate in the Administration Department and vented our dismay that he could be in charge of us but have no experience living overseas himself. The laughing and whining were therapeutic, but we all knew that the bottom line was that if any one of us was really so unhappy we could leave. Since each of us was bilingual we had other options—all of us, in varying degrees, wanted to be there.

One day I warned my English-speaking colleagues about being attacked by the company's EX-O Patrol. EX-O stood for "Excellent Office."

EX-O was a company-sponsored group that was dedicated to improving efficiency in the office. From time to time they rallied around various themes. One promotion encouraged everyone to do away with excessive copying; another set up guidelines to make people limit their storage space by throwing away old data. EX-O posted an "Excellent Office" sign on those departments that lowered copy costs by a certain percentage or reduced excess storage by a certain number of centimeters.

I hadn't paid much attention to EX-O until one day when a patrol member approached me at my desk. He had a clipboard and a list of all the items that an employee should have in his or her desk. The list included one pencil, one red pen, one eraser and one ball-point pen—color optional. He told me that items such as scissors, glue, staplers, and white-out should not be kept in individual desks but rather in a communal box so that everyone could share.

Theoretically I could appreciate his idea. Nobody really needed four pair of scissors in her desk, but when the EX-O officer asked me to open my drawers I felt invaded. That was when he discovered the hoard of erasers that I had scavenged from the secretariat supply closet. I had hoarded a generous handful of the clean white eraser cubes in their trademark blue-and-black wrapping because the erasers lying around the public relations office, if you could find one, were dirty and had been rubbed into stumpy round balls that couldn't be firmly grasped.

I relinquished my supply of fresh, unblemished erasers to the officer but requested that I be able to keep my own bottle of white-out. I argued that since I made so many mistakes in Japanese I was constantly using it. Finally he gave in and allowed one bottle of white-out to stay in my desk, citing efficiency as the reason. I guessed that I had ruined my department's chance of being distinguished as an "Excellent Office."

* * *

Mr. Amamiya approached me one day to talk about an assignment.

"I have a special project for you," he said. "But you must keep this quiet; it's a secret assignment."

"What's the secret?" I asked.

"There is something called X-day; have you heard of it?"

I shook my head.

"Well," he said practically in a whisper, "it's something rather unpleasant to talk about, but it's part of our job to be prepared for it. X-day is the unknown date of Mr. Honda's death."

"Is he sick?" I asked with surprise, remembering how healthy he had seemed at his spring party.

"Oh no. It's nothing like that. This is really quite difficult. You see, it's not that we're anticipating his death anytime soon, and of course no one wants to prepare for that day, but the reality is that Mr. Honda is an important man. When he passes away the whole world will want to know about it. It's our job to be prepared to handle requests for information in order to best represent Mr. Honda and his memory."

Mr. Amamiya explained that there was already a lot of information about Mr. Honda in Japanese. Over twenty books had been written about him, but only two had been translated into English.

"When Mr. Honda's co-founder Mr. Fujisawa passed away last year, we were unprepared. None of our major executives had died before, and we weren't ready for the demand for information from the international press. What I want you to do is start preparing documentation in English on Mr. Honda, his life, and his work. Someday this information will be very useful, but it's extremely important that you be discreet. Don't leave any documents out on your desk or tell anyone what you are doing. Someone could easily misunderstand and it would appear terribly disrespectful. Many people wouldn't understand that doing this job is a way we can honor Mr. Honda."

Mr. Amamiya gave me the books he had and a list of

contacts. He asked me to keep him posted on my progress but told me to research and write as I liked. Finally—a job that engaged me. I just wished it wasn't in preparation for such a distressing event.

I frequently received requests from my colleagues to proofread and explain English documents. Sometimes people at the company I didn't even know showed up carrying a folder and smiling bashfully. The more desperate employees were so eager for my help they promised to treat me to lunch or a drink if I'd read and explain letters from customers, speeches, and product information.

Some of the material made no sense but was often hilarious. There was one safety tag that had already been mass-produced and was supposed to be attached to seat belts. The caption in English read, "Caution. Be sure to hold seat belt by hand after from the seat locking device as illustrated before folding up the seat back or seat back locking devices might bite seat belts." Another one explained that the "Cool Ventilation System" would "clear any displeasure out and increase the comfortableness in head." I only wished there was such a device.

The phone rang one afternoon and I answered it with the usual greeting, "This is the Public Relations Department." The caller mumbled his name and organization, and although I didn't hear him clearly, I gathered that he was a reporter from one of the Tokyo newspapers. Before I had a chance to say the usual *"Itsumo osewa ni natte orimasu,"* a formal way of saying thanks for the call, the caller said, "Give the phone to a man."

"I'm terribly sorry," I said, not believing what I had heard. "May I ask who is calling?"

"Give the phone to a man," the caller growled with irritation.

I felt my neck and ears getting warm. I was sure the caller didn't know that I was a foreigner; he simply knew I was a woman. I again politely requested his name.

"Give the phone to a man!" he demanded in a loud voice.

Mr. Amamiya was standing nearby and noticed that I was having some difficulty. The last thing I wanted to do was hand him the receiver. I covered the mouthpiece and said to him, "I don't know who it is, but he says he wants to speak to a man."

"I'll take care of it," he said, taking the phone. "Hello, this is Amamiya," he said. The caller must have been someone recognizable, because Mr. Amamiya immediately began apologizing profusely and bowed as he talked. A female colleague who had witnessed the event came over. "I'll bet I know who that is," she said. "He's the one who is always rude to women. Don't feel bad; it's happened to me too."

After he got off the phone Mr. Amamiya said, "Oh, don't worry about him. Some of the reporters are so temperamental."

I wanted to say that it wasn't a matter of temperament, it was discrimination. I wanted to tell Mr. Amamiya that the caller had made me feel worthless and that his tolerance of a "temperamental" reporter was just as bad as being discriminatory himself. But Mr. Amamiya and the woman had gone back to work. No one seemed to think it was wrong that a reporter would refuse to talk to any women in the office. I didn't want to look like a cry-baby, so I didn't say anything. I didn't think anyone would understand.

There was another type of discrimination tolerated by my new colleagues that seemed incongruent with being an international public relations office—discrimination against all foreign reporters and a few Japanese reporters who didn't represent the mainstream press. Because Bret worked mainly with the English-speaking journalists, he heard their complaints every time we held a news conference, one for the Japanese reporters and one for the other reporters. The first meeting was always held in Japanese, and only members of the club of journalists who covered the Keidanren, or Federation of Japanese Economic Organizations, were allowed to attend. The second meeting would be bilingual and open to everyone. The Keidanren press club was an old and prestigious group made up of the mainstream Japanese media. They wouldn't admit foreign members, and also prohibited the fringe Japanese news groups from joining.

The Keidanren club exerted pressure on companies like Honda to have the advantage of a members-only press meeting which allowed them to receive information before the others. The consequence of not complying was that the powerful members might choose not to write about the event or, worse, write unflattering articles.

The journalists' club system had originally helped the Japanese media gain power in Japan, but now their rules were clearly out of date. The Tokyo Foreign Correspondents' Club had over two hundred working members, some of whom were fluent in Japanese. But no matter how fluent they were, the Public Relations Department always treated them differently from the Japanese Keidanren club reporters.

After a month and a half of observing, news clipping,

and doing secret research for X-day, I was asked to join the project team for the Integra long-lead event. Mr. Amamiya explained that a long-lead was a preview of a particular product to magazine journalists. Ten journalists from America were going to be given a three-months'-early look at the new Integra so that their articles about it would be published at the same time the car was released to the public. Since this car was expected to be a big seller in the United States, Honda had invited journalists and photographers from the top five automobile magazines, *Car & Driver*, *Auto Week*, *Road & Track*, *Automobile*, and *Motor Trend*.

The release of any new product to the public usually generated great excitement in the auto world. The media constantly speculated about who was doing what. For journalists, having the inside story meant prestige so they were always looking for new information. Magazines like *Car & Driver* frequently published grainy spy-photos of mystery cars and often preempted the public relations effort altogether.

Companies like Honda went to great lengths to protect the security of a new product, sometimes totally covering a vehicle with brown wrapping and adding false pieces so that it couldn't be accurately photographed. The test course at the Research and Development center had an alert system that would warn drivers when an airplane or helicopter flew overhead. When the alarm sounded and red lights flashed, the driver would duck for cover under a roofed structure so that the car couldn't be seen or photographed from the sky.

During the two-day long-lead event the American journalists would get a chance to see the Integra, drive it at the Research and Development center, and talk to the engineers who had designed it. Preparations for the event had been going on for months, but now that it was only weeks away, the project group was concerned with immediate details. Perhaps it was the skill that I had demonstrated through the clipping of news articles, or maybe Mr. Amamiya just thought I'd feel more included if I had an actual job, but for whatever reason, I was entrusted with the job of coordinating name tags for the event. I didn't even have to make them; I just had to make sure that our subcontractor did.

Azuma was a small public relations firm that did project work for Honda on a regular basis. One of their representatives spent so much time in our office that it was a week before I realized that he wasn't a Honda employee. When I approached the Azuma man to inquire about the name tags he told me that Azuma sub-subcontracted the work out to another, smaller company called DAN. I called the DAN company and made an appointment for their representative to come to headquarters.

The name tag supplier from DAN was a young man who looked like he had just graduated from high school. He wore large square glasses on his chubby face and an ill-fitting suit. He always appeared to be a little confused and looked around himself a lot as if to see if he had dropped something. Privately, I called him Mr. Dan.

To Mr. Dan, I represented the whole of the Honda Motor Company, and it was his job to make me happy. From our first meeting he was uptight and uncomfortable, and so intent on pleasing me that words of apology continually poured from his lips. He was sorry that he didn't speak English or that he was taking up too much of my time. He seemed to be on guard whenever we spoke, never for a moment relaxing enough to take a deep breath.

His behavior directly reflected the hierarchy between companies in Japan. Mr. Dan was under Azuma, which was under Honda. I wished he could relax and have a conversation without hyperventilating, but there was no way for him to see me as separate from the company. I knew this for certain when one day he referred to me as the personification of the company and called me "Honda-san."

Every week Mr. Dan would visit the headquarters building and we would discuss the progress of the name tags. When I had first given him a typed list of the participants' names, we had gone over the spellings one by one. The next week he brought me a sample of what the cards would look like.

"This is the name card," he said, displaying the white card between his chubby fists. He demonstrated how the card would slide into the plastic holder that would be clipped to the coat of the wearer.

"You see, if you need to make a name change you can change the entire card. I'll make sure to include several blank ones."

It took all my self-control not to laugh. Mr. Dan took it all so seriously. The cards would be ready in two weeks, he assured me. I wondered what could possibly take so long.

I felt like an impostor at the long-lead, standing outside on the test course with a clipboard hugged to my chest. It was a warm March day, and it was pleasant to be outside. We had reached the test-driving stage, and the reporters were taking turns driving the cars on the maneuverability track with its hairpin turns. After having successfully delivered the name tags, I had been observing the three main groups of participants since the morning: the engineers, the public relations guys, and the American journalists.

A group of half a dozen Japanese senior engineers stood near the track looking as stiff as their plastic pocket protectors. They wore matching white uniforms and looked uncomfortable being exposed to natural light. A smaller group of junior engineers hovered behind them. They looked on guard, just as Mr. Dan had been around me. The whole group looked uniformly unapproachable.

The public relations men were a little more relaxed. No one wore uniforms. A few American employees from the Los Angeles Public Relations office had come with the journalists and were talking with the Tokyo Public Relations men.

The most relaxed group of people were the American journalists. They were dressed in jeans and sweaters and looked like they were having a blast. They compared notes and took turns driving. These men loved cars. They loved to drive them, talk about them, and write about them. Being flown to Japan for a two-day binge of car information was one of the best things about their jobs.

I stood around hiding behind my clipboard and hoping that no one would ask me anything more technical than "How many miles per gallon does the Integra get?" I had read the press information, but I felt totally out of my league. I wondered what it was that I could do.

Later in the afternoon the head of Research and Development, Mr. Kawamoto, arrived at the track. I noticed that my colleagues from Public Relations stopped laughing and maintained a formal distance. Mr.

Kawamoto was one of the highest-ranking men in the company.

I watched him join the senior engineers, who suddenly seemed even more uptight. They greeted him by bowing and speaking softly, acting just like the junior engineers.

I knew Mr. Kawamoto from the tenth floor. We had often said hello to each other when he was in the office. He spoke English well and seemed to intuitively know that I was frustrated with my duties as a secretary. I hadn't seen him since my job transfer, so I walked over and said hello.

"Oh, Rora-san. I see you've escaped from the secretariat." He asked me how it was in Public Relations. We joked and laughed while my colleagues looked on from a distance.

Mr. Kawamoto introduced me to some of the senior engineers. They were interested to find out that I had worked on the tenth floor. We spoke in Japanese and I learned their names and specialties. I discovered that although none of them had talked with the reporters they were eager to do so.

I took one of the engineers to meet the American Public Relations guys and the reporters. Others followed. There were a few bilingual people around to help the groups talk, but it turned out that the engineers and the reporters really spoke the same language of cars. The language was so technical and specialized that they seemed to understand each other due simply to their high level of knowledge.

Throughout the rest of the test drive and photo session I floated among the groups, calling everyone by name and helping to make connections. I discovered that everyone looked at me as part of his group—whether as a fellow Public Relations employee, a fellow American, or fellow Honda person. I felt like a kind of mascot that everyone wanted to claim.

Later that night we all gathered for dinner in a traditional Japanese restaurant where people sat on the floor around sunken tables. The three groups of people sat with their colleagues. I armed myself with a bottle of hot saké and moved among the tables. It was easy to squeeze in, pour drinks, and talk in order to find out who wanted what information and who could supply it. I easily cajoled particular members to move to other tables. They wouldn't make the move on their own, but they didn't resist when I pushed. They talked about cars and talked about themselves. Bottles of beer and saké helped ease the process, and by the end of the evening there weren't three groups any more.

I felt like this event was an extension of co-hosting the international party at the Suzuka convention. By helping these gear-heads and reporters connect, I had found something that I could do that seemed to matter. It gave me a feeling that I'd never had from serving a perfect cup of tea or coordinating correctly spelled name tags.

Before the reporters left the next day we gathered in front of the Research and Development building to take a picture. I stood in the back with my colleagues from headquarters. The reporters sat in front next to Mr. Kawamoto and the senior engineers in their white uniforms. When the picture was taken I didn't even think about making the secret hand signal to myself. This time, my private and public selves were aligned.

Salaryman

12 IT WAS 9:00 P.M. ON A TUESDAY EVENING AND the office was quiet. A few men on the seventh floor worked alone or in small groups. When "Camp Town Races" had played over the loud speaker at 5:40 P.M. to announce the official end of the workday, almost no one left, not even the women, who were permitted to work only twenty hours of overtime a month as compared to forty for the men. But by 9:00 P.M. most of the desktops had been cleared off and people had gone home. I would normally have also gone, but I was waiting for a phone call from the New York office, where it was only 8:00 A.M.

Mr. Amamiya was working at a table with two other men from our department. The only other person in the office was Mr. Inoue, a sub-manager in my section. He sat only a desk away from me. I noticed Mr. Inoue slowly going through his papers and starting to clear off his desk.

"I'm tired. Time to go," he said, more to himself than to me. He repeated the phrases while he got ready, as though he were trying to persuade himself to go home. Finally he put a stack of papers in his briefcase and snapped it shut.

"Sorry to be leaving before you," he said, using the common phrase people used when they left the office. I could tell that he was uncomfortable about leaving.

"See you tomorrow," I said.

He walked behind the desk partition to the closet, got his coat, and went out the glass door leading to the elevator hall. I shook my head wondering what made it so hard for him to leave. There weren't any major events that week, and almost everyone else had already gone home.

Suddenly the glass door swung open and Mr. Inoue, wearing his coat, marched back into the office. He went straight to his desk and popped open the briefcase. "Oh, I've got so much to do," he said, again as if talking to himself. He sighed, as though both exasperated and resigned, took off his coat, and went back to work.

"No, you don't," I wanted to argue. I felt like telling him to just go home, but I already knew that he wouldn't. I got two hundred yen from my stash of drawer-change and bought us each a cup of instant coffee.

Mr. Inoue reminded me of my host father during my year as an exchange student. My host father always left for work before I got up in the morning and was rarely home by the time I returned from judo practice at 8:00 P.M. He regularly worked on Saturdays. We hardly saw each other, and when we did we almost never spoke. The highlight of our relationship occurred on a Sunday afternoon when he took me to see where he worked as an engineer. It was an automobile parts supply company that made electronic door panel parts. He took me on a tour of the plant and explained what happened at each stage of manufacturing. I had never seen him so animated as when he took one of the finished electronic door parts in his hand and pointed out the detailed craftsmanship. My host father seemed much more comfortable at work than I had ever seen him at home, where he acted like an awkward visitor who didn't know how to turn on the rice cooker or fill the bath. He said more to me in that day than he did the rest of the year combined.

My host father and Mr. Inoue were both "salarymen"—a generic phrase like "office ladies" used to describe the majority of men who work and earn a salary, usually at a large company that they join after graduating from high school or college and stay with throughout their careers. Although Honda employed engineers, lawyers, accountants, and salesmen, all of them were considered salarymen.

The salarymen at Honda wore white shirts and dark suits. They were underweight and seemed to live on cigarettes and instant coffee. Salarymen were married, had 1.5 children, and lived in an apartment or small house in a suburb located an hour and a half from Honda. They worked many hours a week and turned their salaries over to their wives, who were responsible for the home and children. A salaryman's domain was not his home, but his work.

At least once every week, on a designated day, representatives from the Honda Employees Union would walk throughout the headquarters forcing salarymen to go home. It was called "go-home-early day," or *teiji no hi* in Japanese. The gang of union representatives canvassed the intelligent building floor by floor wearing uniform armbands and carrying a megaphone from which they issued gentle but insistent encouragement. The number of designated go-home-early days was negotiated by the union each year. In January the union handed out a plastic wallet-sized calendar. Workdays were in black, vacation days were in red, and *teiji* days had a red circle around them.

I suspected that if Honda didn't have go-home-early days, many salarymen would never eat dinner at home. Overtime was a regular part of working life. If, for some reason, someone had to leave right at 5:40 P.M., he would apologize to everyone before leaving.

But overtime wasn't the only way salarymen demonstrated extraordinary commitment to work. It wasn't unusual to skip meals and breaks or stay up all night at the office working on a project. My colleagues had a kind of perseverance that eluded me. They seemed to almost thrive on hardship and self-sacrifice, and always without complaint.

Salarymen had an abundance of a virtue exhibited by most Japanese people I knew—*gaman*. This is a combination of patience, endurance, and self-restraint under unfavorable or even painful conditions. When children on the train complained of being hungry, the mother's advice was "*Gaman shinasai*. Be patient." When the judo team had shown signs of fatigue at the end of a grueling practice, the captain would yell out "*Gaman shiro!* Be strong, endure!" It was *gaman* that kept people from screaming out as they were shoved into contorted positions on crowded subway cars, and kept them from dashing across an empty street when the sign said, "Don't walk."

Gaman was in some ways the opposite of selfishness, and salarymen were the kings of selflessness when it came to the company. It wasn't unusual for salarymen to go on last-minute business trips, even overseas, or to be transferred from one office to another with no explanation. Sometimes even long-term foreign postings were decided at the last minute. Men went overseas alone, leaving their families in Japan while they worked. There was even a word to describe these transplanted men—*tanshinfunin*.

The virtuousness of *gaman* explained why my colleagues in the secretariat preferred to silence their complaints about Ms. Mori. Complaining was not cool; it was selfish. It was as though the more *gaman* one exerted, the more virtuous he or she could be. But exerting *gaman* was not just an individual act. I didn't really know there was such a thing as group *gaman* until I worked on a project with the Finance Department.

The eighth-floor Finance Department was second only to the tenth floor in conservatism and exceeded the tenth floor in dullness. Number-crunching accountants sat silently at their desks with balance sheets and calculators. No one laughed or even stood up to stretch. It was as though they walked to their places in the morning and chained their feet and personalities to their desks.

I sat with Mr. Hirokawa at one of the Finance Department's conference tables, which was so clean it looked as though it had never been used. Although more than fifty people worked only a few feet away, there was almost no sound. The only distraction in the entire room was an electronic board with green numbers that displayed world currency rates and Honda stock prices.

Mr. Hirokawa slid a gold pen back and forth between his fingers. He was the section chief of international finance and had been a frequent visitor to Mr. Chino on the tenth floor, so I knew him well. Mr. Hirokawa wore colorful ties and European-cut suits that made him look much more sophisticated than most of the salarymen at headquarters. His fashionable appearance and slight paunch told me that he had done more than work during his five-year assignment in Paris.

He had asked me to meet him to discuss a big upcoming project. A large group of American automobile analysts would be coming to Japan to visit Honda and other car companies. It had been decided that I would help out when the analysts arrived.

Honda Motor stock had been traded on the New York Stock Exchange since 1979, and auto analysts regularly visited Tokyo to talk with executives so that they could make reports to investors. But, as Mr. Hirokawa explained, they had never had more than one or two analysts visit at a time.

"There will be forty of them," Mr. Hirokawa said. "And since they will be visiting other companies, including Toyota and Nissan, we want to make a very good impression on them while they're with us. The schedule includes a meeting with executives and a factory tour, but the special event is that we're taking them to the Formula 1 race in Suzuka."

The Formula 1 race at Suzuka was the Indy 500 of racing in Japan. Honda owned the racetrack as part of the Suzuka Circuit Race Track and Amusement Park, and it was the only Formula 1-sanctioned track in Japan. Hundreds of fans with general-admission tickets camped outside the track for days prior to a race.

Mr. Hirokawa told me that I wouldn't need to be involved in the preparation but that they need me to help accompany the analysts while they were in Suzuka. He introduced me to two young members of the Finance Department who were in the project group—Mr. Sumita and Ms. Takahashi. I had met Mr. Sumita before. He had spent his teenage years in New York and used phrases like "ya know" and "I dunno" which made him easy to listen to. He wore large-framed glasses and had long, floppy hair like a sixties rock star. He was also tall and outwardly confident—unusual characteristics for the eighth floor.

Ms. Takahashi was an office lady like me. She wore her hair pulled back in a tight, unforgiving bun which accentuated her severe appearance. Her skin was pale, and she wore heavy, dark eye makeup. Her voice was soft and she seemed hesitant to speak too much, as if fearing that she might offend someone.

The day before the analysts arrived, Mr. Sumita, Ms. Takahashi, and I caught the bullet train to Suzuka. We rode in the reserved car with our compact overnight bags overhead on the luggage rack. A young woman wearing a sea-foam green uniform came down the aisle pushing a cart of snacks and beverages and chanted a sales pitch like a rhythmic sutra: "Canned coffee, orange juice, oolong tea." Bags of rice crackers, chocolate bars, and boxed lunches filled the two-tiered cart.

The Suzuka Circuit Race Track and Amusement Park was located in the same area as the Suzuka factory where Honda manufactured motorcycles and cars. The amusement park had many facilities, including the large convention halls where the quality-circle convention had been held. Since the race was only days away, the circuit hotels and facilities were full. We were allocated a small meeting room for the analysts and executives. It was simple and unorganized. The beige walls seemed to be there by accident. There were rectangular tables and chairs scattered around the room.

We spent the day organizing—arranging the tables first one way and then another and setting up a reception table with name tags and name plates. In the front of the room we arranged a display of the most recent innovative car parts, with a description of their function and where the technology had come from.

Ms. Takahashi and I checked and cross-checked the name tags against a master list of analysts' names. We counted and recounted chairs, tested the overhead projector, and ran through the slides. At least one hour was spent discussing how and where to hang four framed posters of the four generations of the Accord, and another hour trying to figure out a way to display the model year on the posters.

At 5:00 P.M. the room looked like a professional conference room. At 7:00 P.M. it hadn't changed, but we were all still there, ostensibly making it better. We hadn't had a break all day, and I was tired and hungry. I wanted to leave, but I didn't even know where we would be staying. Eventually we would all go to dinner, but I had no idea of when that would be.

Half an hour later Mr. Hirokawa decided that he was satisfied with the room, and we finally got ready to leave. I wondered whether we would go first to the hotel or straight to dinner. Part of me just wanted to spend the evening alone, relaxing and taking a bath. After traveling and being cooped up all day, I wanted some time to myself.

Mr. Hirokawa, Mr. Sumita, Ms. Takahashi, and I piled our bags into the trunk of a taxi and climbed in.

The hotels near the circuit must have been full, because the taxi drove all the way back to the train station even though I hadn't noticed any hotels near there. Mr. Hirokawa paid the driver while we retrieved our bags.

"Where is the hotel?" I asked Mr. Hirokawa.

"All the places around here are full," he said, and turned in the direction of the station.

I felt impatient and hungry and annoyed. With all the planning involved in this event, why hadn't someone reserved four extra hotel rooms?

"Then where are we going to stay?" I asked.

"Osaka," he replied, and started climbing up the stairway to the train station.

"Osaka?"

"Yes, we're going to Osaka."

I couldn't believe it. Osaka was two hours away.

There was no time to complain or ask any more questions because a train was about to depart. We got our tickets and boarded the local train. Our car was nearly empty, so we all sat in separate aisles. I put on my Walkman and slouched into the seat. Osaka. Unbelievable.

The local train chugged along and stopped at every station, and my hunger and frustration grew incrementally with each stop. I would have paid triple for a bag of crackers from the snack lady in the sea-foam green outfit, but there were no vendors on this train.

It was 10:00 P.M. when we finally checked into the hotel. Mr. Hirokawa told everyone to meet in the hotel restaurant for dinner in ten minutes. If I hadn't been so hungry I would have stayed in my room.

When I went down to the restaurant I wasn't surprised that it was French, but I was surprised at what I found at the table. Mr. Hirokawa had taken off his jacket and loosened his tie and he was studying the wine list. Ms. Takahashi had changed and wore a bright red-and-blue scarf. They sat with Mr. Sumita around the table laughing.

"I'm gonna have a beer," Mr. Sumita said.

"I think I'll have wine. Anyone else?" Mr. Hirokawa asked.

The group ordered and settled into a rather lively discussion of the day's events. Ms. Takahashi was more talkative than I had ever noticed, and everyone seemed to relax in a way that I had never before seen. It was as if everyone had forgotten that we had spent more than five hours on trains and another ten hanging posters, moving tables, and counting name tags.

We retired to our rooms right after dinner and made plans to meet early in the morning to catch the train back to Suzuka. The next day when we got back to the conference room we checked all the details again. The finance manager arrived, followed by five Honda executives. After lunch the analysts showed up on a chartered bus.

Once everyone arrived the day went quickly. The executives made speeches and answered questions. We took the analysts on a tour of a highly automated, prototype assembly line that would be used to manufacture the NSX sports car. It was around dinner time when we took them back to their hotel and got back on the train to Osaka. This time it was before 10:00 P.M. when we ate dinner and discussed plans for the race-day.

"We'll leave Osaka on the 8:00 A.M. train," Mr. Hirokawa said. "Make sure to bring your bags because we won't return."

He explained that we would pick up the analysts at their hotel with two buses. Everyone would get on the buses and drive to the racetrack. It was impossible to get tickets for over forty people all together, so the analysts would be split up into groups of four or five people, including one Honda employee who would be responsible for that group.

"The racetrack will be very crowded," Mr. Hirokawa emphasized. "It's important to stay together during the race so that everyone can get back to the bus on time when it is over. It will be very difficult to leave Suzuka quickly because of the crowds. Most fans stay overnight and leave the next day, but we must get the analysts back to Tokyo."

He told us that because of the massive number of people, the taxi ride to the train station, which normally took twenty minutes, would take hours. It was actually faster to walk. But they had devised a plan to drive our group to another station an hour away where we could catch the bullet train. The departure time was set, and tickets had already been purchased. The key would be getting all forty analysts back on the bus and out of the Suzuka traffic in time to make the train.

When we got to the racetrack the next afternoon, I understood what kind of crowds Mr. Hirokawa meant. Entering the grounds was like walking into a state fair on the busiest day. People stood around looking for other people, studying the program, or eating. It was impossible to walk fast or in a straight line, so I navigated a circuitous route for the four analysts with me. Walking by food and drink stands, I smelled fried noodles, and saw people eating grilled octopus on skewers and drinking beer.

After listening to all the warnings about leaving on time, I felt enormous pressure to keep to the schedule. It was hard to relax even after we got to our seats. We had a clear view of a small section of the racecourse. Looking directly across the track, I could see an open field where thousands of people sat on the ground.

I paid more attention to my watch than I did to the race. It was difficult to keep all the cars straight when they were driving so fast anyway. I kept my eyes on the two red, white, and blue Honda cars driven by Ayrton Senna and Satoru Nakajima. As soon as the checkered flag came down I started to hustle my group out of the stands. Carefully retracing our steps, we moved past the food stands that were now surrounded by overflowing garbage cans. When we got to the parking lot I panicked. The two buses we had left had multiplied into an entire lot of buses, and they all looked the same. Just as I was about to turn around to find help, I saw Mr. Sumita waving at us with his arm high in the air.

We got everyone on the buses and made it to the station in time, but at the last minute there was some confusion about finding enough seats for all the analysts. We boarded the train and then ran around the different cars making sure everyone had a seat. By the time we finished checking, the train had begun to move, and I found myself standing in between two passenger compartments in a tiny space near the bathroom with Mr. Sumita and Ms. Takahashi. We stood facing each other with our bags sitting between our feet.

"So everyone has a seat?" I asked, wondering where our seats were.

"Yup. They're all taken care of," said Mr. Sumita.

Ms. Takahashi nodded with obvious relief.

"What about us?" I asked.

"Well, there weren't enough reserved seats, so we have non-reserved ones," Mr. Sumita said.

"Shouldn't we go find them?" I suggested.

"I don't think that will do much good," he said. "The non-reserved section is already packed and people are standing in the aisles."

I listened to him without fully registering the meaning. Then it sank in. We would be standing for three hours in this small nook between cars, watching and smelling people go in and out of the bathroom, all the way home. My feet ached and my head hurt from translating all day. I wanted to sit down and buy some hot oolong tea from the snack lady. I didn't want to *gaman* any more.

I saw that Mr. Sumita and Ms. Takahashi were just as tired, but they didn't complain. Instead they piled our bags up so we had more room. Ms. Takahashi found a newspaper and spread it on the floor so we'd have a place to sit, and Mr. Sumita got three cans of lukewarm tea. Joking and laughing, we persevered together, all the way back to Tokyo.

By the end of March I was feeling restless. My work in public relations had been a huge improvement over the secretariat, but striving to be a successful salaryman at headquarters left me feeling unsatisfied. I had been thinking about the long-lead event and how good I had felt using my skills to help people connect.

The next three-month segment of my training was scheduled to begin in April. I had been in touch with Mr. Yoshida on a weekly basis, sending him faxes about my work, but I hadn't told him that I was dissatisfied. He had been faxing me back with vague details about the remaining nine months of training. It was generally understood that when I left public relations I would visit other departments that would help me understand the company and have relevance to my job when I returned to America—but that was also vague. Honda's largest American facility was in Ohio, but it was just as likely that I would be sent to one of the satellite offices in Los Angeles, New York, Detroit, or Washington, D.C. Mr. Yoshida had been promoted and moved to the Los Angeles office, so there was a good chance that I would go there.

I had decided that I was tired of being a trainee and tired of waiting for chance opportunities to have meaningful work. I didn't like sitting around and observing without a specific goal. My experience at the Integra long-lead and the quality-circle convention left me yearning for work that made me feel useful. I wanted more significant responsibility, and I knew where I could get it—the factory.

The Sayama factory acted as the "mother factory" to the Ohio plant. Since the Ohio automobile factory start-up, Americans had been traveling to Sayama for short-term training. The Sayama factory was accustomed to training small numbers of Americans, but recently, the numbers had increased significantly. The Ohio plant had started a new program to train over a thousand associates in Japan and was sending them over in large groups.

News about the Americans in Sayama had filtered through the English-speaking grapevine. I heard reports of disillusioned associates frustrated with the working and living conditions. Even senior managers weren't shy about saying they hated coming to Japan. Over the months, more Americans had cycled through the factory and returned to Ohio with horror stories about being treated unfairly and the intolerable living conditions. Going to Japan was a burden.

I had visited the Sayama plant as an informal translator for Scott Whitlock, the American plant manager of the Ohio factory. He had come to Japan to check the progress of the training. We talked all day with both American and Japanese staff and got a clear idea of some of the problems. Communication was the biggest one, and both the Japanese and Americans were responsible.

Distrust was rampant on both sides. The Americans didn't like coming to Japan because they felt lost and stupid. The Japanese employees resented all the extra work it meant for them every time an English-speaking employee was assigned to their department.

Scott and I had dinner and discussed the problems. I told him that many of the things the Americans complained about made sense, considering the traditional attitude toward hospitality in Japan. Japanese hosts tend to completely care for their guests. They feel they must accommodate every need and would consider themselves inadequate hosts if their guests had to do things for themselves. Accordingly, the Japanese administration department in Sayama arranged all transportation, provided all meals, and generally tried to anticipate and fulfill every need the Americans had, rather than teach them how to do things for themselves.

By being polite and taking care of daily needs, they inadvertently took away the American associates' independence, because the associates had to depend on the Japanese administration for everything. These Americans were used to controlling their lives and their work. In Ohio they functioned as competent adults who successfully managed people and executed decisions. When they couldn't do something as simple as buy a train ticket or order a meal, they felt powerless, ineffective, and sometimes even depressed. The key to helping them was teaching them how to do things on their own, to give them at least the perception of control over their lives.

The foreign experience intimidated people. Some associates had never even traveled outside the Midwest before coming to Japan. A majority did not have a passport before their assignment, and had minimal knowledge of Japan.

In the workplace, language problems caused further resentment. Because many Japanese had very limited English skills, directions often sounded like orders. "Why don't you observe this area today?" might come out as "You stay here."

All Japanese students study English starting in junior high school, but they focus almost exclusively on reading and writing. By the time a college graduate goes into the working world, he or she has studied English for ten years, but because of the myopic textbook approach, men and women who could read the *New York Times* cannot even hold a simple conversation about the weather. For most Japanese, face-to-face conversation is the most difficult of all English skills.

In the factory there was no time to waste in ineffective communication. Rather than laboriously thumb through a dictionary in hopes of finding the right word, some Japanese associates just left the Americans out of work projects. Still under pressure to complete their jobs successfully, the Japanese workers often avoided fearful and problematic communication situations.

Scott listened to me in a way that Mr. Yoshida never

had. I jokingly told him that the only thing I had really learned in Japan was how to get along with middle-aged Japanese men. He replied in all seriousness that I had developed a valuable skill. He encouraged me to ask Mr. Yoshida to assign me to the Sayama factory.

Sayama seemed like another step away from my glamorous international career, and I didn't know if I wanted to leave Tokyo. Then Scott confided in me that plans were being made to send workers from Ohio on long-term assignments with their families. The information was highly confidential, which appealed to my desire to be taken seriously. Scott had a way of making me feel important and that my ideas mattered. He needed someone like me at the factory now. I agreed to try.

I sent Mr. Yoshida several urgent faxes asking him when he would be in Japan and when we could meet. I told him there were things I wanted to discuss. As I waited for him to confirm a date, my mind raced with ideas and I got more excited about going to the factory. I studied books about overseas employment and, with data provided by Scott, prepared to make a convincing argument. I was desperate to be taken seriously by Mr. Yoshida and wanted him to think I had developed useful skills. I was determined to make a change.

When Mr. Yoshida finally got to headquarters in late March, we met in the coffee shop on the sixth floor. It was late afternoon and I had been anxiously waiting for him all day.

I asked him to elaborate on his ideas for the rest of my training and my job in the U.S. He outlined his plan that I spend time in the North American Sales Department, maybe visit the Research and Development Center and perhaps one of the factories. After I finished training he thought I might end up with him in Los Angeles working in public affairs.

I told him that it was helpful to know what he was thinking because I had been feeling rather confused and unsure of what he had planned. I also told him that I was dissatisfied with my training and that I spent the majority of my time just watching things and not being included unless English documents had to be proofread. I told him that I wanted to use my ideas and abilities.

He was concerned that I hadn't been included by my colleagues in public relations work. He thought maybe people didn't know how to interact with me and work with me except as it related to English. I agreed with him and told him what Paul Kennedy, author of *The Rise and Fall of the Great Powers*, had recently written in a newspaper article about Japan's foreign relations: "It is not technology or finance, but respect for, and cultural understanding of, others and psychological understanding of itself [that is of importance]." This quote seemed to justify all that I felt about the importance of people and their experiences and why Mr. Yoshida should send me to the factory.

Then I told him that I wanted to go to Sayama and really do something, not just observe and correct English. I explained what Scott and I had discussed and told him that I thought I could really help the administration in dealing with such large numbers of Americans. Mr. Yoshida said he hadn't planned anything like that for me, although he could see there was a need. The idea of nine more months of office observation made me sick to my stomach. I could feel myself getting upset. He wasn't listening.

"I really think I can do something useful in Sayama.

It's very important that I feel like I'm contributing," I said, feeling as though I were almost pleading. Still he didn't seem to understand. My throat got tight, and I felt my eyes welling up with tears. If I said another word I would start crying.

I turned away from the table and tried to regain my composure. Mr. Yoshida was startled. I had never behaved like this in front of him before, but I couldn't help it. When I calmed down, Mr. Yoshida asked me what I thought I would learn in Sayama. He wondered how I could be a part of the group at Sayama if I had felt alienated by my experiences at headquarters.

I felt sure that I could do more in Sayama than in North American Sales where I had nothing but language skills to offer. I told him that I had a better chance of becoming part of the group because Sayama needed someone like me. I identified with the frustrations of the American employees, and from my own experience as an exchange student and working at headquarters, I knew that part of the solution was learning how to do things on one's own.

I told Mr. Yoshida about the anxiety of my first subway ride in Tokyo as an exchange student and how I'd looked at the Japanese-English map every two minutes to confirm my location. When I emerged from the subway station and realized that I had successfully reached my destination, I practically yelled with joy. It wasn't so much reaching the right place that made me feel so good, I explained to him, but that I had negotiated my own way in an unfamiliar place. I asked him if he remembered having such an experience when he had first gone to America by himself.

I must have struck a chord, because Mr. Yoshida

seemed to change his mind mid-sentence. He said that he would arrange a position for me at Sayama and that once I got there I could decide how much time I would spend there. He said he would visit me in Sayama on his next trip to Japan and asked me to come up with a plan for making communication between American and Japanese employees better.

At the end of the two-hour meeting, I was exhausted but satisfied: I had just gained the same kind of control that the Americans at Sayama needed. I was on my way to the factory.

The Factory

13

A RAW EGG IN ITS SHELL ROLLED AROUND IN a small blue-and-white dish. I picked up the egg and whacked it sharply against the edge of the table and let the gooey contents plop into the bowl. I poured a stream of dark soy sauce over the bulging yellow yolk and then swished it around with my chopsticks. The mixture was soupy and brown, and I poured it over a bowl of steaming rice. Once the heat of the rice congealed the egg I started to eat my breakfast.

I was sitting in one of the Sayama factory's four cafeterias on my first day of work, April 3. The cavernous room was dim and smelled vaguely of the weld shop. I sat by myself trying to eat without noticing that almost all of the one hundred male workers in the cafeteria, wearing grungy, white coveralls, were watching me with great interest. I was the only woman and the only American, but I ate just like them.

I unwrapped a packet of dried seaweed. There were four paper-thin, dark-green pieces, each about a quarter of the size of a dollar bill. With my chopsticks, I picked up one of the seaweed rectangles, dunked it lightly in soy sauce and placed it on top of the sticky rice. Steam softened the seaweed, and I scooped up a mound of eggy, seaweed-covered rice and plopped the whole thing into my mouth. Picking up a bowl of miso soup in my palm, I stirred it once with my chopsticks. Pebble-sized crumbs of tofu swirled to the surface of the dark-brown, savory broth.

Until my decision to eat breakfast under scrutiny in the cafeteria, I had been pleased with the transition from Tokyo headquarters to the Sayama factory. The best thing I had done was to visit the factory a week earlier to meet my new boss in the Training and Welfare Section of the Administration Department. Mr. Yoshida had arranged for me to work in this department because they were responsible for the American employees in Japan.

I had come to visit before my assignment started because I knew that having Mr. Yoshida secure a desk for me wasn't enough. I was an outsider in every way: an American, a woman, and someone from headquarters. It was likely that I would be seen as a threat, and I wanted to avoid any repeats of my experience with Ms. Mori.

When I visited a week before, I had found the Training and Welfare office on the second floor of the Administration Building. The second floor was the size of two basketball courts and filled with people and desks. Just as at headquarters, the sections were divided by low beige cabinets and empty tables. Gray metal desks in each section were grouped together in groups of six or eight on a white linoleum floor. The orderliness reminded me of a sterilized hospital room.

My new boss, Mr. Takahashi, sat at a desk set apart

from the others. He stood up to greet me. He was tall, and I noticed that his white uniform pants came down only to his ankles. His face was youthful but his hair was graying. He wore glasses and parted his hair on the side. I couldn't help thinking that he bore a remarkable resemblance to my Uncle Justin.

I told Mr. Takahashi about my work experience at headquarters and that I looked forward to learning many things at the factory. "I've only worked at Honda for a year and a half, so I still have so much to learn. I don't know if there is anything I can do here, but if there is something I will try very hard. But I really think that I can't do anything."

As these words came out of my mouth, another narrative played in my head. "I understand the communication problems that are going on here. I have worked in Ohio; I speak Japanese; I have worked at headquarters. I can help make a difference." But I knew I could only make a difference if I was an accepted member of the group. That was my first priority.

For the first time, I felt like I was really in control of my language—not just the words, but the nuances. I understood how useful the numbing, solicitous phrases could be in easing introductions. *Osoreirimasu*—I'm sorry to bother you. *Ojama shimasu*—I'm interrupting. *Oisogashii tokoro, gomen nasai*—I'm sorry, you must be so busy. I used these phrases liberally, but rather than feeling submissive or obedient, I felt smart. The phrases gave me ample space to humble myself and show respect, and they padded the sharp, awkward moments of first encounters.

Mr. Takahashi and I talked about the hundreds of Americans who were training at Sayama. Mr. Takahashi said that the Training and Welfare Section sometimes felt overwhelmed. The main responsibility of the section was the seven thousand Japanese employees in Sayama. I realized the enormous burden it was to play host to an extra couple hundred Americans. The more we talked the more he reminded me of my Uncle Justin, and not just in appearance; the fact that he was intelligent and unassuming also brought my uncle to mind.

"I heard you graduated from Waseda University," Mr. Takahashi said.

"Actually, I didn't graduate from Waseda," I said, trying to downplay my connection to the prestigious university. "I was just an exchange student."

"I also graduated from Waseda," he said.

"Oh, really?" I was startled.

"Well, that was many years ago."

"So you are my senior," I joked, and bowed my head. "Do you remember this? *Miyako no seihoku Waseda no mori ni.*" I sang the phrase. Mr. Takahashi recognized it and started swinging his arm to the beat. "Ah. The Waseda theme song!"

"I want to introduce you to another Waseda man," Mr. Takahashi said. "Arinami!" he called out to a young man about my age who had been sitting with his back to us.

"*Hai!*" he shouted like a cadet in basic training, and leapt to Mr. Takahashi's side.

"This is Mr. Arinami," Mr. Takahashi said. "He handles all the administrative needs of the American associates. You will be working together, so perhaps Mr. Arinami can tell you about his work."

"Yes, I understand," Mr. Arinami replied politely.

Mr. Takahashi returned to his desk and we sat down

at the table. Mr. Arimani's eyes bulged slightly, as if straining to watch my every move. He clasped his hands tightly in front of him on the table. I noticed that his light-blue polo shirt was buttoned up snugly around his neck. In the pocket of his pressed uniform was a white plastic pocket protector with evenly placed pens and pencils. His skin looked pale, as though he hadn't been outside during the daylight hours. We would have been about the same height, except that his thick black hair stood out stiffly adding at least an inch to his height.

"Please call me Laura," I said in Japanese.

"Thank you," he said stiffly. "My name is Arinami but please call me Koji." He pointed to a round, plastic name tag that was pinned to his uniform.

"Why are you called Koji?" I asked him.

"It's a nickname I made up because the American associates have a hard time with my last name."

"I had a nickname too. In college people called me Kiki because I thought it would be easier than Laura," I told him.

Koji leaned forward a little and said, "Actually, I was born in America—in Hawaii. I'm Japanese, but I've got two passports and an American middle name, it's Peter. You can call me Peter." He spoke as though he were making a confession.

"So you speak English?" I asked.

"Well, I've forgotten many things. But I can speak a little," he replied, again in Japanese. I had the sense that both Koji and Peter were a bit shy.

"May I ask you a favor?" he said in English.

"Sure."

"My English skills are very poor and I would like to improve. May I speak English with you?"

"Of course."

"But I want you to correct me."

"Only if you'll do the same for me in Japanese," I said.

Koji told me that he had recently returned from a three-month research tour of the factories in Ohio and was in the process of updating a guidebook for Japanese employees who worked there. I told him that was the kind of thing I hoped to work on for the Americans in Sayama.

Koji asked me about my living situation in Sayama. Honda had a policy regarding relocation: housing would be provided for an associate only if the new location was outside a two-hour radius of headquarters. The company considered a two-hour train ride from Tokyo to Sayama commutable, so the administration at headquarters was not responsible for providing accommodations for me in Sayama.

I didn't know how long I would be working in Sayama and I didn't want to give up my apartment in Tokyo, but riding the train four hours every day seemed ridiculous. Koji said that he could probably find a room for me in one of the dozen or so company dormitories where Honda employees lived. That way I could live in Sayama during the week and return to Tokyo on the weekends. I told him it sounded like a great idea, and he agreed to have something ready by the time I started at the factory on April 3.

As I scraped up the last bits of rice and egg from my breakfast bowl, I wondered what kind of place Koji had found for me to stay. Wherever it was, I hoped it would be a place where I could fix my own breakfast from now on. I dumped my bowls in the cafeteria wash bin and went to start my first day of work.

I met Koji in the Training and Welfare Section. He told me it was almost time for the morning meeting and asked me to follow him. We joined a stream of people who walked outside. A group of about fifty stood in a concrete courtyard near an aqua-blue water fountain in front of the building. Exercise music played over the loudspeaker and everyone stretched, even the women. The air was dewy and fresh, and it felt good to move around.

When the exercises were over the group gathered in a tight circle. A young man stepped forward and greeted everyone, *"Ohayō gozaimasu!"* *"Ohayō gozaimasu!"* the group replied, and bowed in unison like a troupe of trained soldiers.

The leader called the meeting to order and asked the general manager of Administration to make announcements. Then the Safety Manager gave a report from the previous day. Other announcements were made that I didn't really follow. Then the leader asked if anyone else had anything to say. Koji stepped forward, and I felt my palms start to sweat. "I would like to introduce a new member of the Training and Welfare Section," he said. "Ms. Laura Kriska will work with us to help take care of the American associates. She worked at headquarters in the secretariat and in Public Relations. Her Japanese is very good."

Everyone stared at me, so I smiled. Koji asked me to say something. I stepped forward and bowed. *"Hajimemashite. Watashi wa Rora desu."* I told the group that my Japanese was terrible and that I had only been in Japan for a short time, so I hoped they would be patient with me and teach me many things. *"Dōzo yoroshiku one-gaishimasu,"* I said, using the customary first-time greet-

ing, and bowed again. The entire group returned the
bow and chanted *"Yoroshiku onegaishimasu."*

At the end of the meeting a young woman sprang out
in front of the group and held out a clipboard for everyone to see. There was a single phrase written on it in
large letters. The meeting leader pointed at the clipboard and recited the phrase in a loud, perky voice:
"Tsukue wo kirei ni shimashō!—Let's keep our desks tidy."
The group snapped to attention and pointed to the clipboard. Koji stood next to me with his arm stretched all
the way out and his pointer-finger erect. I felt awkward
but I raised my arm and loosely extended my forefinger.
"Tsukue wo kirei ni shimashō!" the group yelled, affirming
that yes, they would attempt to keep their desks tidy.
The meeting was over; the workday had begun.

The first thing I had to do was get a uniform. I didn't
mind wearing one this time because everyone at the factory, men and women, wore the same white polyester/
cotton uniform. A young woman took me to the ladies'
room to try it on. I could see that she wore pale pink
socks to match the pink blouse that she wore under the
uniform jacket. She also wore flat white tennis shoes and
a pink bow around her ponytail.

"I think it fits," I said when I stepped out of the stall,
even though the hem of the pants barely reached my
ankles and the sleeves were above my wrists. I felt sure
that my arms and legs were longer than those of any
other woman in the factory.

"Button the top button," the young woman said as
though talking to a child. I yielded to her instructions
even though I wanted to resist.

"Button the sleeves too," she instructed.

Part of me wanted to scream, "I'm agreeing to wear

this potato sack; at least let me decide which buttons to button!" But again I yielded and followed her rules. There was no reason to resist. The uniform culture had certain parameters, and she was simply helping me understand them. With a smile I looked at her in her cheery, pink outfit and said, *"Hai, wakarimashita."*

Koji set me up at a large metal desk right next to his. We sat at an island of six desks with four young men in the department. There were two more islands in our section, plus Mr. Takahashi's desk which floated unattached nearby. There was a pad of writing paper in my desk, and I noticed that all the common supplies were in a box in the middle. I asked Koji where I could get some pencils, pens, and a pad of Honda facsimile paper.

Koji looked slightly disturbed. "Follow me," he said.

We walked through a maze of desks up to the front of the room where four women in uniforms sat behind the reception counter.. Koji approached the counter hesitantly and one of the women looked up. They all looked like high-school students, and none of them smiled. Koji talked with the woman in a soft, low voice. Behind her I could see a fax machine; it was the only one on the whole floor. The woman studied me, then nodded her head. We followed her to a supply cabinet which she unlocked with a key that hung from her wrist.

The cabinet was neatly organized with boxes of pens and stacks of paper. She extracted one pencil, one pen and handed them to me. When she turned to lock-up the cabinet I said, "What about some fax paper?" I felt Koji wince beside me and heard him clear his throat. The woman paused and then opened the cabinet door. I watched her pull out a tablet of fax paper with the Honda logo from one of the shelves. Just as I was about to reach for the tablet and thank her, she carefully tore off a single page and placed it in my outstretched hand.

The factory culture was noticeably different from headquarters in many ways, not just in the frugal use of office supplies. Most people in the office wore tennis shoes and had T-shirts on under their uniforms. Only the general manager wore a tie with his white jacket. The women seemed very young; most of them were just out of high school. I noticed that people spoke more casually than at headquarters; they didn't use formal greetings when they answered the telephone.

I spent the morning setting up my desk and writing out some of the objectives that I wanted to talk over with Koji. When the lunch bell rang at noon I followed Koji and his colleagues upstairs to a cafeteria. It was different from the one where I had eaten breakfast. Hordes of factory workers, wearing their work gloves and dirty uniforms, rushed into various lines around the room. Food was dispensed from counters along the perimeter. Each counter seemed to distribute a different kind of meal, but the sounds of dishes and moving chairs and hungry chatter distracted me. I couldn't tell which line led to which meal, so I got in line behind Koji and followed along.

I ended up with an enormous plate of curry rice sitting next to Koji and the other men from our department. I was grateful for a peaceful moment and ate my meal in silence while the others slurped and talked. Someone offered me some green tea. Banners hung around the room with slogans in large block letters: "Quality UP! Let's Meet our Production Goals!" On one wall, below the colorful signs was a calligraphy drawing in a simple, black frame. The phrase read, "If we don't have safety, we don't have production." The signature read "Soichiro Honda."

After I finished my lunch Koji leaned over to me and said, "You should eat lunch with the women too." My stomach tightened. "Don't tell me who to eat with. I'm an adult. I'll decide!" I wanted to shout. I didn't like being classified by gender, and I felt hurt that maybe Koji didn't want me to eat with his group. But when I looked around the room I saw that the men and women ate in completely separate groups. There wasn't a single mixed-gender group in the room of over five hundred people. I managed a half-smile and said, "Yes, what a fine idea."

In the afternoon I went with Koji to watch the official entrance ceremony for Honda's new recruits. We walked into a gymnasium filled with chairs and eight hundred fresh high school graduates in brand new white uniforms. Each one of them wore a maroon-colored arm band that said *Shinnyūshain*—New Employee.

The plant manager took the stage and made a rousing speech, challenging the new recruits to work hard. He welcomed them into the Honda Family and wished them good luck in their new roles in society. A young man with a crew cut marched on stage as a representative of the new employees. He spoke in short, powerful spurts like a military cadet and formally accepted the challenge and the opportunity to grow through Honda.

Suddenly there was a loud noise from behind where Koji and I stood in the back of the gymnasium. Six men dressed in red, white, and blue outfits ran down the center of the gym.

"It's the Honda cheerleaders," whispered Koji.

The men ran up on stage and stood in formation.

Large white letters spelled out HONDA on their red sweaters. One man had a blue and white bass drum strapped to his chest. He beat the drum while the others performed a drill team cheer. It was like being transported back to a high-school pep rally, and I felt the pride and excitement of the moment. The cheerleaders instructed the recruits to sing the company song. All eight hundred stood in matching rows of white uniforms and maroon armbands. With the drum pounding the rhythm, the new kids shouted out the verse. Their earnest voices filled the auditorium, and the drumbeat reverberated off the walls.

Life in Sayama

14 I FOLLOWED KOJI DOWN A DIRT ROAD THAT led between the two-story buildings of the Honda Terrace House complex. There were eight block-shaped buildings, four on each side of the road. Each building contained five connected apartments. Shoulder-high bushes and chain-link fences separated the backyards. Laundry hung from the balconies like tattered, long-forgotten party decorations. Wild grass and weeds grew through the chain-link fences and over abandoned tires left on the road.

The buildings were the color of aged plaster; rust and dirt marks bled down the walls from corrugated roof tops. There were aluminum bars over the upstairs windows in each apartment. The front of each building was identical—five reddish-brown doors, five exposed water meters, and five gas meters prominently displayed next to each door.

Koji opened the heavy, steel door of apartment three, block one, and stepped into the concrete entryway. He wiggled out of his sneakers and stepped up onto a dark, wooden floor. The apartment smelled old and moldy and I was reluctant to take off my shoes. Koji explained the smell by telling me that no one had lived in this apartment for two years.

"Well, here it is," he said glancing around hopefully. There was a tiny porcelain sink at the end of the foyer and next to it a door. "I think that is the toilet," he said.

I opened the door and found an old-fashioned toilet room with a porcelain squat-toilet fixed in a raised wooden platform. But over the porcelain hole was a plastic toilet converter with a lid and seat, which turned the Japanese-style toilet into something resembling a Western-style one. I laughed and Koji seemed embarrassed. On the lid of the plastic contraption was a green sticker with written instructions and stick figures demonstrating how both a man and a woman should use the plastic seat by sitting, not squatting.

"Shall we look at the rest of the apartment?" Koji asked, eager to move on.

The foyer led to a four-mat tatami room which was completely empty. The walls were white and the tatami bare. Heavy curtains made of a dull gold material hung from the ceiling to the floor, covering a sliding glass door that opened into the backyard. Koji struggled with the door until it clattered noisily over its track and banged open against the frame. The narrow backyard was so overgrown with leafy vegetation that I couldn't see the ground. In the far corner were two motorcycles carelessly turned on their sides; weeds covered the wheels and threatened to completely camouflage the machines.

Next to the living room was a narrow wooden floor space with a stainless steel sink against the wall. The countertop was made of the same dull stainless steel. Underneath it were cabinets covered in yellowing paper that peeled brown at the edges. There was a hookup for gas but no burners, just an old tin kettle with a bent lid. Overhead were two more cabinets that were missing their doors and from which the shelves had fallen.

Two steps away from the kitchen sink was an opaque glass door. Koji slid open the door to a small bathroom. Water pipes snaked up the side of the dirty-white walls. A blue plastic *ofuro* Japanese-style tub sat in the far left corner; next to it was a water heater with a dingy metallic vent that shot up through the ceiling.

"The gas won't be on until tomorrow," Koji said. "So right now there is only cold water." He stepped down onto blue plastic slats—a raised platform over the concrete floor. There wasn't room for both of us, so I looked in over his shoulder. I could see dark mildew creeping over the edges of the platform. An old yellow plastic stool and a slimy pink bucket stood in the corner. Koji showed me how to fill the tub from a long-necked faucet that produced only cold water. The waist-high faucet could be placed over the tub or over the platform. Once the tub was full, the gas could be turned on to heat the water in the tub.

A narrow stairway led upstairs to a small landing with a room on either side. There was a six-mat bedroom to the right of the landing. This room also had a floor-to-ceiling sliding glass door. A neat stack of folded futon mats and blankets stood in the center of the wide-open room. Koji told me it had been leased for me. It was the only furniture-like item in the place. To the left of the landing was a smaller, three-mat room that had a window with aluminum bars on the lower half.

Koji left me in the apartment, promising that the gas would be turned on by the next day. I quickly surveyed my new space. All the walls were white; the floors were old light brown tatami. There was not a single piece of furniture. I had two books, one bag of clothes, and three times the space of my Tokyo apartment.

Before I unpacked my clothes I felt the urge to scrub every surface of the apartment, but the only cleaning item around was an old broom with mucky, broken bristles. I went to the supermarket and came back carrying three bags of scrub brushes, window cleaner, disinfectant, sponges, a new broom, and a new bucket, stool, and platform for the bathing room. In bare feet and wearing my exercise clothes, I cleaned the whole place.

I swept the floors, wiped the tatami with a damp sponge, and scoured every floor and closet space with cleaner. The worst part was the bathroom, where years of mold, hair, and sludge had been festering on the concrete floor underneath the plastic platform. The platform was so disgusting that I picked it up with the old broom handle and threw them both out into the jungly mess in the backyard.

I couldn't complain because I had little choice. It was either the Honda Terrace House or four hours on the train every day. The apartment was spacious and simple. With a few additions from Tokyo I thought that apartment three, block one, might eventually feel like a home. I would try to think of it as my place in the "country."

Since I didn't know how long I would be staying, I was reluctant to ask for more than a place to sleep. But if this was going to be a place where I could live, I at least needed a refrigerator. The next day, after thanking him for arranging the apartment, I asked Koji if there was any possibility of getting one. He told me that the person to talk to was the manager of the Honda Terrace House, who happened to be a member of our Training and Welfare Section. Koji explained that all the dormitory managers in Sayama were part of our group even though their daily responsibilities were outside the office. And it just so happened that later in the week our entire section would be having a party. Koji thought that the party might be a good time to bring up my request with the manager.

The party was both a welcome party for me and a farewell party for a woman who was leaving to have a baby. On Wednesday evening after work we walked to a pub-like restaurant in town. I left my shoes in the disorderly pile in the entryway and climbed a narrow stairway to the second-floor party room. About forty of us gathered in the large space that looked well-worn, with dingy marks on the walls and rough spots on the tatami.

A row of low tables circled the room and blue floor cushions ringed the tables. Piles of wooden chopsticks sat next to large trays of cold fried chicken, pork cutlets, and shredded cabbage. Tall bottles of beer and short bottles of soda were lined up along the center of each table.

After everyone arrived we filled each others' glasses and stood up for the toast. Mr. Takahashi said a few words to welcome me. Then he spoke about the woman who would be leaving. She smiled shyly and held her glass of orange soda in front of her protruding belly. Before we could toast he asked a few others to speak. The foam in my glass settled while I listened to the speeches. Finally Mr. Takahashi issued the final "*kanpai,*" or cheers, and we drank.

Koji grabbed a full bottle of beer and said, "This may

be a good time to meet the dormitory manager." I put down my chopsticks and followed him to the other side of the room. A group of seven gray-haired men sat cross-legged at a table, drinking saké and smoking. Koji and I kneeled down to greet them. He introduced me to Mr. Hiratsuka, the manager of my dormitory. I smiled and introduced myself. Mr. Hiratsuka looked intrigued while his cronies moved away but watched us closely.

I held up the bottle and offered him a drink. He grinned and picked up his already full glass. He tipped back his head and drained it in one gulp. He watched me with damp eyes as I filled his glass. Then he took the bottle and offered me a drink. I held my glass with two hands and he poured. I took a sip and the old men nodded with approval as though I had passed a test.

None of them spoke English, but they seemed very interested in me. "Please meet my friends," Mr. Hiratsuka said, and they all stood up. Even in stocking feet I was taller than any of them. I greeted each one of them in Japanese and learned their names. They insisted on shaking my hand.

"She's like Marilyn Monroe!" one googly-eyed man said.

"I'm never going to wash my hand again," another exclaimed and giggled like a drunk.

Like a proud father, Mr. Hiratsuka showed me off to his pals as if to say, "Don't you wish you had a pretty foreign lady living in your dormitory!"

I told Mr. Hiratsuka that I was very happy to be living in the Honda Terrace House.

"Did the gas work?" he asked. "Koji asked me to make sure it was on."

I assured him that I'd had hot water since Tuesday.

"Good, good," he said. "And everything else is all right."

"Oh yes. Very good," I replied and offered him more beer.

"But it's such an old place," Mr. Hiratsuka said, accepting the refill.

"But it is fine and three times bigger than my apartment in Tokyo!" I insisted. Mr. Hiratsuka filled my glass again.

"It's very good. However," I said nodding and sipping the brimming glass.

"What?" he asked.

"Oh, it's really nothing," I said.

"What is it? Do you need something?" he said.

"Well, there was just one thing I thought of, but of course, I may not be here for very long, so it might be unreasonable."

"What is it? Tell me."

"Well, I was thinking about a refrigerator, so I can keep milk and some food."

"A refrigerator?" he said.

"Yes. I'm sure it would be too much trouble. It's really not important."

"I'll see what I can do."

On Thursday evening I came home from work and walked into my apartment. Everything seemed the same until I went into the kitchen. Next to the stainless steel counter was a miniature refrigerator. It was bright kelly-green, and had white handles. I opened the door and felt a swoosh of cold air. On the other side of the counter I found two gas burners that had been hooked up to the gas outlet. I turned the knob and a blue flame leapt up from the metal ring.

Suddenly I had an image of Mr. Hiratsuka and the other white-haired managers in a huge storage room of mutant home furnishings: glass-topped tables with chipped corners, neon-colored beanbag chairs, and eight-track stereos. Where the items came from was as mysterious as how they got into my apartment while I was gone. But I was happy to have the fridge, and I accepted that some things would remain a mystery, beyond my control.

On Friday afternoon I got a call from the guardhouse. "There has been a delivery from headquarters for Ms. Laura," the gruff voice told me. I had been expecting this call and went immediately to the front gate of the factory. Two guards stood outside looking curiously at my red mountain bike. There was a tag attached to the handlebar with my name on it.

"Great!" I said and thanked them. I could tell they were hoping for some explanation. But I was feeling so clever and pleased with myself that I couldn't tell them the story without sounding boastful. I hopped on the bike and rode back to the office.

When I got back to my desk I called my old assistant manager from the Welcome Plaza. Before leaving for Sayama, I had gone to see him about a favor. He was responsible for coordinating transportation of motorcycles and cars between the factories and the display at the Welcome Plaza. When I explained that I wanted to transport my bike to the Sayama factory he had offered to put it on the next truck.

"It's here," I told him. "Thanks."

In the following weeks I got used to a smooth, comfortable rhythm in Sayama. Every morning I ate cereal at home and read the English newspaper. I would get on my bike and ride to a pay phone to make calls to friends in Tokyo before going to work. In the evenings I exercised at the Honda sports center and rode my bike home. I usually had dinner at the same family-style restaurant, where I ate rice and grilled fish and read comic books. Despite the inconvenience of having no phone, no mail, and no television, I was content with my simple, salaryman life, mainly because, for the first time since working for Honda, I had real work to do.

Every week a new group of Americans arrived; sometimes there were more than two hundred. Koji spent much of his time just trying to coordinate hotel rooms for all of them. Sayama had only one hotel, so Koji had to find rooms in nearby towns. I listened to him negotiate room costs with the hotel managers and make apologies for sudden schedule changes. On a large piece of cardboard, he wrote the names and capacities of all the hotels. He was forever juggling the numbers and locations, erasing his previous plans to accommodate an extension for ten Paint Department employees or finding rooms for seventeen assembly workers who suddenly moved up their arrival date by a week.

At first I just sat in on the new arrival orientations and went to meetings with Koji. I also studied his guidebook and looked at the materials that were developed for Japanese employees going to America. His guidebook was comprehensive and thorough. It included diagrams of local airports, enlarged pictures of American coins, directions for how to drive on the right side of the road, and basic language lessons. Most of these things would have been helpful in reverse for the Americans in Japan, but the information was not available in English.

I listened carefully to the material provided in the orientation meetings. Although it was presented in English, the information was not always useful. The safety manager gave a speech in Japanese that Koji translated. He also handed out a one-page safety sheet with basic rules translated into English. Safety in the factory was the most important concern for everyone, but these workers already knew basic safety. They needed more than translated factory rules.

One thing that hadn't been considered was the personal safety of each American associate outside the factory. We had no plan or system for helping an employee who got sick or lost. Koji and I talked about the worst-case scenario and developed an emergency identification card that we would ask all employees to fill out and carry with them in Japan. The card gave the phone number of the factory and information about the person. It was bilingual and could be used if someone got lost.

During the orientation Koji also passed out maps of Tokyo in English. But there was no information about Sayama. I had never even seen a Japanese map of the area, so one afternoon I left the office with a clipboard and drew a map. The town was small and centered around the train station, which was about a ten-minute walk from the factory gate. I walked by an open field with a playground and a rusty swing set. There were a few small, one-story homes on the narrow streets, but most of the residents lived in dormitories or small apartment buildings farther away. The air had a sweetish smell from a nearby confectionery factory.

I made note of the post office, banks, stores, restaurants, and twenty-four-hour convenience stores. There were two phone booths near the station that could connect international calls. I wrote down the names of the noodle shops and drug stores, an eyeglass shop, a sporting goods store, and the hardware store. The town had all the basics; they just needed to be identified. As soon as I finished drawing the map, Koji made copies and started handing it out.

Things in the Training and Welfare Section were going well. I discovered that as long as I ate lunch with the women in our group every once in a while, no one seemed to mind that most of the time I ate with Koji and the other young men in our department. The office ladies were sweet and friendly, but I found it hard to relate to them. Although they were only a few years younger than me, we seemed to look at the world in such different ways. Most of our conversations centered on their hobbies, which included learning to wear a kimono and flower arranging.

I felt much more comfortable around the men because we could talk about work. I think they found it odd that I had voluntarily come to the factory from headquarters. Some of the men had joined Honda directly after high school and had earned jobs in the office only after working years in the factory. Men like Koji had started after college and were ambitious to move on from office work at the factory to headquarters.

As I spent more time with them, they seemed to warm up to me and included me in their conversations. We talked about baseball and sumo and argued about the current favorite, Chionofuji, who had been my favorite player since I had first seen sumo on television. Every day after lunch the gang of six or seven men at our table played a game of rock-scissors-paper; the loser had to buy drinks from the coffee shop for everyone. Since I sat with the group, the loser always bought me a drink too, even though I didn't play the game. One day they asked me to play. I sensed that the stakes had risen—no more free drinks. If I wanted in, I had to play the game, and I did.

I knew how to play rock-scissors-paper, but I didn't play it as fast as my colleagues. They knew the game so well that it took them only seconds to evaluate a circle of fists, palms, and split fingers to determine if there was one winner or if we had *aiko desho*, a tie. Like speed-chess players moving their pieces over the black and white checked board, my colleagues completed each round in seconds.

Jan-ken-pon, ready-set-go, was the phrase used to start each game. We played a series of rounds; each round eliminated one player. Since we started out with six or seven players, we often tied and immediately played again until there was one winner. We played as many games as it took to determine who was the winner in that round.

"*Jan-ken-pon*," pause, "*aiko-desho*," pause, "*jankenpon*," "*aikodesho*." Each game of the round went faster and faster. The others assessed the whole group in the time it took me to understand if I had beat the guy next to me. But rather than look stupid, I relied on the reactions of my colleagues to tell me whether I had won or lost, whether to play again in this round or move on to another, minus the winner. I was even the last to recognize when I won the round.

It was bound to happen; one day I finally lost all seven rounds. I could tell a few of the guys felt a little guilty, as though I shouldn't have to buy everyone drinks. One guy even tried to give me money, but I insisted on paying for it myself. Like a good loser I took their orders and bought the beverages in the coffee shop. I carried a heavy metal tray of iced coffee and coke back to the table and served up the glasses. But rather than feeling like a loser, I felt I had won.

I started interviewing American workers to find out what it was like for them in Sayama. They were open with me from the beginning. I earned their trust simply by being from Ohio. They admired the fact that I could speak Japanese; I was different and yet one of them. I had worked on the line in Ohio. We knew each other's high schools and sometimes had mutual acquaintances. I could have been their next-door neighbor. In this way, I had a clear advantage over Koji and the other Japanese in communicating with them.

The Japanese had a reputation, in Japan and America, for excluding American workers. I had seen how easy it was for good intentions to get scrambled up in unclear language and careless expressions. Many Japanese felt embarrassed that they could not speak English, especially after having studied it for so long. They felt ashamed when the few words they tried didn't work, so rather than try something again and risk further embarrassment, they shut up altogether. When the Americans got the silent treatment, they felt as though they had done something wrong and were being punished. They felt ostracized and frustrated because they couldn't do their jobs if no one talked to them.

Each meeting with the American associates gave me new insights. I made a note to request a few spare extra-large uniforms from the Ohio factory to have on hand for emergencies. Smaller people could borrow uniforms from the Sayama plant, but the big men were out of luck. Other people confessed their frustrations at not being able to do things on their own and feeling like they weren't being trusted. A few felt as though there was some conspiracy against the Americans to keep them from learning how to do things like ride the train. One man I talked to was practically in tears because he had promised to call his wife on their anniversary and he didn't know how to use the phone.

I typed out directions for making international phone calls, reading the train maps, and buying tickets. As soon as the directions came out of my computer, they went to the copy machine. It was the beginning of a guidebook that I knew would take some time to complete. I called Mr. Yoshida and told him I would be in Sayama for at least three months.

I had moved the futon into the children's room to sleep because the master bedroom seemed too big. The weather had become warmer, so I usually left the windows open when I slept. One night I awoke to a swishing, flapping sound in the curtains. Swish. Flap, flap. Swish. The curtains were moving, then something flew into the room. It was a bat.

I leapt from the futon and crawled out of the room with my head low, slamming the sliding door shut behind me. Sitting on the landing between the two bedrooms, I tried to think. My heart was pounding but my urge to scream had passed. What could I do? Would the bat fly back out the window, or were the curtains in the way? Didn't bats have some kind of radar that helped them find exits? Or did that radar malfunction in small spaces? My mind was too hazy to think.

I stumbled down the dark, narrow stairwell and turned on the light in the living room. The floor was completely bare. My jean jacket hung from a nail on the wall and a damp towel hung next to it. I couldn't sleep here, so I found the broom, turned off the lights, and crept back up the staircase.

The bat was thudding against the walls. In the darkness I went into the master bedroom and opened the sliding glass door all the way, hoping that the bat would understand my plan. Holding the broom over my head, I slid open the door to my bedroom and crawled in. The bat flew in furious circles. I moved away from the open doorway and swished the broom in the air without standing up. The bat flew out the open door and into the master bedroom. I followed quickly and shut the master bedroom door. My adrenaline was pumping, but there was nothing else to do but listen to the bat fly in bigger circles and thud against the walls. I crept back into my futon and fell asleep.

When I woke the next morning I listened for sounds in the next room. It was quiet. Preparing for the worst, I crouched by the door with the broom held firmly in front of my face. Peering cautiously through the stiff bristles, I slowly slid open the door. The gold curtains fluttered slightly with a breeze, and sunshine filled the empty room.

Culture Lessons

15 "SOYBEAN-PASTE SOUP, SQUID TENTACLE AND cucumber salad, buckwheat noodles in hot fish broth with seaweed, simmered kelp with lotus root." Translating the daily lunch menu into English did not always produce the results I hoped for. The American employees would not eat Japanese meals because the ingredients were a mystery. Using cookbooks, I tried to make the dishes sound appealing, but sometimes my fellow Ohioans were even more reluctant to try the Japanese food once they understood the contents.

Since translating the menu did not solve the food problem, I met with the factory cafeteria manager, Mr. Hamaguchi. He was a large man with tight, black permed curls, and he looked like someone who could have easily ended up a convict but somewhere along the way discovered the joy of food. He smiled often with an expression that made him look as though he had just had something good to eat when no one was looking.

Mr. Hamaguchi told me that he had visited the Ohio

factory the year before to teach the American cooks how to prepare Japanese food.

"Now they serve Japanese meals in the cafeteria every week," he said with great satisfaction. I guessed that he'd had a good experience in Ohio because he kept referring to a cook named Jean and smiling a lot.

I explained to Mr. Hamaguchi that many Americans had problems with Japanese food. "It's not that they don't like it; they won't even try it." I told him how many of them just ate cookies and chips from the snack shop. It seemed like every week someone got sick and missed work because of a poor diet. We'd had to take one man to the hospital because for days he had eaten only peanuts hoarded from his plane trip.

We talked about making a Western-style lunch. "If we can get them to trust the cafeteria food with a Western lunch, maybe they'll try the other food," I suggested.

"I want to make food that they will like," Mr. Hamaguchi agreed.

We discussed a few ideas for the lunch. Mr. Hamaguchi said he had some ideas of his own, but he wanted an American opinion before serving it. We made arrangements for a taste test later in the week.

Four stainless-steel domes sat on the table in Mr. Hamaguchi's office. He unveiled the dishes. Three of them were different combinations of the same ingredients: cold yellow eggs, white bread, and unnaturally pink breakfast meats. A small mound of dry cabbage salad and a slice of fruit decorated each plate. The last platter looked promising with a meat-patty sandwich and fried potatoes, convincingly close to a hamburger and French fries.

Mr. Hamaguchi looked on anxiously and waited for a response. I realized that my original expectations had been much too high. Requesting a Western-style lunch from Mr. Hamaguchi, manager of an industrial cafeteria in Japan, was like ordering sushi at McDonald's. Mr. Hamaguchi's meals looked as strange to me as McSushi would to a Japanese. I gently explained that in America, people usually ate eggs, toast, and sausage for breakfast. Then I praised the appearance of the hamburger. Appearance alone could lure the Americans to try the food.

Another American associate, Mark, on a short-term assignment from Ohio, came along to be the American taster. I doubted my ability to taste objectively after nearly two years in Japan. Mark took a bite of the hamburger and chewed thoughtfully. "Good," he said, giving the thumbs-up sign. "Good hamburger!" Mr. Hamaguchi glowed.

I tried a forkfull of the cold scrambled eggs and took an obligatory bite of one of the mini hot dogs. The French fries tasted better than the eggs, but Mark detected a slight fishy aroma. Mr. Hamaguchi said he would investigate.

A few days later Mr. Hamaguchi kicked off the first Western-style lunch in the cafeteria. The hamburger and French-fry combination sold out by the end of the first lunch shift. Like a proud entrepreneur, Mr. Hamaguchi beamed at his successful enterprise, and arranged to increase the number of lunches for the following day.

I saw Mr. Hamaguchi the next afternoon hovering near the Western-style lunch counter expecting another sellout. But he looked disappointed and confused—only a few lunches had been purchased. When I got a closer look I understood why.

On a large white plate were two sandwich halves with the crusts cut off. There was a single slice of salami in one half of the sandwich and a thin layer of tuna salad in the other. In the corner of the plate was a sprig of parsley and a few slices of sautéed onions. Mr. Hamaguchi would have had better luck trying to sell mint juleps at a pool hall.

He looked defeated, so I bought one of the meals, but it hardly made a dent in the surplus. After lunch, Mr. Hamaguchi and I discussed the meal. I explained to him that factory workers were not the type to eat dainty finger sandwiches. He told me that part of the problem was that he had instructed one of the cooks to make the meal, and his image was different from the cook's image. Mr. Hamaguchi had pictured a layered, submarine-style sandwich with batter-fried onion rings.

I encouraged him to keep trying and reminded him of his hamburger and French-fry success. He seemed to regain some of his enthusiasm, and as he started to walk away exclaimed, "Next I'll try pizza!"

I spent time talking with American workers from different departments including Weld, Assembly, and Paint, and discovered that their concerns about work were secondary to the problems of just being in Japan. A big part of their frustration was feeling like they had no access to things that everyone else understood: the train station, restaurants, and newspapers. The incomprehensible Japanese characters gave even comic strips a mysterious quality. Many places in Sayama, within walking distance of the factory, seemed strange and unapproachable. One of my objectives was to teach people how to negotiate these seemingly unmanageable places. My job was to demystify everything from the weekly lunch menu to the train schedule.

The Sayama factory had a sports facility located within the factory complex near the main entrance. On the outside of the four-story concrete building was a perplexing English phrase, DO SPORTS, painted in large, red letters. Inside, the building had a basketball court, a weight room, a jogging track, and a sauna. There were volleyball nets and ping-pong tables and even a wood-paneled martial arts room.

Honda also had a clubhouse located ten minutes away from the factory. It looked like a large house and had rooms for playing board games, watching television, and reading the paper. There was also a small garden and a hot-spring bathing room for associates to use during their off-hours.

As with Mr. Hamaguchi, I arranged meetings with the managers of both the sports center and the clubhouse to talk about how to make the facilities more accessible to the Americans. They were both eager to do what they could to make visitors feel welcome and apologized for not being able to do it themselves. I paired up with each manager to translate the rules and hours. We made bilingual equipment sign-out sheets and posted signs around the buildings in English. I added the information to the ever-growing orientation packet that each associate received on his or her first day at Sayama.

Koji and I kept each other informed about our work and often worked together. I would bring him an idea that I had learned from the American associates, and he would negotiate with his Japanese colleagues to get it done. We tried hard to be bicultural and understand all sides of an issue, but sometimes it was too difficult to communicate directly, and cultural stereotypes got in our way. The Americans were viewed as loud, disrespectful, impatient, and slow to admit mistakes; the Japanese were seen as disingenuous, ambiguous, shy, and slow to make decisions.

Sometimes we relied on our nicknames to help us communicate. We would leave messages for one another and sign it Peter or Kiki. It was as though these names helped us look at a problem through the other's eyes. Like spies sharing secrets from opposing sides, we used our code names to communicate what was too difficult to say.

Koji and I argued one day about a situation with an American associate who was on a six-month assignment. Koji had heard that the associate was arranging to have his wife and mother visit during the company vacation, and he was upset because the associate had not told him of these plans.

I happened to know about the plans because the associate had asked my advice about places to travel. I told Koji that I didn't think it was his, or the company's, business to know the associate's vacation plans.

Honda's overly parental policies had always annoyed me. When Japanese workers at the factory planned a trip during vacations, they had to show their travel plans to their bosses for approval. If the boss thought the plans were too ambitious, he'd suggest a change that the employee was obliged to follow. If an employee got into a traffic accident, the company punished the employee by requiring him to sign a document promising that he would not drive for a certain period of time.

I explained to Koji that his interest could be interpreted as invading the associate's privacy. Koji told me that he didn't want to intrude, he wanted to be responsible. "What if there is an emergency and the associate needs our help? Wouldn't we be better prepared if we knew who was visiting and when?" Koji asked. "If the associate were in America, I'm sure he could handle an emergency, but since he is in Japan, it's the company's responsibility to help." I could see that Koji felt strongly that it was his duty to prepare for an unlikely emergency, and I had to admit he had a point. I talked with the American associate, who didn't like the situation but reluctantly agreed to mention his plans to Koji.

Koji and I made plans for a video series. We filmed the first one in the cafeteria and explained in fifteen minutes how to buy lunch tickets and get a particular meal. On camera I explained how painted lines on the floor each led to a particular food counter—the orange line led to curry rice, yellow to the meal of the day, red to noodles, and blue to the healthy meal of the day. The video turned out well, so we advanced to the train video. Since it was a little more complicated, Koji asked me to write a script.

We planned to film the video on a Wednesday morning. But before we left for the train station, Koji made a call to make sure it was all right. The answer was no. We were told to contact the railroad's head office in Tokyo. They told us to submit a formal request including an outline of our plan. When Koji made a second call, the person in charge refused him. I thought we should just go to the station and film what we could before we got kicked out, but Koji persisted. He spoke with the railroad representative again, and I listened as he used his best negotiation skills. He was a pro. He talked about the large number of Americans visiting Sayama and how the video would help ensure their safety on the trains. He even mentioned something about good international relations. Finally, after we promised to go during non-peak time, we got permission.

The next day we walked to the station carrying the video camera and an easel with an enlarged map of the train system. I was all ready to start shooting when Koji announced that we would have to introduce ourselves to the station master. We went to the office and commenced a round of introductions, bowing and exchanging business cards with men in blue uniforms. There was more talking and explaining. Koji was patient and answered their questions at length. When we finally got started, one of the managers followed us, sometimes acting as a human barrier to prevent any stray passengers from getting in our way.

One evening after work I ran in to a group of the American associates on the train. I recognized them from an orientation meeting I had helped Koji with earlier in the week. They had just been to dinner and were all excited to show me something. One of the guys unfold-ed a copy of the English map of Sayama that I had made.

"Look," he said and pointed to the map. He had pen-ciled in a box on an unmarked street. "We found a restaurant that serves cooked seafood and Budweiser beer!" I congratulated them on their find, feeling equally excited. It was the first time I had seen this happen. They had gone beyond the map we had given them and were making Sayama their own.

Koji and I often heard stories from the associates about their adventures and misadventures. Sometimes they acted like little kids after their first fishing trip and embell-ished the stories as if it were an initiation or contest.

"I bought a donut thinking there was chocolate inside," a man said. "But when I took a bite I found sweet bean paste instead."

Another man recounted a surprise in the bathroom. "While I was using the john a little old lady walked in with her mop and started to clean as if I wasn't even there."

The more adventurous people took trips to Tokyo on the weekends and came back with stories of seeing expensive jewels at the Mikimoto Pearl shop in the Ginza area, or walking into a neighborhood festival and being mobbed by kids who wanted their autographs. "One old lady was fascinated with my beard," a burly man from the weld shop told me. "Normally I wouldn't consider this, but I let her touch it."

By the end of June I had seen and heard of many positive results from our work, but I still felt there was so much to do. Koji had asked me to help develop a training class for Japanese associates in Sayama who were preparing to go to America. I was interested in the project and pleased that he had included me.

My ideas about supporting Americans had expanded to include the long-term associates that Scott had told me about. I started to think about what it would mean to have children and spouses here. Where would they live and go to school? I made arrangements to interview Japanese women in Sayama who had lived in Ohio, thinking that they might have good insight into life as a Honda spouse in a foreign place. I had been keeping Mr. Yoshida posted on my work with weekly faxes, so when I told him that I wanted to extend my stay for two more months, he agreed.

I started to work on the training class for Japanese associates going to America. Like some of the Ohio factory workers who had never been out of the Midwest before coming to Japan, many of the men bound for Ohio seemed ill-prepared for international travel, not to mention working overseas. They were country men who had worked for Honda since high school. They smoked, spoke rough Japanese, and had bad teeth. They were also highly qualified at what they did, and the Ohio factory needed their expertise.

They often went for short, one- to three-month assignments. When they were in Ohio they wore the local white uniform with two red patches, one of which said "Honda of America, Mfg." and the other "J.T." for Japan Trainer. Koji explained that because of their unfamiliarity with English and American customs, the J.T.s had earned a reputation for being rude and aloof. Koji wanted to teach a class about the unwritten rules of behavior, and he thought it would be more meaningful if I helped explain these rules. We consulted surveys, interviewed people, and read books to come up with a list of nineteen things to avoid in America.

1. Shaking hands with a weak, flimsy grip.
2. Looking away from the person to whom you are speaking.
3. Covering your mouth with your hand while speaking.
4. Responding by loudly sucking air.
5. Saying "yes, yes" when you don't agree.
6. Not being clear between "yes" and "no."
7. Saying "I'm sorry" for no particular reason.
8. Using a contradictory negative: "Don't you have any money?" "Yes, I don't have any."
9. Smoking indiscriminately.

10. Picking your ear or nose in front of others.
11. Adjusting belts, trousers, and clothing in front of others.
12. Making excessive noise while eating.
13. Relentlessly encouraging others to drink alcohol.
14. Misbehaving while drunk and using it as an excuse for poor behavior.
15. Not considering others at an entrance/exit.
16. Ignoring others when you pass in the hall.
17. Not participating in group meetings.
18. Touching other people.
19. Not treating women equally.

I stood up in front of a class of two dozen scruffy-looking men. A few of them were sleepy and unshaven because they had just come off the third shift. Most of them looked uninterested in sitting in a classroom for the next hour. I could see that the prospect of going to America seemed like a burden to them.

We passed out the list, and Koji started by explaining in Japanese that one of the first things that they would notice about America is that people greet each other by shaking hands, not bowing. Koji nodded to me. I approached one of the men sitting at the front table and held out my hand. He stared at me as though I had offered him a pistol. "Please shake my hand," I instructed. He grabbed my hand with a quick, loose wiggle and then stuck his hand back under the table.

"You shake hands like a fish!" I exclaimed, and the whole room erupted in laughter. The man smiled sheepishly. "Try it again but more firmly," I said. This time he had a stronger grip, but I could tell that he had never shaken hands before. "Very good," I said, praising his handshake. He grinned. I went around the room shaking each person's hand and asking them to practice with each other. They seemed to like the activity, but they didn't know how to do it very well. Some did not shake; they just held the other person's hand. Others didn't know when to let go.

Koji and I went down the list, sometimes demonstrating and telling funny anecdotes. Everyone laughed when Koji pretended to tuck his shirt into his pants with exaggerated gestures or pretended to pick his nose. But when we got to the points about touching other people and treating women equally, Koji became very serious. He explained that not only were expectations different at work, but that the consequences were different too. He told stories about J.T.s who had gotten themselves and the company into a lot of trouble by not following the rules. These men had little experience with women in the workplace, other than as secretaries and little old cleaning ladies who walked into the men's bathroom without hesitating. But Koji made it clear that inexperience would be no excuse for bad behavior.

*   *   *

The days in late July were clear and sunny. After lunch I would sit outside on the brick patio with the sleeves of my white jacket rolled up and watch my forearms turn pink. Sometimes there would be a few others outside—men who hunkered down on their haunches and smoked.

One day a group of about two dozen young men and women from the Administration Department came outside. Two men unraveled a rope, at least twenty yards long, and stretched it along the brick sidewalk. Six men and women lined up along the rope. The man at each end held the rope with two hands and crouched low to the ground. "One, two, three," they yelled and swung the rope around. The group jumped but somebody missed and the rope stopped swinging.

I asked one of the women on the sidelines what was going on.

"We're practicing Team Jump Rope," she said. "It's for the Sayama Festival."

I had seen signs for the upcoming annual event that was like a carnival for employees and their families. The woman told me that the record for the Team Jump Rope was held by the Assembly Department. Last year they jumped five consecutive times with fifteen people.

I watched the group prepare to jump again and I felt an impulse to join them. They stood close together, their uniformed arms almost touching. I saw a woman from my office. Her long hair was pulled back with a barrette. "One, two, three," the group chanted as the two end-men prepared to turn the rope. They jumped together as the rope landed with a lethargic slap on the patio; the young woman's hair swung wildly across her back. The rope turned again and I heard another successful slap.

Each time the group made more than one successful turn, more people joined the jumpers. At the next break I stepped in line. "One, two, three," the rope swung around, and we jumped together.

Feeling like part of the group was the next most important thing for American associates after feeling like they had some control over their lives. It was true of my experience as an exchange student and at Honda. I recognized some of the things that had made me feel like part of the Sayama gang, like playing rock-scissors-paper with the lunch crowd, the way Koji used my nickname, and including me in helping to train the Japanese workers.

Koji and I interviewed people in the factory and came up with a short list of things the Japanese staff could do to make American workers feel like part of the team. They were just small things, but they seemed to make a difference.

1. Add Americans' names to the daily roll call.
2. Add Americans' names to circulation lists.
3. Include Americans when passing out handouts and announcements, even if they are in Japanese.
4. Give American team leaders a Japanese team leader armband.
5. Ask American team leaders to assist in safety and clean-up checks.

Even after four months in Sayama I was acutely aware that my standing with the group was not secure. I constantly paid attention to my verbal language, my body language, and my behavior. Sometimes I had to compromise because I didn't want to risk alienating myself.

One night I was sitting at the computer working when Mr. Takahashi came over and told me I should go home. I had been so involved in what I was doing, I hadn't noticed that all the women had already left. Mr. Takahashi said that if I didn't go home people would worry about me.

I felt resentment welling up. His comment didn't have anything to do with being worried. Leaving by 7:50 P.M. was a Sayama rule for women. I felt angry because telling me to go home, just because it was

8:00 P.M., made me feel like my work was unimportant. With that single comment he was able to totally discount the value of my work.

"Why will people worry?" I asked him. I was curious to see how he would answer without discriminating.

"A woman could have an accident late at night and that would be terrible," he said quietly. I could tell that he didn't want everyone around us to hear.

I wanted to tell him that was the stupidest thing I had ever heard, but I knew he had little choice but to come up with such a dumb reason. If I didn't leave it would make him look bad, and he was only following the rules. I said that I would finish up soon and go home. He looked relieved.

Other times, being part of the group didn't require much sacrifice, just awareness and sensitivity. I always tried to join the department coffee breaks which took place after work. I took turns with the other women taking drink orders and running upstairs to the cafeteria vending machines. Mr. Takahashi usually came in and joined us, and we would all sit around a table in an empty conference room and share a box of sweet bean cakes or rice crackers.

I closely observed other Americans to see how they developed a sense of the group. Since most of them didn't speak Japanese, I was especially interested in how they created a sense of "us."

One of the men from Ohio, Mark, who had helped taste-test Mr. Hamaguchi's French fries, seemed to have a natural ability for becoming part of the team. Mark was one of the few non-factory workers. He came from the Administration Department to learn how things were done in Sayama.

Surprisingly, language was one of the ways Mark connected with his Japanese colleagues—not the way he spoke it, but the way he tried to speak it. He dove into the unfamiliar sounds headfirst and let everyone see him flailing and splashing around. He memorized a few phrases and used them at every opportunity, even if they weren't necessarily appropriate. His most successful saying was "*Sō desu ne*. I see." It became a kind of default phrase that he used with his facial expressions to convey just about anything from "I understand" to "I have no idea what you are talking about."

The Japanese weren't impressed with his fluency—he could only say about three things—but they were impressed that he tried even though he made mistakes. Because most of the Americans didn't or wouldn't speak Japanese, even the smallest effort greatly impressed them. They were flattered when Mark asked them questions and tried to learn their language.

One morning Mark asked to be included in the morning meeting and led the group in chanting the daily slogan. He wrote down the four-word slogan and memorized it the day before. When the office lady stood out in front of the whole group with her clipboard, Mark pointed at the slogan and yelled it out. Everyone could see what he was saying, so his mispronunciation didn't matter. The group was so impressed with his effort that they cheered.

During the month he was in Sayama, Mark organized more impromptu after-work dinners than anyone I had met, Japanese or American. He went jogging with some guys on the Honda track team, and on weekends he was invited to take trips to Tokyo and was treated to dinner at his colleagues' homes. He showed that you didn't have to be fluent or knowledgeable about how everything worked in Sayama—you just had to try.

I hadn't realized how much a part of the Sayama landscape I had become until one day when I received an invitation to see the Painting Club exhibition. The invitation was from Mr. Odashima, a manager in the Paint Department. I had gotten to know him at the factory because many Americans worked in his department. I told him I thought it was funny that a man who painted for work would paint for a hobby as well.

Mr. Odashima came from northern Japan; he had a wide, firm jaw and a stocky build. He wore glasses and liked to tell me about his home prefecture, known for its strong soy sauce, pure rice, and beautiful women.

I guessed that Mr. Odashima was a high school graduate, but he spoke English as though he had majored in it. He was forever jotting down English slang words in a tiny notebook he had stashed away among the tools in one of his many uniform pockets. In another pocket he carried a well-used Japanese-English dictionary.

Mr. Odashima smiled and joked and really tried to understand the Americans. He went out with them after work for dinner and sometimes out drinking on a Saturday night. One weekend he invited me, Koji, and Mark to go to see sumo in Tokyo.

The Painting Club had made a temporary studio out of the basketball court in the DO SPORTS building. Partitions were set up so the floor looked like a maze. Fifty or more paintings hung on beige walls.

The exhibit was divided into various media: water colors, ink drawings, charcoal, and acrylic paint. I wound my way through the exhibit, noting that Mount Fuji was the most popular subject. Yellow chrysanthemums were second. I turned a corner, expecting to find the acrylics, and what I saw made me gasp.

It was me. I saw my face—a larger-than-life reproduction of my face in flesh-colored acrylic hanging in a frame on the wall. The face had short auburn hair and wore a light green blouse like the one I had worn to the sumo match in Tokyo. It was hideous. My hideous face was hanging on this wall for all to see. In the lower right corner I saw the name "Odashima."

I tried to examine the painting more critically. Did my skin really look so patchy and dark? Was I really that fat and unattractive? Is this how Mr. Odashima saw me? He had obviously worked hard, and I felt guilty for not liking it. But did he really think I looked like that?

I tried looking at it from a distance and then up close. But from whatever angle, I had the same urge to take the painting off its hook and hide it.

When I walked into the office it became apparent that others had seen it.

"Nice portrait," a woman at the front desk said to me. I nodded and smiled. What could I say? As I walked to the Training and Welfare Section, I felt everyone looking at me with knowing glances.

I greeted Koji. "Did you see it?" I asked.

"You should be honored," he said. I tried to agree. I called Mr. Odashima and told him I had seen the painting.

"It's the first portrait I've ever done. I was working from a photo, from the day we all went to see sumo, so it doesn't look like real life."

I thanked him and said that I was flattered. "No one has ever painted my portrait before."

"I want you to have it," he said.

Permanent Effects

16 IF I CRINKLE MY FOREHEAD WHEN I LOOK IN the mirror I can see a small crescent-shaped scar near my hairline. It used to be hard and white, but now it's just a fading moon. It's from an accident I had when I was just one year old. I climbed up on a chair and then tumbled headfirst through a glass door. My parents told me that the Japanese babysitter who had been with me was more upset by the accident than I was.

They have told me many stories about my earliest childhood in Japan—things that I don't remember. The one that intrigues me the most is about the day after my birth. My father had come to see me for the first time in the nursery at the hospital. He described walking to my mother's room and seeing groups of babies wrapped up in blankets laid out in a row on a rolling cart, waiting to be taken to their mothers. He said they looked like little sausages. All the Asian babies had long, dark hair. I was bald, just like the only other Caucasian baby there, which had been born to a German couple.

As my parents approached the nursery, my mom saw the German couple at the window admiring and cooing to their baby. But when she looked at the baby, she saw it was me and panicked. "Oh my God. They've mixed up the babies! Brian, that's our baby!" My father went to the window and told the nurse his name. He watched her discover the mix-up. "Oh, I've made a mistake!" she said and hurriedly switched the bald babies, apologizing profusely to my relieved parents and the embarrassed German couple.

I have wondered, in an absurd way, what would have happened if the mix-up had gone undiscovered. I would have gone home with the Germans and moved back to a city like Berlin or Frankfurt. Perhaps I would have grown up speaking German and maybe some English. But whatever my life would have become, I still would have known one true thing about my identity—that I had been born in Japan. Sometimes I've wondered why my place of birth has been such a defining fact of my life.

* * *

In September, after six months in Sayama, I made plans to return to headquarters. I had decided that I could finish writing the guidebook in Tokyo. Although I would miss the people and work in Sayama, I wanted to get back to my city life—basketball on Wednesdays, hanging out with Masa and Tokiko, and cooking my own dinner. Research for the guidebook was complete; now I just had to organize and write it, something that I could do just as well at headquarters.

The only thing I didn't look forward to was putting on the old blue polyester uniform. Even though the factory uniforms looked like dumpy flour sacks, I had gotten used to seeing everyone wear the same thing. More than a year had passed since we had talked with Ms. Kawamura and the Special Project Group about changing the uniform policy. When I made periodic visits to headquarters during my time at the factory, I had worn business suits, like the men from the factory when they visited headquarters. No one ever indicated that this was a problem, but now that I was being transferred back I was resigned to wearing the uniform again.

A week before my new assignment in Tokyo was scheduled to begin, the International Administration Department manager called me to headquarters for a meeting. I assumed the purpose was to discuss my job. Since I was working on material for international associates, I would be part of the International Administration Department.

I was met by three Japanese men—the manager, an assistant manager, and a colleague, all of whom I knew. The manager, Mr. Kosugi, was an amiable man with a peculiar propensity for English. When he talked with one of the American associates, he randomly inserted English words into Japanese phrases.

The assistant manager, called Tak, had recently returned from eight happy years in Ohio. Whenever he got the chance, he spoke at length about his family's American life: a two-car garage, neighborhood tennis courts, and a yard. When he was transferred back to Japan he insisted on bringing back a piano they had bought. In their small Tokyo apartment, the piano took up one whole room, and his children could only play during daylight hours so they wouldn't disturb the neighbors.

Both Tak and Mr. Kosugi were pleasant and easygoing, but I disliked the last member. He couldn't have been much older than me, but he acted as though he were my boss. He was responsible for enforcing the rules that applied to international employees like me, and it seemed as though whenever I spoke with him he was telling me I couldn't do something because it was against company policy. Supposedly, he had spent several years on assignment in Europe, but I never heard him speak anything but Japanese. Among the foreign workers, he had a reputation as being singularly impersonal and inflexible, as though he held a grudge against us. We called him Mr. Rules.

The four of us went to the sixth-floor coffee shop and sat knee to knee around a small table. As on my previous visits from the factory to headquarters, I wore a business suit. We chatted for a while and ordered coffee. Mr. Rules began the meeting by telling me what I already knew, that I would be assigned a desk in the International Administration Department. "Working at headquarters is different from working at the factory," he said as though I had never been here before. "We have different starting and finishing times here at head-quarters."

His words made no sense. Had he forgotten that I had worked in Aoyama for over a year? He spoke to me as though I were an idiot.

"The lunch hour is different," he said. "Also, at head-quarters," he continued, "women must wear uniforms."

Suddenly everything became clear and I understood why I had been summoned to this meeting. Since I had been wearing suits when I visited headquarters, Mr. Rules thought that I might continue wearing them when I returned to work in the International Administration Department. His concern amused me because I intended to wear the uniform when I returned. I hadn't even considered not wearing it. The only reason I had worn my suit when I visited was because that's what the men from the factory had done and I was simply following their example.

Mr. Rules continued his condescending lecture.

"The rules state that women must wear uniforms," he said as though that would be the end of the discussion, but I knew from my research into the uniform policy that no written rule existed.

"Oh, that's so interesting," I said, not being able to resist a rebuttal. "I think I would understand so much better if I could see the rule."

All three men simultaneously inhaled sharply. They all knew what I meant—I didn't have to explain that the rule was discriminatory, counterproductive, and just plain ugly.

"Unlike in America, rules in Japan are not necessarily written down, they are understood," Mr. Rules replied snidely.

"Well what if someone doesn't understand the rules?" I continued, giving him the impression that I was not going to wear the uniform. Mr. Rules was getting annoyed, and his tone became more patronizing, but I was not about to give up without making a point. "How can you help someone understand if the rule isn't written down?" I asked.

Mr. Kosugi stepped in. "Rora-san, the uniform policy is being reconsidered. Soon there will be a change."

"When?" I asked.

"Soon," he said.

Tak was sympathetic to my position. After eight years of working with competent women and seeing his own daughter grow up around American girls, he understood my resistance to the policy.

"If you don't wear the uniform, then the other women will wonder why they have to wear it," he said.

"That's the point!" I wanted to shout. "I want them to question the policy too!"

Tak continued with a worried look on his face. "If you don't wear the uniform it will cause much confusion."

I sat back in my chair and looked at Mr. Rules. "My purpose is not to cause confusion," I told him. "My purpose is to do a job. I'll wear the uniform, but I want you to know how I feel about it."

I returned to the headquarters in full uniform and took a desk on the seventh floor reporting to Mr. Kosugi. Working independently on the guidebook project gave me a feeling of wild autonomy. I commandeered a Macintosh computer in the secretariat and moved freely between the seventh and tenth floors. Everyday I bicycled to work, met with the *gaijin* breakfast club, and ate lunch with Ms. Ogi and Ms. Shoji. Except for the uniforms, life at headquarters was better than it had ever been.

I continued to make regular visits to Ms. Kawamura to ask about the uniform investigation. I did not put much stock in Mr. Kosugi's news that the policy was under consideration, but until I returned to America I couldn't give up on the issue completely.

Mr. Yoshida was pressuring me to set a date for my return. But now that I had found a job that was important, I didn't want to leave until it was done. I knew that once I started something new in Ohio I wouldn't be able to do any work related to Sayama. I also knew that if I didn't finish writing the guidebook, no one else would. This was my project and I wanted to finish it.

Since I was now a member of the International Administration Department, it was easy to get involved in other projects. I helped with training for Japanese wives who were going overseas to live and had started to research other areas in Japan where Honda had factories that might host American employees long-term. My colleagues wanted my help and asked my advice about work—not just English grammar.

One evening I made my ritual stop at Ms. Kawamura's desk to ask about the uniforms. She paused when she looked up at me and asked me to go with her out into the hallway.

"I've got some good news," she said quietly. "It's still early, so don't tell anyone, but we are making a formal recommendation to management concerning the uniform policy. We are going to recommend that the uniforms for women become optional."

"When?" I asked.

"This week."

Although I hoped it would happen, I didn't really believe the policy would change. It had been a year and a half since the idea had come up. Finally Ms. Kawamura and her group had come to the same conclusion we had. I wanted to feel excited, but all the waiting and uncertainty made me wary of other unexpected problems or delays.

I didn't say anything to anyone until I heard the buzz around headquarters. Rumors started and unconfirmed reports spread. The quality-circle group members talked on the phone and kept each other updated on the latest news, but no one knew for sure when or what would happen. A few weeks passed without official news.

Then suddenly, on a Thursday afternoon in October, a written announcement was distributed throughout the building. It said, "Starting on Monday, the uniform policy for women will be discontinued. Women are free to choose to wear the uniform or their own clothing."

The quality-circle group members went out for lunch together to celebrate. I typed up a memo with the new policy in Japanese and English and included a logo—a picture of the blue uniform in a circle with a red slash across it. We drank a toast to no more uniforms.

But our excitement was somewhat tempered by the fear of what we would see on Monday. If the women continued to wear the no-cost, easy, familiar uniform despite the policy change, then it wouldn't matter. For the women in the quality-circle group, discarding the uniform was assumed. But what would all the other women do?

On Monday I was thrilled to see a small number of women, like me, who showed up in their own business clothes. A larger contingent of hardliners, like Ms. Mori and all the other secretaries, made no change in what they wore. But the majority of women seemed to be experimenting in stages; they wore the uniform skirt but got rid of the uniform blouse and vest.

All that week uniforms dominated conversations in the cafeteria, the coffee shop, and elevators. Most men acted ambivalent, as though it meant nothing to them either way, but I did hear a few supportive comments. They thought women looked better in their own clothing and that it was a nice change for the office.

I overheard two women talking in the bathroom. I

was in a stall and listened to them discussing the uniform out by the sinks.

"What are you going to wear tomorrow?" one woman asked the other.

"I haven't decided yet," the other replied like a self-conscious junior high school student wondering what to wear to the Saturday-night dance. "Are you really not going to wear the uniform?"

"I think so."

"Even the skirt?"

"I think I'll try wearing all my own clothes."

As the days and weeks passed, more and more women left the full uniform hanging in their lockers. I watched with keen interest the way certain departments would change overnight from uniform-wearing departments to uniform-free departments. I realized that what I viewed as a highly personal choice was really a group decision for some. Ironically, it was possible that some women may have even been pressured into discarding the uniform. Other women switched back and forth between the uniform and their own clothing on a day-to-day basis. And by the middle of November, change reached the tenth floor. Even Ms. Mori stopped wearing the uniform.

* * *

Mr. Amamiya, my old boss from Public Relations, came to see me. "We want you to participate in a special event for Mr. Honda," he said. Mr. Honda had been recognized by the international automobile community earlier in the year by being inducted into the Automobile Industry Hall of Fame in Michigan. The company was going to celebrate the event with a ceremony and a big party at headquarters, and Mr. Amamiya wanted me to be a part of the recognition ceremony with a group of other young employees.

I wore my favorite purple dress for the event. I met Bret, two Japanese men from Public Relations, three of the most beautiful Japanese women at headquarters, and Jenny, the only African-American who worked for Honda in Japan. She had started working for Honda only during the past year, but her photograph appeared in almost every corporate manual that Honda produced. The men wore suits and coats and the women wore skirts, suits, or dresses. We were a handsome group, an idealized version of mixed gender and race.

We gathered in the most elegant room on the six-teenth floor. Large windows looked out over Tokyo, and flowering plants and art work decorated the room. This particular room was famous in the company because Princess Diana and Prince Charles had visited there in 1986. One of the six plush beige chairs with marble arm rests was actually called the "Diana-chair," because she had sat there.

Mr. Amamiya was there carefully coordinating and coaching us. He gave me a bouquet of pink and white flowers that I would present to Mr. Honda. We each took turns pantomiming our greetings and practicing our words.

While we were waiting, Mr. Amamiya congratulated me on something, but I didn't understand what he meant.

"What did you say?"

"Congratulations on your work for the Hall of Fame memorial."

"What are you talking about?" I asked.

"You know, the English material you prepared on Mr. Honda."

I realized that he was referring to the data I had put together for the unmentionable X-day. I had finished the project, but thought that the information had been stashed away in a locked, metal drawer.

Mr. Amamiya explained that part of the material I had written had been used for Mr. Honda's display in the Hall of Fame. My work had been engraved in stone. I'd had no idea.

*   *   *

I had a dream one night after I had been back in Tokyo for about two months. In the dream I was brought into the center of a group of people who looked very much the same. I looked different and was bound like a prisoner. Somehow I got loose and I began to move slowly down a path through the middle of the group. I moved in a way that was natural to me, but it seemed very strange to them. I danced and moved my body and made musical sounds—tapping and singing. It felt very comfortable because I was doing what I knew. The people were fascinated because they had no understanding of what I was doing. They watched me and I continued dancing. It was odd to me that they had never known this joy which I knew.

When I awoke, I wrote the dream down on a piece of scrap paper, knowing that it meant something important, that it signified another part of my relationship with this place. Japan wasn't just my birthplace, but a part of me and who I was becoming.

Growing up in the plains of the Midwest, I had always loved telling people where I had been born. Tokyo had the sound of a distant, mysterious place—deep blue woodblock-print oceans, delicately folded origami cranes, and the blazing red Japanese flag. Tokyo—the syllables clanged brightly compared to the ordinary-sounding places where my friends were born—Marion, Springfield, or Columbus. I would entertain my classmates by reciting the numbers one to ten in Japanese, "*ichi, ni, san, shi, go, roku, shichi, hachi, ku, jū,*" feeling as though the words unlocked a secret which only I could know.

My relationship with Japan had started early with my first steps on a tatami floor and Japanese babysitters shaping the sounds I heard and coded in my brain. My parents helped me continue the journey. They had four newlywed years in Japan where they explored new territory and learned to juggle soft new syllables across their meat-and-potato tongues.

When they returned to America, they decided to get involved by hosting Japanese families who were temporarily living in Ohio. On American holidays the Japanese mothers would dress their children in matching outfits and bring them to our house to hunt for Easter eggs or decorate Christmas cookies. The mothers usually brought rice dish in a black-and-red lacquered tray.

One time the Japanese food included a dish of sliced cold octopus. Each slice of the rubbery white meat was ominously edged with dark maroon tentacles. My father teased me and told me that if I ate it I would grow more arms during the night. I watched in horror as he ate the meaty slices, certain that I would wake to find an eight-armed father at the breakfast table.

In college, my relationship with Japan became personal; I explored the country and reinvented myself. I was Kiki instead of Laura, practiced judo instead of cheerleading, and spoke Japanese in place of English. I climbed Mount Fuji during a typhoon, hitchhiked around the snow-covered northern island of Hokkaido, drank bitter green tea wearing a three-layered purple kimono, and ate raw horse meat and liked it.

When I came to Japan to work for Honda, I brought a colorful landscape of images that crackled and sparkled in my memory. But once I started working, I felt as though I had suddenly and unexpectedly veered onto the dark side of a planet where there was no light. I trudged through the darkness, not realizing that I had just stepped into a deeper valley than I had ever experienced before. It was a valley that I would have encountered anywhere—the result of growing up and becoming an adult— but the valley seemed darker because I was in a foreign place. When I finally learned to negotiate the depths of this landscape I discovered a joy that I had never known.

I kept extending my return date to America, explaining to Mr. Yoshida that my research and writing were taking longer, especially since other projects kept coming up. What I couldn't tell him, and what I hardly recognized myself, was that my life in Japan had become the life I had anticipated when I first came to work at headquarters.

Every day my work engaged my mind, stretched my thinking, and challenged me to learn. I knew how things worked, and I had done enough English-language favors that I had contacts on every floor. My friends like Ms. Ogi, Ms. Shoji, Masa, and Tokiko were supportive, fun, and generous. I had worked so hard to reach this point, I didn't want to just leave it.

I managed to postpone my departure to the end of December and spent almost every night of that last month attending dinners and farewell parties. I packed up my photo albums and pottery for a sea shipment and sold my purple racing bike to a friend. I gave the old red mountain bike to Masa. The lease company came and reclaimed their furniture.

On my last day of work at Honda I visited people and said good-bye with bows, handshakes, and a few awkward hugs. "I'll work hard not to let my Japanese get rusty," I told everyone, using an idiomatic phrase that would have paralyzed me with confusion two years earlier.

I went to the tenth floor to pack up a box of files, but I was distracted. I wanted to say something to Ms. Mori, but I wasn't sure what. Ever since I had left the secretariat we had treated each other with distant civility, but I felt like we never resolved our feud.

I went to the supply closet to get some packing tape and when I turned around, Ms. Mori was there. No one could see us. She had something to say too.

"Mori-san," I said. She looked me straight in the eye. Her mouth was drawn; she almost looked sad. Suddenly my mouth felt dry and I was anxious and trembling. I felt rushed and pressured to say something meaningful. Why hadn't I ever said anything before? The intensity of my regret surprised me, and I felt sorry that I hadn't done more.

"I've been wanting to say something," I began. My throat was tight and my eyes stung around the edges. "I really learned a lot from you."

"I'm sorry," she said and bowed her head.

"No. I'm sorry," I said, my eyes were full of tears. "I didn't understand so many things," I tried to explain.